Global Leadership **Lineage**

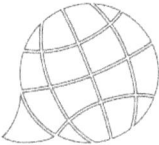

CCBS Press

Title: Global Leadership Lineage
Subtitle: Cross-cultural empirical analyses of leadership styles and practices
Author: Sander Schroevers, Chris Higgins, and CCBS/GBS researchers
Contact: Sander Schroevers, Amsterdam, Netherlands
Copyright holder: Cross-Cultural Business Skills
Year: 2025
Imprint: CCBS Press
ISBN: 978-90-79646-65-4

Global Leadership Lineage

Cross-cultural empirical analyses of leadership styles and practices

Amsterdam University
of Applied Sciences

CCBS-Press
First edition 2025
ISBN: 978-90-79646-65-4
NUR: 812
Editorial managers: Christopher Higgins, Aynur Doğan, Sander Schroevers
Inner and cover design: SH69T Studio, Amsterdam, Netherlands
Cover graphic: AI-generated (OpenAI), supervision: Sander Schroevers, 2025
Text copyright: Alejandro Hernández Arbizú, Alex Maas, Amelie Foroutanian, Amicie de Montalembert, Aparajita Bhattacharya, Artem Nozhenko (Артем Ноженко), Ayoub Benniss, Benjamin Abd El-Malek, Benjamin Daniel, Bibiche van Ooijen, Busra Demir, Claudi Elberse, David Caramelo, Deandre Burnet, Dennis Grimme, Dex den Hoed, Deyhane Vos, Diederick van Walsem, Diego de Kom, Diego Muñoz Carvajal, Dilawar Raja Khan, Dolf van Coeverden, Eefje Hurkmans, Ennio Eckardt, Eunseo Kim (김은서), Fadi Algemise, Fahim Faqiri, Faissal Mehdaoui, Fatih Tutucu, Floris de Vreese, Gabriela Peixoto Gonçalves, Georgina Kasteleijn, Ghalia Ghalib, Ghislaine Rojer, Ghita Belhaj, Guido Boogaard, Haider Hussain, Hanna Hunya, Ihsan Yilmaz, Ilias El Aidi, Iliass Zwiggelaar, Iman Hossainpourian Taheri, Iman Loonat, Isa Beau Veldhuis, Isa van der Laan, Jack Maher, Jacob Osman, Jesper Linnenkamp, Jette Arts, Jordy van der Tak, Joshua Tubiana, Julia Langelaar, Julie Boiteux, Kaan Birinci, Kaan Kara, Kadir Çivi, Kanokphon Sophaphon (ใสภาพร กนกพร), Karmen Hiis, Karsyn Keetch, Kees-Jan Lagemaat, Kevin Boom, Kimon Bletsis (Κίμων Μπλέτσης), Kristina Kovshova (Крістіна Ковшова), Kyah Bedano, Leandra Carsilia, Leonardo Ghelli, Levent Bálint, Lia Lačen, Lindsey Houwaard, Luc Brandsen, Luca Junge, Luuk Hagoort, Mahnaz Daneshgar, Manisha Thurairajah, Marco Lorenzo Ovalles, Mare Slop, Mariam Jvarsheishvili (მარიამ ჯვარშეიშვილი), Marit van de Kamp, Marwa Boujada, Maureen van der Greft, May Hassan, Mees Verkerk, Meric Eminoglu, Mika Nagtegaal, Mina Zakian, Nadia Appia-Kubi, Nadine Blijham, Naeb Tekeste, Nick Olchov, Ouiam Dahman, Pim Warmerdam, Raoul van Dort, Raymond van den Bos, Remco Sluik, Rens Langeveld, Rodi Beikzadeh, Rosa Blom, Rosa Guenbour, Sam Kluft, Sara El Fargoussi, Saviero Landveld, Sedef Caliskan, Sekou Dicko, Senne Bakker, Sepehr Abdoli, Serkan Dural, Shanice Weidum, Sharnelle Power, Sieb van der Laan, Sita den Besten, Špela Kukovič, Su Kwan Jung (정수관), Sylvana Koopman, Tammara Bokhorst, Teun Schouten, Tiia Kallio, Tugay Öztürk, Wester Klerk, Yannick Dankbaar and Zoi Zormpas.

Table of Contents

Preface 6

About CCBS 7

Methodological approach 8

Country profiles 9

Angola 15

The Bahamas 27

Estonia 38

Finland 50

Greenland 63

Kenya 76

Kosovo 88

Macedonia, North 101

Morocco 111

New Zealand 124

Slovenia 137

Thailand 149

Bibliography 163

Preface

Welcome to the latest edition in our ongoing series of empirical cross-cultural analyses of global leadership styles and practices. Our title underlines a key premise, namely that every style of leading has a lineage: a chain of teachers, traditions and turning points that quietly shape what is seen as 'good leadership' in each society. This book is the result of collaborative research by 120 students on the 'Cross-Cultural Business Skills' and the 'Global Business Skills' electives (minors), which are hosted by the University of Applied Sciences Amsterdam. Over the course of a single semester, these students have empirically investigated leadership styles and practices across multiple countries, through employing a combination of research methods. More specifically, the students performed desk-based literature reviews of local scholarship, in conjunction with generating both quantitative and qualitative data through conducting a survey and interviews with thousands of local business professionals and cross-cultural scholars and practitioners. The quality of the contributions in this edited collection are thus, above all, a testament to the perseverance and collaborative work ethic of everyone involved, and, moreover, provide rich and colourful insights. First and foremost, we would like to take this opportunity to thank all the individual co-authors for their determination to complete their respective analyses. Moreover, we also wish to extend our upmost gratitude to all the survey respondents and interviewees for being gracious enough to provide insight into the prevailing leadership styles and practices in their country. To the reader, we hope this book finds you well and perhaps, dare we say it, sitting in a convenient airport lounge waiting to board a flight to one of the countries explored in this book, with locally-informed insights into cross-cultural leadership, eager to apply them in practice.

Aynur Dogan, Sander Schroevers & Christopher Higgins

About CCBS

Since 2010, Cross-Cultural Business Skills (CCBS) has sought to educate bachelor students in both the fundamentals of cross-cultural business skills and specific research methods. CCBS/GBS are elective courses ('minor') established and taught by Prof. Dr.Hc. Sander Schroevers, Aynur Doğan MA and Christopher Higgins MA at the Amsterdam University of Applied Sciences (the Netherlands).

Educational approach
At CCBS/GBS we believe that effective learning takes place through sharing and engaging with first-hand experiences. For this reason, we challenge our students to produce new knowledge from a localised perspective. Often this involves conducting research in an unknown language, alphabet or cultural milieu, which, in turn, helps out students develop fundamental skills for the contemporary interconnected world. Our main objective is to co-create country-specific bodies of knowledge, which we generate through carrying out both expert-interviews (video and audio) with native professionals and scholars and in-depth analyses of local academic and trade literature. In order to create a truly international classroom experience, we try to host students from across the globe. Moreover, we attempt to connect our students with a broad range of representatives from the business, media and diplomatic sectors, through hosting professional symposia in the school. All CCBS-learning materials (print, digital and video) are 100% bespoke. We are honoured by the fact that we have consistently received the university's highest evaluation scores over the last ten years, and that Sander was elected as teacher of the year at the FBE-faculty.

About CCBS Global Leadership research
CCBS Global Leadership is our ongoing academic research project for the Amsterdam University of Applied Sciences, which directly informs the cross-cultural business material taught on the minor. Every six months, CCBS researchers survey C-level executives around the world. Our analytical gaze is focused on five main areas: management, meetings, leadership, recruitment and expatriates. Since conducting the inaugural international poll in 2012, the CCBS global-fact-tank has conducted interviews in 167 trade nations, with more than twenty-five-thousand professionals. Thank you!

Methodological approach

Three modes of data collection were employed to generate the insights published in this book. Firstly, insights into the cultural aspects of leadership were gathered through country-specific literature searches, in both peer-reviewed academic journals and in-country books, which served as the foundation for the subsequent research. Secondly, a global online survey on leadership was conducted with qualified respondents from each country (CCBS Survey, year). Expert sampling was used to identify the survey respondents, in conjunction with snowballing techniques, which were subsequently introduced to target a population who are often difficult to reach. In total, over 25,000 respondents participated in the CCBS survey; however almost one-third of these surveys were not used, because they were not fully completed, or their background or sometimes IP-addresses did not match our target group. The survey was created in English and subsequently translated by competent bilinguals, who were either research collaborators or supervised by them. The present study made use of translations into Albanian, Arabic, Chinese traditional, Danish, Dutch, Estonian, Filipino, Finnish, French, German, Hungarian, Italian, Macedonian, Mongolian, Portuguese, Romanian, Russian, Serbian, Spanish, Slovenian, Swahili, Tajik, Thai and surely: English. Evaluations of translation accuracy were completed by using back-translation or parallel translations, where possible. The Albanian, Arabic, Dutch, French, Russian, Serbian and English version were rolled out in multiple countries. The questionnaire comprised 27 items, both multiple-choice and open-ended questions, which provided descriptive information on national-based views on leadership.

The respondents answered the psychometric multiple-choice questions on five or six-point Likert scales, which were anchored by terms ranging from 'not at all' to 'a lot'. All the qualitative data provided comprehensive knowledge into the topic of local leadership styles and practices. The multinational survey and interviewing were conducted between 23 September and 10 December 2025. The findings that emerged out of this research have not been presented prior to the publication of this book. Thirdly, in addition to the survey respondents, a selection of 23 leadership experts were also interviewed for the present study. These audio and video recorded interviews lasted between 15-60 minutes on average, and were transcribed verbatim (a selection of these will be published on the YouTube and Spotify channels of the CCBS minor, where permitted).

Country profiles

Empirical studies have revealed that the relationship between certain kinds of motivating leadership behaviour and work outcomes systematically varies from culture to culture. As noted by the Global Leadership and Organizational Behavior Effectiveness (GLOBE) Research Program: "to date, 90 percent of leadership literature reflects US-based research and theory". The American-centric nature of extant literature is a profound problem, insofar as it fails to account for how leadership theories, styles and practices operate across national frontiers. This is important, because as the number of countries expand, so do the differences. It is for this reason that I have always been fond of Peter Drucker's quote: "Management is doing things right; leadership is doing the right things". That is to say, leadership encompasses the human element of business, whereas management is often about systems and processes. For the purposes of writing this paragraph, I conducted a quick check on Amazon.com for the number of books with the word 'leader' in their title, which produced an incredible 60,000 results. Similarly, a quick search on ProQuest (one of the databases we recommend to students for accessing scholarly journals) resulted in almost a million hits for 'leadership'. Evidently, there is extensive research informing us of how leaders' communication styles are profoundly influenced by the geographical region in which they are operating. Regrettably, some business leaders overlook local managerial and cultural practices, and instead acquiesce to management-styles that are grounded in Western concepts, which, in turn, undermines the performance of their organisation. Given that ineffective managers risk costing organisations notably large sums of money, there is an emergent trend among both human resource professionals and senior executives to adopt more localised leadership styles and practices.

Chapter makeup

This book consists of country-specific chapters, which each describe at length the leadership styles and practices within their respective country. All country profiles were written in a standard format, in order to allow for a clearer identification of points of similarity and divergence across the different business cultures. Most of the country profiles in this book contain the following sections:

- Country introduction,
- How the indigene characterise leaders,
- Survey results and what local respondents say,
- An in-country YouTube review,
- A transcribed telephone interview with a local leadership scholar,
- A summarised video interview with a local cross-cultural trainer,
- A description of an in-country best-selling book on leadership,
- Understanding hierarchy in the chapter's country,
- How to achieve leadership empathy in that particular culture.

I will briefly introduce each of these sections in turn below.

Local leadership analysis

The more I work abroad, the more I realise that it takes more than just a survey to examine and classify national cultures. More specifically, there is too much cultural heterogeneity and nuance, which substantially impacts upon how one effectively operates in a particular country, but yet simply does not fit within prevailing academic constructs on this topic. Notwithstanding the many good Western-centric books on a variety of countries, what is invariably obfuscated in these texts is the local perspective. The need to address this lacuna in the field by prioritising localised perspectives became pivotal to our approach to investigating country-specific leadership styles and practices. This approach comprises gathering data from indigenous sources, including: (i) survey-results and what local respondents say, (ii) a local leadership scholar, (iii) a local cross-cultural trainer, (iv) and an in-country best-selling book on leadership. While having to conduct research sometimes in other languages and even scripts has proven to be incredibly challenging for some of our students, it has undoubtedly produced rich local-based data that provides insight into how leadership styles and practices are enacted in these selected markets.

Understanding hierarchy in a country

Most of the trends in Western leadership across the twentieth century were centred on moving away from hierarchical command-and-control processes. To this end, both management literature and business school education began to introduce a more egalitarian and facilitative style of leadership. For example, we started to see open-plan office architecture and 360-degree feedback. However, it is important to note that there are profound cross-cultural differences with respect to how authority is viewed. In India, for example, the teaching staff are addressed by Madam or Sir, while I also observed on occasion students standing up when their 'senior-lecturer' entered the classroom. Conversely, on my own Dutch course (CCBS - the authors of this book) local students address me by my first name, and at times feel free to contradict me in front of the class.

Relational hierarchy
Eight out of ten Swiss survey respondents (CCBS Survey, 2021) reported that employees greeted their leaders by their first name. This low-level of hierarchy results in equal and harmonious relationships between superiors and their employees, which are based on mutual trust. Being acutely aware of someone's relative level of authority is of critical importance in a country such as South Korea. This is because it determines how colleagues interact with each other, including choosing between the many different linguistic levels of politeness. For example, organisations tend to have far more levels of management compared to some other countries, each of which have their own corresponding forms of address. Hence, the informal way in which business is conducted in Australia, for example, would likely completely confuse the average Korean employee. This would especially be the case for those Korean workers who have attained senior positions within their organisations, and are wholly accustomed to VIP treatment.

Power Distance
The words Hierarchy and Power Distance are often used interchangeably. The latter can be defined as "the degree to which members of an organisation or society expect and agree that power should be stratified and concentrated at higher levels of an organisation or government" (House & Javidan, 2004, p. 12). Countries that have scored high Power Distance values in either Hofstede or Trompenaars' respective research, believe that power dispenses agreement, social order, and role stability, and, hence, should be concentrated within those in the upper echelon of organisations. In high power distance cultures, leader-subordinate relationships are characterised by paternalism, whereby a leader assumes a parental role and feels obligated to provide support and protection to subordinates under their care (Yan & Hunt, 2005). Many of the country profiles in this book reference their country's Power Distance Index score (PDI), as measured by Dutch cultural scientist Geert Hofstede. However, the value score in and of itself cannot fully explain how hierarchy operates within a particular culture. For example, despite Greece and South Korea both having equally high PDI values (60), leadership is enacted in a fundamentally different way in both countries. Therefore, in this book we attempt to account for such cultural contingencies by conducting culture-specific qualitative research, including interviewing local cultural experts.

How to achieve leadership empathy
This section addresses a specific people-oriented leadership requirement: empathic soft skills. Here, empathy is defined as a leader's capacity to relate to the feelings and experiences of their employees. Empathy is an altogether broader category than sympathy, and, in fact, several researchers consider empathy to be both a key part of emotional intelligence and a critical element of being an effective leader (Bar-On & Parker, 2000). Of course, the ability to successfully build and maintain relationships has long been regarded as a fundamental managerial skill; however, in accordance with the Center for Creative Leadership, the point being made here is that, in some cultures, empathy is more important to job performance than other aspects of leadership (Gentry, Weber, & Sadri, 2016). In addition to this, the way empathic understanding is expressed varies dramatically from country-to-country. Above all, empathy touches upon a leader's understanding of role requirement. To understand its importance across different cultures, several questions in our online survey (CCBS Survey, 2020) pertained to the specific expectations that local leaders had towards empathy. Furthermore, each team attempted to interview local experts, scholars and cross-cultural trainers on the country-specific ways in which empathy is effectively utilised. To cite an example: whereas in Nordic countries empathy is partly established through low-key and modest behaviour, Latin countries prefer a warm, personal and 'simpatico' approach, while, conversely, South Koreans value a courteous leader who, above all, attempts to save face (Kibun). It is well-established that how we connect with people is dependent on our cultural background, and, as such, the ability to be empathetic is especially important for leaders working across cultural boundaries (Alon & Higgins, 2005). The results of our CCBS survey (2020) reflect this, insofar as a large majority of the respondents from the different cultures examined in this book agreed with the statement that a manager should actively spend time on the personal wellbeing of their team members. When one compares the actual country scores (Dell, Eriks, 2018), South Korea and Ukraine score significantly lower on empathy than countries such as Uruguay and Portugal, due, in part, to the fact that Ukrainian and South Korean leaders generally prefer to keep more personal distance from their employees. However, it is important to stress that having empathy for others is not the same as demonstrating empathy; this is because staff expectations may vary considerably across culture in terms of: (i) the amount of verbal attention employees require; (ii) the praise and encouragement expected by staff; or (iii) the daily routine of managers. When managers increase their awareness of the cultural context in which empathy takes place, it often has a direct impact on employee performance, the organisational climate, and the quality of the productive working relations between leaders and employees.

Concluding Remarks

It was Darwin who first showed us the supreme value inherent to diversity. With this in mind, both the increased cultural heterogeneity of today's workforce and the increasingly global footprint of contemporary organisations transforms the styles and practices through which we lead teams. This calls for leaders with an ability to decode cultural differences and adjust their leadership-style to fit the cultural milieu in which they are operating. In summary, I hope that our findings contribute to increasing the richness of extant leadership literature, alongside aiding professional leaders to recalibrate their skills and mindsets in a manner advantageous to themselves, their employees, and, above all, the organisations they serve.

de Baas

ප්‍රධාන විධායක නිලධාරී
தலைமை நிர்வாக அதிகாரி

Big-man

प्रबन्धक

Chief Executive Officer

Gerente general

Manajer umum

Generálny Riaditeľ

المدير التنفيذي

総監督

Président Directeur Géneral

Consejero Delegado   генеральний директор

MAIN DUDE

Angola

Isa van der Laan, Deyhane Vos, David Caramelo, Gabriela Goncalves & Eefje Hurkmans

Angola, or the Republic of Angola as it is officially known, lies on the western coast of Southern Africa and borders Namibia, Zambia and the Democratic Republic of Congo. Amongst other things, the country is distinguished by its considerable cultural and ethnic heterogeneity, which includes major groups such as the Ovimbundu, Kimbundu and Bakongo. Portuguese functions as the official language of the country, in conjunction with a wide range of other local dialects (Silva et al., 2015). Since securing its independence in 1975, Angola has undergone extensive political and socio-economic reconstruction, supported by reforms aimed towards both strengthening the state's capacity and improving public administration (Horta, 2020). Urban growth, particularly in the city of Luanda, has transformed social structures and contributed towards shifting expectations regarding community life, governance and participation. Within this evolving socio-political context, traditional authorities (*autoridades tradicionais*), especially *sobas* (local chiefs) and *régulos* (community chiefs), continue to shape governance patterns and community norms, influencing, amongst other things, how authority is perceived within contemporary institutions (Ferreira, 2025). Our interview with Dr. Rosa Lutete Geremias, a specialist in organisational behaviour and leadership development, underscores that managers in Angola often combine *chefia* (managerial authority) with interpersonal attentiveness, by, for example, offering discreet guidance and upholding respect and relational harmony (Geremias, 24 October 2025). These practices are in alignment with broader socio-cultural preferences for indirect communication, social cohesion and sensitivity to relational dynamics (Silva et al., 2015). Extant research further indicates that Angolan employees value leaders who demonstrate charisma, competence and cultural awareness, whilst, simultaneously, maintaining clear hierarchical expectations (Silva et al., 2015; Cunha et al., 2016). Collectively, these insights indicate that effective business leadership in Angola relies largely on leaders' ability to integrate traditional norms with adaptive and context-sensitive managerial approaches, as will be explored further in the proceeding chapter by drawing on primary and seconday data sources.

How Angolans characterise leaders?

Leadership in Angola is shaped by the country's complex history, cultural traditions, and social structures. Centuries of Portuguese colonial rule, followed by a prolonged civil war, have culminated in a society that, above all. values unity, order, and deference to authority (Hofstede, 2025). Angolan culture is strongly collectivist in nature, with individuals' identities closely tied to their families and wider communities. Within this context, leaders are regarded as protectors and decision-makers, who, ultimately, are responsible for maintaining stability and continuity within organisations (Mbigi, 2005). Cultural expectations of leaders emphasise moral integrity, ethical conduct, and concern for the collective good, with leaders moreover being expected to act as role models, who demonstrate honesty, modesty, and a commitment to the welfare of their teams rather than focusing solely on personal gain (Sibanda, 2023; Mbigi, 2005). Whilst authority is respected in Angolan organisations, empathy and emotional intelligence are also highly valued. Effective Angolan leaders listen attentively, remain approachable, and balance decision-making with care for employees' well-being. Our interview with Dr Rosa Lutete Geremias provided us with further nuance regarding Angolan business leadership. She informed us that transformational leadership is rare in the country, with transactional and aversive styles being altogether more common in Angolan organisations, historically. She proceeded to explain how Angolan leaders frequently emphasise control and seniority, particularly in conservative regions where age and status often carry more weight than competence. As she put it, *"feedback is more easily experienced as criticism or a personal attack"* (Geremias, 24 November 2025). Furthermore, she underscored the influence of traditional local leadership structures, such as *sobas* and *régulos* (local and community chiefs), whose authority is grounded in personal relationships, reciprocity, and moral responsibility. These practices continue to inform modern managerial behaviour, blending hierarchical respect with relational care (Geremias, 24 November 2025).This framing of Angolan leadership was corroborated by the results of the CCBS Survey (2015-2025), which indicated that Angolan employees value leaders who balance authority with interpersonal sensitivity. Gender remains a salient factor in perceptions of what constitutes effective leadership in Angola, according to Geremias who explicated that, *"whilst women leaders often excel in relational and empathetic skills, they still face structural and cultural resistance that undermines their authority"* (Geremias, 24 November 2025). Although hierarchy is central, leaders often combine authority with relational care. Managers may consult trusted colleagues informally before making decisions, particularly on issues affecting team cohesion or community expectations. Furthermore, employees tend to appreciate leaders who provide clear guidance, whilst, simultaneously, demonstrating concern for their well-being, which is emblematic of the requisite balance between authority and empathy required in Angolan leaders (Lerutla & Steyn, 2022). In summary, Angolan leaders are characterised by a blend of authority, ethical integrity, and relational awareness. Leadership is strongly embedded within the prevailing social and cultural norms, where respect for hierarchy coexists with the expectation that leaders act morally, listen attentively, and protect collective interests. Interview insights, supported by survey observations, suggest that although hierarchical and transactional tendencies persist, relational and empathetic leadership is recognised as being essential to organisational effectiveness in Angola.

Survey results and what local respondents say

In order to gain a deeper understanding of leadership practices and organisational culture in Angola, a group of local C-level executives and senior professionals with extensive managerial experience were invited to participate in the CCBS Survey (2015-2025). The survey data, which combines data from different periods of data collection, provides valuable insights into Angolan perceptions of what constitutes effective leadership, how hierarchical organisations are, employee expectations of leaders, and the extent to which traditional leadership norms continue to influence organisational behaviour. The most salient findings emerging from the survey are discussed in turn below. First, the vast majority of the respondents indicated that a strong charismatic personality is essential for effective leadership (78.3%), followed by high intellectual capacity (69.6%) and access to the right professional networks (62.3%) (CCBS Survey, 2015-2025). These findings underscore the importance placed on personal authority and social capital in leadership roles. Resourcefulness was also cited as important by nearly half of the respondents (49.3%), whilst good political connections were deemed to be significant for 47.8% of respondents. When asked what employees expect from their leaders, the most common responses were visionary thinking (71%), powerful decision-making (75.4%) and good listening skills (68.1%) (CCBS Survey, 2015-2025). Organisational experience (78.3%), technical competence (73.9%) and market knowledge (66.7%) were identified as the primary sources of respect (CCBS Survey, 2015-2025). The survey also shed light upon specific organisational practices. For instance, a considerable number of the respondents indicated that leaders typically receive privileges, such as, for example, dedicated office space and transportation. In addition, 24.6% of the respondents reported that confronting subordinates during staff meetings is very characteristic of their behaviour, thus reflecting a direct and sometimes forceful approach to performance management. The qualitative responses provide additional depth and nuance to these quantitative findings. Several of the respondents underscored entrenched hierarchical norms, noting *"great respect for authority"* and that *"wrong decisions are not questioned"*. Others yet still described Angolan leadership as *"dictatorial"*, *"old-fashioned"*, and characterised by *"abusive supervision, authoritarianism and narcissism"* (CCBS Survey, 2015-2025). Beyond these observations, the survey revealed that hierarchy and authority remain central to leadership culture. Whilst many leaders emphasise direct engagement with employees, traditional norms maintain a symbolic distance, reinforcing structured interpersonal boundaries (CCBS Survey, 2015-2025). Communication preferences drew varied responses from the respondents: whilst a majority of respondents preferred direct feedback, some indicated that indirect criticism remains culturally embedded, reflecting the persistence of relationally cautious communication patterns (CCBS Survey, 2015-2025). The respondents were also divided on the issue of the level of gender (in)equality with respect to attaining senior-level leadership positions in Angola, with only a minority recognising equal opportunities for men and women to attain senior positions, thus signalling enduring traditionalism within the organisational culture there (CCBS Survey, 2015-2025. Overall, the survey depicts Angolan business leadership as combining charisma-based authority with respect for hierarchy and meritocratic credentials. Whilst, on the one hand, employees value decisiveness, vision, and relational attentiveness, on the other, leaders continue to operate within rigid frameworks that privilege authority and seniority. Emerging expectations for listening, compromise and competence suggest a gradual shift towards more relationally aware and balanced leadership, albeit within a context that remains strongly hierarchical and grounded in tradition.

Local leadership analysis

Rosa Geremias: an Angolan leadership scholar

Dr. Rosa Geremias is a professor and researcher in human resources and organisational behaviour. She has worked in both Portugal and Angola and her research is focused mainly on leadership, psychological capital, work–life balance, job stress and burnout. She holds a PhD in Organisational Behaviour and has published many scientific articles on these topics, as well as taking part in international academic networks and receiving several awards for her work. Because she has studied Angolan organisations and employees for many years, she can be regarded as one of the main experts on business leadership in the Angolan context (Geremias, 24 October 2025). In this interview, we asked her about the prevailing leadership styles in Angola, regional differences across the country, the level of gender (in)equality with respect to accessing leadership positions, and the main challenges that foreign managers might face when working in Angola. At the beginning of the interview, Dr. Geremias explained that Angola is a very diverse and multicultural country, so it is hard to talk about just one "*Angolan leadership style*" (Geremias, 24 October 2025). Despite this, based on her research, she explained that transformational and inspirational leadership are not very common yet in the Angolan context. She proceeded to argue that "we automatically discard the inspirational and *transformational leadership... because it is not part of the common culture*" (Geremias, 24 October 2025). Within many organisations, leadership is more transactional and aversive. Leaders tend to focus on control and on punishing mistakes, by, for example, cutting salaries, removing benefits or even dismissing employees when goals are not reached (Geremias, 24 October 2025). Later in the interview, she emphasised that leadership is also strongly connected to hierarchy and seniority within the Angolan context, especially in more conservative regions, where age and status often count more than competence. This is quite different from many Western leadership theories, Geremias informed us, which ordinarily emphasise participation, empowerment and more equal relationships between managers and employees (24 October, 2025). In response to our question about the level of gender (in)equality within Angolan organisations, Dr. Geremias opined that Angolan society is still very patriarchal, and that women therefore remain under-represented in leadership roles. Although, she added, there are quota policies at the political level, these changes come *"from above"* and do not yet reflect a broader cultural change in everyday life. Allied with this, issues such as early pregnancy and limited access to education also make it harder for many girls and young women to reach the level of qualifications that are often needed for leadership positions. Rosa illustrated this reality by stating that "*it is very easy to find girls from 12 to 15 years old, all with childeren* [in Angola]" (Geremias, 24 October 2025). This means there are still relatively few female leaders who can act as visible role models. Towards the end of the interview, Dr. Geremias underlined that Angola has a sensitive feedback culture. In many Western organisations, feedback is seen as a normal and even positive tool for learning and development. However, she concluded the interview by stating that, feedback in Angola is more readily experienced as criticism or a personal attack. Consequently, if managers do not pay close attention to how they give feedback, then this can damage trust and relationships with their employees. With respect to the future of Angola, she believes that one of the biggest challenges is to "*humanise*" leadership in Angola. To this end, in her estimation, organisations must invest more in training, career development and the long-term well-being of employees, rather than focusing almost exclusively on productivity and short-term results (Geremias, 24 October 2025).

Angolan Social Media Review

In order to capture contemporary Angolan views on business leadership, four local practitioners active on LinkedIn and the media more broadly were analysed: Amália Djaló Morato, Belarnício Muangala, Gabriel Praia and José Rocha (Djaló Morato, n.d). A first theme that emerged centres on people-centred leadership and well-being. Behavioural analyst and soft-skills trainer Amália Djaló Morato, who is involved in initiatives such as *Liderança Feminina em Angola*, defines well-being at work as employees' physical, emotional and psychological health, stressing that workers must feel respected, fulfilled and emotionally supported within Angolan organisations (Djaló Morato, n.d.). She links effective leadership in Angola to promoting emotional intelligence, so that employees can manage stress, build positive relationships and maintain productivity (Djaló Morato, n.d.). Next, visionary and developmental leadership emerges in the posts of Gabriel Praia, founder of CIT – *Clube de Inteligência e Treinamento* and the Fórum RH Top Talks Benguela (Praia, n.d.). Reflecting on a forum themed *"Liderança Visionária: do Legado à Inovação"*, he presents leadership in Angola as being about building networks of dialogue, innovation and collective learning about people management and human capital, emphasising continuous learning and collaboration amongst professionals (Praia, n.d.). Third, the importance of strategic, reform-oriented leadership in Angolan organisations was discussed in interviews with Belarnício Muangala, founder and CEO of Fly Angola (Muangala, n.d.). Discussing the aviation sector, he openly criticises the State's dominant role and lack of incentives, arguing that without fair competition and private investment the industry cannot deliver its potential for citizens and the economy (Muangala, n.d.). Here, leadership is also about advocacy: speaking up to change structural conditions in Angola as a whole, not only running one company (Muangala, n.d.). Finally, corporate leadership in the form of social dialogue with youth was discussed by José Rocha, who is the CEO of Deep Ocean Integrated Solutions in Angola (Rocha, n.d.). Commenting on a partnership with media figure Weza Solange, he referred to it as *"a milestone"* and *"a strategic step"* to strengthen the brand and show that the oil sector can communicate transparently and creatively with society, particularly with young Angolans (Rocha, n.d.). Angolan ladership, here, is framed as being about connecting industry, innovation, sustainability and the country's future generations (Rocha, n.d.). When viewed together, these voices show Angolan leadership discourse shifting towards being more people-centred, visionary and socially engaged: caring about employees' well-being and emotional intelligence, investing in human capital and networks, whilst also challenging structural barriers and building bridges between business, society and youth (Djaló Morato, n.d.)

In-country leadership bestseller

One of Angola's most relevant books on leadership and human resource management was written by Edson Maurício Horta in 2020 and is entitled *Estratégia e Gestão de Pessoas em Angola* (Strategy and People management in Angola). Horta is an Angolan academic and public administrator with experience in governance, public management, and human capital development (Rodrigues, 2016). In his book, he explores how Angolan organisations can strengthen their performance by moving away from traditional, administrative management models and instead viewing leadership as a strategic function. As noted in the book, *"the new approaches to people management in organisations considers people as critical success factors […] therefore, the managers must not only know the goals but also participate in the development and implementation of major strategic decisions"* (Horta, 2020, as cited in Morato, 2021, p.113). This perspective underscores how important inclusive, participative leadership is in Angola's social and economic environment. The book integrates leadership theory with the economic and cultural realities of Angola. Horta believes that effective leadership in Angola requires being adaptive, focusing on the people as the main factor, and building trust. He warns that imported management models often fail to match Angola's culture or economic situation; therefore, he urges leaders instead to adapt approaches to local needs whilst, simultaneously, encouraging performance and innovation. One aspect of this is that Angola is characterised by a high level of power distance, which *"generates on followers a set of reactions of submission and dependence, but also of conformity, subservience and adulation"* (Cunha et al., 2016, p.684, as cited in Ana Maria Rocha et al., 2024). This highlights the need for Angolan leaders to manage authority carefully, maintaining clear hierarchy whilst limiting the negative effects associated with high power distance. Horta argues that these cultural dynamics require strategic management, especially placing the right people in the right positions. Horta further explains that reform in Angola requires more than merely changing structures; rather, it means changing how public servants think and work. Strong leadership, political support, and ongoing training are needed to overcome resistance and improve both the efficiency and effectiveness of public administration (Horta, 2021). Overall, *Estratégia e Gestão de Pessoas em Angola* offers practical recommendations for leaders in Angola to adapt their approaches within a rapidly changing environment, outlining that genuine leadership depends on strategic thinking, inclusion, and the ability to place the right people in the right positions to strengthen organisations (Horta, 2020).

Local leadership book		
Title	*Estratégia e Gestão de Pessoas em Angola*	ESTRATÉGIA E GESTÃO DE PESSOAS EM ANGOLA
Author	Edson Maurício Horta	
Publisher	Mayamba	
Year	2020	
ISBN	9789897612398	

Angolan leadership YouTube review

This section reviews a video featuring host Helder Filipe and guest Dr. Pedro Félix Manuel Zola, who are both drawing upon their direct experience of leadership within the Angolan organisational context. Filipe presents himself as a mentor focused on mindset and personal development, whilst Dr. Zola, vice-director of Population Services International (PSI Angola), brings substantial organisational leadership experience within Angola to the mix (Helder, 2025, 3:20). His rise from junior commercial assistant to executive illustrates a leadership trajectory shaped by practical exposure to Angolan workplace structures and expectations. The discussion explores leadership in Angola as a mindset that is centred on communication, humility, and service, rather than merely holding authority (Helder, 2025, 14:10). Zola underscores mentorship, perseverance, and self-improvement as crucial skills for navigating the Angolan business environment, noting that upward mobility often requires initiative and resilience (Helder, 2025, 6:45). He proceeds to define leadership in Angola as corresponding to the ability to communicate effectively, inspire others, and act with integrity, emphasising that self-leadership, managing one's own decisions, emotions, and actions is foundational within the Angolan context (Helder, 2025, 33:48). Both speakers advocate for a shift from self-serving leadership towards leadership approaches that prioritise service to others, noting positive developments in recent years particularly within Angola's private sector (Helder, 2025, 50:02; 1:33:57). The second video features Ágata Rosa Santos, an Angolan entrepreneur with over twenty years of experience in marketing, corporate management, and social responsibility. In this video, Santos stresses the importance of a people-focused leadership approach within the Angolan context, encouraging leaders in the country to recognise and develop employees' strengths whilst providing them with honest guidance. As they put it: *"Better people make better companies"* (Ágata, 2025, 34:06). Ethics and integrity are central to this endeavour; she draws from her father's example, insisting that all employees must be treated with professional respect within Angolan organisations (Ágata, 2025, 36:54). Adaptability and resilience are other key traits in Angola's leadership context. Santos shares how she successfully tackled unfamiliar roles, such as starting a factory without prior technical knowledge, demonstrating the importance of courage and flexibility in the process (Ágata, 2025, 58:07). She integrates social responsibility into her leadership approach by supporting community projects that empower local populations, illustrating how leadership in Angola can extend beyond organisational success to also generate societal impact (Ágata, 2025, 46:23).Viewed together, these discussions reveal that leadership in Angola is defined less by titles and more by mindset, ethical conduct, personal growth, and the ability to empower others.

Understanding hierarchy in Angola

Hierarchy in Angola is deeply rooted in both precolonial traditions and the legacy of colonial rule, resulting in a complex structure that connects customary authority with modern institutions. Traditional figures such as *sobas* and *régulos* continue to play influential roles in local governance, mediating between communities and the state, particularly in matters concerning land, justice, and conflict resolution (Aragão et al., 2025). Their authority is grounded not in bureaucratic command but rather in kinship, reciprocity, and moral legitimacy. Leadership within these systems is both paternalistic and relational, based on a moral obligation to preserve social harmony and collective well-being rather than on formal power. In terms of decision-making, leaders ordinarily confer with a select group of reliable advisors. Moreover, since it may be seen as disrespectful to authority, open disagreement or public criticism is uncommon within Angolan organisations (Vilakati, 2021). As a result, subordinates frequently express their opinions in an indirect manner using cautious language. This dynamic fosters an atmosphere in which loyalty and hierarchy are essential, and where deference is shown through discretion and obedience (Hofstede Insights, 2024). Cunha et al.(2016) argue that the country's leadership culture reflects ambidextrous dynamics, balancing the preservation of authority with the need for participation and innovation. This duality is deeply embedded within Angolan workplaces, where respect for hierarchy coexists with an emerging preference for more collaborative practices. One of our interviewees, Dr. Rosa Lutete Geremias, emphasised that hierarchy varies across regions and social settings. She explained that in the northern provinces, leadership remains conservative and strongly tied to age and social status, whereas in Luanda and other urban areas, a younger and more cosmopolitan generation of leaders promotes greater openness and inclusion (Geremias, 24 October 2025). Furthermore, she informed us that, despite these regional differences, many Angolan leaders continue to rely on transactional or aversive approaches, reflecting enduring patriarchal and centralised traditions (Geremias, 24 October 2025). Such models typically privilege control and compliance over dialogue and development. However, a growing awareness of the benefits of human-centred leadership is gradually beginning to challenge these patterns, as empathy and emotional intelligence become increasingly valued in management practice in Angola (Chimbunde & Neneh, 2024; Cunha et al., 2016). Indeed, Geremias explicated that leaders who succeed in combining authority with empathy are able to maintain hierarchical respect whilst, simulatenously, fostering inclusion (24 October, 2025). Silva et al.'s (2015) research supports this evolution by demonstrating that Angolan organisations operate within a collectivist and high-context communication environment. Respect for elders and authority figures remains fundamental, and decisions are frequently made through consultation within hierarchical structures. Managers must therefore exercise sensitivity, insofar as feedback and disagreement are often perceived as personal rather than procedural. The ability to navigate such dynamics requires emotional tact and an understanding of cultural expectations. Leaders who achieve this balance can foster trust and cohesion, which are essential for effective performance in a collectivist setting (Silva et al., 2015). Chimbunde and Neneh (2024) demonstrate that leadership styles significantly affect employees' motivation and organisational commitment. Leaders who combine authority with psychological support encourage stronger loyalty and performance amongst staff. Conversely, Moura et al. (2024) find that overly authoritarian leadership erodes motivation and trust, particularly in Angolan organisations transitioning towards more participatory models. Geremias noted that leaders must be sensitive to the cultural expectation of hierarchical respect, whilst, simultaneously, encouraging constructive participation, a balance that is crucial for sustaining effective organisations (Geremias, 24 October 2025). Gender also remains a defining aspect of hierarchical relations. Despite policy efforts to increase women's representation, Geremias argued that access to authority often results from administrative enforcement rather than cultural acceptance. Leadership remains largely male-dominated, with women leaders frequently encountering resistance rooted in traditional gender norms. Nevertheless, Geremias observed that their empathetic and relational approach is gradually influencing perceptions of authority, suggesting that Angola's hierarchical system is evolving towards greater balance and inclusivity (Geremias, 24 October 2025). In conclusion, hierarchy in Angola embodies a synthesis of traditional authority, colonial bureaucracy, and emerging participatory leadership. The persistence of relational values such as empathy, respect, and loyalty ensures that leadership remains grounded in human connection. Yet, as education, gender equality, and globalisation continue to transform the organisational landscape, Angolan hierarchies are becoming more flexible and inclusive. The future lies in leaders who can integrate the wisdom of tradition with the ethical and empathetic demands of a modern society.

How Angolans achieve leadership empathy

Angolan business leadership practices are deeply influenced by a collective orientation, where respect, loyalty, and social harmony are of paramount importance. According to Aragão et al. (2025), the legacy of customary authority continues to influence leadership behaviour even within contemporary organisations. Traditional leaders such as *sobas* and *régulos* (local chiefs) have historically governed through personal relationships, reciprocity, and moral responsibility rather than rigid authority. This relational model persists today and informs the way Angolan managers interpret empathy as an essential component of effective leadership (Aragão et al., 2025). Empathy within Angolan organisations is often expressed through paternalistic concern and interpersonal care, with managers viewing employees not merely as subordinates but rather as extended members of a professional family (Silva et al., 2015). Research indicates that successful Angolan leaders demonstrate ambidextrous capabilities, namely the fact that they must balance task orientation with human sensitivity, which allows them to integrate empathy into decision-making without compromising authority or performance (Cunha et al., 2016). For instance, Dr. Geremias, explained that Angolan managers often hold private consultations with employees to discuss challenges or mistakes, offering guidance and support, whilst, simultaneously, maintaining formal authority. Leaders who show understanding, patience, and flexibility in this way are therefore more likely to inspire commitment and cooperation, particularly in hierarchical environments where power distance remains high (Geremias, 24 October 2025; Silva et al., 2015). Leaders who exhibit compassion and emotional awareness foster higher organisational commitment and motivation amongst employees (Chimbunde & Neneh, 2024). Empathy enables leaders to identify emotional needs, manage stress within teams, and promote a sense of belonging. Conversely, aversive and toxic leadership undermines trust and intrinsic motivation, which underscores how decisive empathy is in building healthy leadership cultures (Moura et al., 2024). However, Dr. Geremias also stated that empathy can be constrained by hierarchical norms, insofar as younger or female managers may feel less authorised to express emotional openness, and that these dynamics are reinforced by structural and cultural barriers (24 October, 2025; Horta, 2021). Silva et al. (2015) emphasise that communication in Angola is predominantly high-context, which means that empathy is conveyed more through tone, gesture, and attentiveness than through direct verbal feedback. Consequently, empathetic leaders are those who can interpret unspoken cues, recognise collective emotions, and respond in ways that preserve dignity and respect. The emphasis on community, rather than individuality, requires leaders to understand the emotional climate of their teams and maintain balance between authority and care (Silva et al., 2015). Empathy is also emerging as a strategic asset within the context of Angola's evolving business environment. As globalisation and digitalisation introduce new organisational models, empathetic leadership helps bridge generational and cultural gaps within the workforce. Younger professionals, particularly in urban areas such as Luanda, increasingly value inclusive and participatory forms of management. This generational shift encourages leaders to adopt a more consultative and human-centred style, integrating traditional respect for hierarchy with modern expectations of equality and collaboration (Rego & Lopes, 2023). Despite this aforementioned progress, several barriers to empathetic leadership remain in Angola. First, the persistence of patriarchal norms limits women's participation in decision-making, whilst empathy is sometimes perceived as a sign of weakness within male-dominated environments. Dr. Geremias stated that whilst women leaders often excel in relational and empathetic skills, they still face structural and cultural resistance that undermines their authority. Overcoming these challenges requires both organisational reform and cultural evolution, ensuring that empathy is recognised as a form of strength rather than vulnerability (24 October, 2025). In conclusion, leadership empathy in Angola emerges out of a unique synthesis of cultural heritage, social values, and organisational adaptation. It is achieved not through imported management models but through an evolving reinterpretation of traditional ethics within modern contexts. Angolan leaders achieve empathy by combining paternalistic care with professional integrity, listening with authority, and structure with compassion. As the country continues to modernise, empathy represents more than an interpersonal skill; rather, it symbolises a bridge between the nation's collective identity and its aspirations for equitable and humane leadership.

The Bahamas

Karsyn Keetch, Sepehr Abdoli, Deandre Burnet, Fahim Faqiri & Luca Junge

Situated in the tropical Western Atlantic, the Bahamas consists of over seven hundred islands and cays in total. Indeed, as a result of its subtropical climate and geology, it is considered to be one of the most distinctive regions in the Caribbean (Buchan, 2000). Besides its many beaches, Bahamian culture is characterised by rich customs and traditions, such as, for example, the *Junkanoo*, which is an annual street parade with vibrant costumes, music, and dancing that influence the social identity of many Bahamians (Greenidge, 2009; Grand Bahama Museum, 2025). Tourism continues to be the main driver of the Bahamian economy, accounting for approximately 60 percent of its GDP, in conjunction with offshore finances and fisheries (Thomas, 2017; Statista, 2024). Nassau operates as the financial centre of the Bahamas, whilst its relative proximity to the United States strengthens the nation's bonds with the outside world. At the same time, its dependence on external markets threatens the country's chances of surviving global economic recession or environmental degradation. In response, both business and political leaders have been actively striving to strike the requisite balance between pursuing economic opportunities and ensuring sustainability (Wright et al., 2018). Bahamian business leadership is heterogeneous in nature. On the one hand, the University of the Bahamas seeks to foster broader leadership competencies and encourage future leaders to think beyond traditional national parameters (Tooms, 2010). On the other hand, within the business sector, research demonstrates that transformational leadership, particularly within the tourist industry, promotes greater employee satisfaction and higher service quality, thereby underlining people-centred practices in a service-based economy (Gooden & Preziosi, 2004). The Bahamas is also undergoing digital transition, with the increasing internet and mobile usage reshaping social, economic, and political engagement (Kemp, 2025). Leaders are experiencing a double burden, therefore: the need to sustain and benefit from international connectivity whilst protecting their unique national Bahamian culture. The following chapter proceeds to unpack the underlying processes of business leadership styles and practices in Bahamians, utilising both primary and secondary data collected from experts and professionals in The Bahamas.

How Bahamians characterise leaders?

In the Bahamas, leadership is best described through personal character, involvement in the wider community, and trustworthiness. Research on Caribbean leadership has demonstrated that Bahamians prefer leaders who are fair, inspirational, and people-oriented over those who command strict authority or exercise transactional leadership styles (Mujtaba, 2010). In this respect, leaders are expected to set an example for those they lead by operating in a moral and ethical manner. These attributes are highly valued in The Bahamas, where interpersonal harmony, community, and respect for one another are basic cultural attributes (Alapo, 2017). Given that the Bahamas are small islands comprising close-knit communities, the kind of leadership that inspires and is fair to its people fits the prevailing cultural orientation regarding the importance of relationships over organisational structures. Or, phrased otherwise, most Bahamians believe that leadership is about service to the people rather than seeing it as a means to attain and wield power over others (Gooden & Preziosi, 2004). This explains why good leadership in The Bahamas is often associated with the ability to inspire others, communicate effectively, and unite people (Gooden & Preziosi, 2004). This view is reflected in the results of the CCBS Survey (2025), insofar as the respondents consistently ranked qualities such as being a good listener, eloquent speaker, consensus seeker, and powerful decision maker as being the most valued leadership traits for Bahamian leaders to possess. Moreover, the respondents also emphasised the importance of strong organisational experience, market expertise, and technical competence as key foundations for credible leadership in the country. Charisma and access to influential networks were also cited as important assets, which serves to underscore the prevailing belief that effective Bahamian leaders require both personal influence and strategic social connections in order to succeed (CCBS Survey, 2025). These preferences are also emblematic of the aforementioned close-knit nature of the islands, where reputation and personal relationships carry significant weight in the workplace and strongly influence perceptions of leadership effectiveness. According to Alapo (2017), leaders in such cultures, where family and social relationships are important, are inclined towards focusing on the well-being of the in-group and sharing responsibility (Alapo, 2017). The Bahamas also scores averagely on uncertainty avoidance according to Hofstede's cultural framework; this implies that leaders prefer clear rules but are flexible enough to accommodate change when necessary (Hofstede, 2001). This goes some way to explaining why industries such as tourism, finance, and logistics can thrive here, where leaders often must adapt to changes in the international environment. This need for adaptation is reflected in the day-to-day pace of major industries. As Mendel G. Samuel, a senior manager at Atlantis Bahamas, informed us in our interview with them, the organisational culture in The Bahamas operates *"very close to Florida and Miami"*, which is to say that there is a fast-paced rhythm and rigorous expectations that defy stereotypes of an often assumed relaxed *"island-style"* work culture (21 November, 2025). Consequently, then, Bahamian leaders appear to operate at a crossroads: on the one hand, they must uphold local traditions of personal connection, whilst, on the other hand, they must meet and maintain high standards, particularly within large organisations influenced by US business models. This confirms that Bahamian work culture is shaped as much by its geopolitical proximity to the US as by local social values. With respect to the latter, respect is very important in the Bahamas, and leaders realise it by inclusive decision-making, concern for workers' welfare, and engaging in polite, open communication—all attributes of the nation's relationship-oriented and collectivist culture (Greenidge, 2009; CCBS Survey, 2025). For example, in our interview with them, Dr. Jason Styles underscored a critical pillar that defines Bahamian leadership, namely the commitment to being accessible and listening to people, along with the capability to make firm decisions (Styles, 19 November 2025). This serves to illustrate the importance of consulting with staff whilst, simultaneously, balancing authority and responsibility. Further support for this comes from the CBS Survey (2025), where the respondents reported that qualities such as being a good listener, fostering inclusion, and attending to employee welfare are amongst the most valued traits for Bahamian leaders (CCBS Survey, 2025). These examples demonstrate that respect in Bahamian leadership is not merely procedural but deeply relational, reflecting a culture in which interpersonal harmony and collective responsibility guide organisational behaviour. Leadership based on respect and cooperation is valued particularly in the Bahamas because it furthers social cohesion in a small, closely knit society where good relations with others are important (Greenidge, 2009).

Survey results and what local respondents say

In order to gain insight into the prevailing leadership skills and practices of Bahamian leaders, as well as the organisational culture and level of gender (in)equality in the country, the CCBS Survey was administered to C-level leaders. This allowed us to gain empirical insights from the extensive knowledge and experience of the Bahamian business leaders who participated. The most significant results emerging from the survey are summarized in turn below. The first significant finding is the emphasis on employee well-being. All of the respondents were in agreement over the fact that managers should actively support the personal welfare of their staff, which, as noted by our interviewee, is reflective of a relational leadership style grounded in interpersonal trust (Styles (19 November, 2025). Dalton Forbes, a consultant and trainer, noted that Bahamian leaders *"prioritise maintaining respectful and supportive relationships within their teams"* (CCBS Survey, 2025). Secondly, decision-making emerged as a key theme in the data. Specifically, the respondents reported that Bahamian managers typically stand by their decisions and rarely reverse them, with missed deadlines being taken seriously and often viewed as failure (CCBS Survey, 2025). An Aviation Planning Manager explained that because Bahamian leadership is shaped by political traditions *"where decisiveness and authority matter greatly,"* firmness and clarity remain key traits (CCBS Survey, 2025). Third, communication in Bahamian workplaces tends to be locate somewhere in between a direct and indirect approach. This is evidenced by the fact that public confrontation of subordinates in meetings was deemed to be uncommon, whilst criticism or corrective feedback was said to be generally delivered in private, thus reflecting a cultural preference for maintaining harmony and respect within the team (CCBS Survey, 2025). Fourth, hierarchy and organisational structure were perceived as being flexible. For example, as one Higher Education professional informed us: influence in Bahamian organisations often flows through personal relationships and social networks, rather than strictly following formal chains of command (CCBS Survey, 2025). There were varying perspectives on the level of hierarchy within Bahamian organisations: some respondents felt leaders should be addressed by their title, whilst others indicated that first-name communication is acceptable. Privileges such as separate offices or transportation also differed across sectors, suggesting that expectations are context-dependent (CCBS Survey, 2025). Finally, the respondents consistently emphasised the specific combination of skills and personal qualities that are required for effective leadership in the Bahamas, namely organisational experience, market expertise, listening skills, eloquence, decisiveness, charisma, and access to networks, reflecting a broad and multifaceted understanding of leadership (CCBS Survey, 2025). Overall, the findings depict Bahamian leadership as relational, decisive, and shaped by both cultural traditions and contemporary expectations.

Local Leadership Analysis

Dr. Jason Styles: a Bahamian leadership scholar
Dr. Jason Styles currently serves as Chair of the School of Business at the University of The Bahamas. His background spans leadership, human resource development, and over a decade of teaching and administrative experience. At the beginning of the interview, whilst discussing the realities of leading within a

Bahamian institution, the expert (19 November, 2025) explained that leadership on the islands is deeply relational in nature. In his words, *"leaders here strive to balance professional respect with personal connection,"* which reflects the small-community nature of Bahamian workplaces, where people often know one another outside the job. Working in a university setting, he tries to approach leadership with consultation and openness. Dr. Styles described surrounding himself with colleagues who have more institutional experience, saying he listens carefully to their advice before deciding on major changes. Still, as he noted, there are moments when firm decisions are required to meet policy and accreditation standards: *"Sometimes leadership has to act, and everyone has to move with it."* This balancing act, cooperation paired with responsibility, is a recurring theme in his experience. Styles described Bahamas as having a workplace culture that respects hierarchy, but not in an overly rigid manner. For example, whilst titles may matter to some, others are more relaxed about this and address leaders by their first names (19 November 2025). He proceeded to explain that informal influence, personal relationships, and social trust often shape decisions alongside formal rank. He acknowledged that this dynamic can occasionally lead to challenges such as cliques or perceptions of favouritism, especially within a close-knit society in which everyone is connected to someone who *"knows somebody."* A major priority for Styles is creating a climate of inclusion and mutual respect. He provided simple but telling examples—such as organising food for faculty meetings across different islands—to ensure staff feel recognised: *"I want people to feel part of the success."* This relational and supportive approach aligns with broader cultural expectations that Bahamian leaders must maintain cooperation with others, offer guidance privately, and show care towards their teams. When considering the future of leadership in The Bahamas, Styles reported that he believes that expectations are shifting. Younger generations, particularly Millennials and Gen Z, want transparency and evidence behind decision-making. As he put it, *"They will Google you... they will fact-check everything."* Whilst this can create pressure, he views it as an opportunity for improvement because it encourages leaders to stay informed, reflective, and open towards new ideas. Taken together, Dr. Styles' reflections present Bahamian leadership as practical, people-focused, and still evolving. Authority remains important, but so does approachability. Leaders are expected not only to manage performance but also to build trust and support their communities. For Styles, the heart of leadership lies in relationships—understanding others, communicating honestly, and helping the group progress together (Styles, 19 November 2025).

Bahamian Leadership Social Media Review
Social media also increasingly is fertile ground for collecting data on business leadership, including Bahamian business leadership. Contemporary Bahamian perspectives on leadership underscore themes of capacity-building, service, purpose and collective empowerment. Executive coach Amad Rashad Thompson frequently emphasises leadership as a discipline rooted in personal capacity rather than overcommitment. In several LinkedIn posts, Thompson (2025a) argues that many emerging Bahamian leaders stagnate because they take on excessive operational tasks, positioning themselves as *"the glue"*, rather than developing the strategic space required for promotion. Conversely, he frames effective Bahamian leadership as centring on the ability to delegate, set boundaries and prioritise thinking over doing. In a second post, reflecting on a national panel discussion, he stresses that the Bahamas *"can no longer afford incremental change"* and that the country instead requires leaders with the courage to innovate and build a future-ready workforce (Thompson, 2025b). A more spiritual and values-driven lens is offered by Marlane Knowles, who associates leadership in the Bahamas with purpose, clarity and inner steadiness. Her posts frame strong Bahamian leaders as individuals who move with intention and embody confidence, peace and conviction (Knowles, 2025). Although devotional in tone, her message aligns with an emerging cultural preference for leadership grounded in personal integrity and emotional resilience. Leadership coach Patrice G. Taylor promotes a servant-leadership approach within the Bahamian context. In a widely shared LinkedIn video, Taylor (2025) insists that leadership success in the Bahamas is measured through the growth of one's team. She argues that Bahamian leaders must therefore mentor individuals *"from where they are"* and foster hope regarding where they can be, reinforcing a people-first leadership ethic. Finally, business leader Sir Franklyn Wilson reflects on Bahamian leadership through the historical legacy of economic empowerment. Specifically, Wilson (2023) underscores how collective discipline, cooperation and intentionality enabled the Sunshine Boys to reshape national economic participation. His perspective underscores a longstanding Bahamian belief in leadership as a communal, purpose-driven endeavour. The unifying idea across these varied social media perspectives is clear. Contemporary Bahamian leadership is increasingly viewed as a practice of empowering others, driven by strategic vision, personal integrity, and an unwavering commitment to national progress.

In-country leadership bestseller
Becoming a Leader by Dr. Myles Munroe is one of the most influential Bahamian books on leadership. Munroe was a Bahamian pastor, orator and leadership expert who wrote for people in small nations who wanted to lead but felt limited

by history or foreign models (Munroe, 2009). He argues that people fail to lead because they never discover purpose. He writes, "*There is leadership potential in every person*" (Munroe, 2009, p. 13). Leadership starts when a person understands why they were born. Munroe explains Bahamian leadership in practical terms and does not focus on corporate titles. Rather, he describes leadership as an influence that comes from purpose, vision and character. He states that "*leaders are ordinary people who accept or are placed under extraordinary circumstances*" and that those circumstances reveal their potential (Munroe, 2009, p. 19). This is relevant for The Bahamian context, where many people work in tourism, church, or public service and still want to build something of their own. Munroe emphasises that you do not need anyone's permission; you can lead right where you are. He lays out a clear path for doing so: begin by discovering yourself, then capture your vision, and commit to the principles and values that will guide your journey. Fourth, empower others. Fifth, manage priorities and prepare successors (Munroe, 2009). Each part is written in simple language. He explains that without vision people copy others, but with vision they guide others. Additionally, he also links discipline to purpose. If you know what you are called to do, then you remove activities that do not serve that calling. Munroe often notes that people from former colonies were trained to take orders, rather than set direction, which creates a sense of dependency (Munroe, 2009). This applies to the Bahamian context as the book challenges current and future Bahamian leaders to shift from waiting for external direction to producing local leaders. It also links leadership to moral and spiritual responsibility. Leaders should serve God and people, and model what they teach. A leader should train the next leader, so the community does not lose progress. *Becoming a Leader* is well suited to the Bahamian context because it connects purpose, faith, and national development through a local perspective.

Local leadership book	
Title	*Becoming a Leader*
Subtitle	How to Develop and Release Your Unique Gifts
Author	Myles Munroe
Publisher	Whitaker House
Year	2009
ISBN	9781629119212

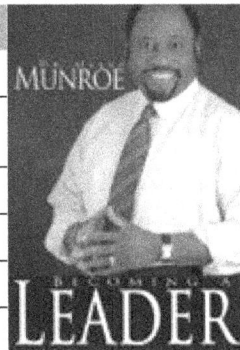

Bahamas leadership YouTube review

Bahamian leadership is not a distant concept limited to the boardroom; rather, it is an existential practice that is deeply interwoven with national development and community well-being. The ideas from local leaders across a diverse range of sectors shows the constant refrain for an inclusive leadership that looks ahead and is resilient. The key message relates to leadership as the agent for the development of the nation and its region. This was powerfully articulated by Gravette Brown, the Chief Innovation Officer at ALIV Bahamas at that time, who stated that leadership in the Bahamas is most effective when *"it is getting different viewpoints from all segments of society"* (Brown, 2022, 0:11). This call for inclusivity is echoed by Michaella Lockhart of the Caribbean Woman in Leadership (CIWiL) during her address at a Bahamian Mock Parliament session. This event was part of the "She Leads" initiative, a program designed by CIWiL to empower and prepare young women for the leadership sector in the Bahamas. In this context, Lockhart's statement that leaders should put forth *"an intentional focus on resolving the issues that stifle the progress of our nation and our people"* (Lockhart, 2025, 4:30), carries significant weight, framing leadership in the Bahamas as a deliberate practice to better the future generation of business leaders. Almost running parallel to the message above is the theme of creating opportunity and fostering innovation through business and political leadership. Prime Minister Davis has insisted that when it comes to *"building a more inclusive economy for all Bahamians, it means creating opportunities and expanding opportunities,"* which in the video is defined as *"opening doors for everyone and building ladders to success"* (Davis, 2025, 0:01). This vision is put to work through voices such as Glacy Brooks, who insisted that economic development is *"the pathway to opportunity, equity, and lasting prosperity."* She called for practical systems to support this: *"we must establish incubators and mentorship programmes where seasoned business leaders can mentor the next generation"* (Brooks, 2025, 36:20 & 38:51). This underscores a preference for a leadership style in the Bahamas that is not merely transactional but rather developmental in its approach. Taken together, these perspectives portray a nuanced picture of Bahamian leadership that is purposeful, empathetic, and committed towards creating a sustainable future of prosperity and resiliency for its citizens.

Understanding hierarchy in the Bahamas

Hierarchy in the Bahamas is shaped by the country's strong emphasis on relationships, community values, and interpersonal respect. Whilst formal ranks exist in organisations, such as, for example, government offices, schools, and large companies, Bahamian workplace culture generally remains deeply influenced by collectivist traditions that prioritise teamwork, harmony, and personal connection (Mujtaba, 2010; Alapo, 2017). As a result, although hierarchical structures provide clarity and order, leadership in the Bahamas is generally less top-down compared to many other countries. Similar to other relationship-oriented cultures, Bahamian organisations recognise formal authority, yet leaders are expected to remain approachable and engaged with their teams. This was corroborated by one of our interviewees, who apropos the leadership of Atlantis President Audrey Oswell, described her as *"very open"* and stating that *"she walks around a lot and speaks openly to no matter who at what level"* (Samuel, 21 November 2025). This behaviour emphasises the Bahamian leadership ideal in which formal position is balanced by deliberate engagement, reinforcing that authority is strengthened by accessibility. The use of titles such as "Mr.", "Mrs.", "Dean", or "Director" is also common and considered to be respectful (Styles, 2022; CCBS Survey, 2015–2020). However, our interview and survey data suggests that are is a degree of flexibility regarding this, insofar as some employees prefer formal addresses, whilst others are comfortable using first names. This reflects a hybrid approach in which hierarchy coexists with accessibility, depending on the organisation, sector, and individual preferences (CCBS Survey, 2025). This flexibility also extends to the preferred communication styles of Bahamian leaders. Samuel noted in our interview with him that *"some people will be indirect, [whilst] some will be direct"*, a variation he attributes to individual emotional intelligence, education and hierarchical position rather than being a fixed cultural rule per se (21 November, 2025). This observation underscores that Bahamian communication norms cannot be essentialised but rather vary according to role, status and interpersonal maturity, which leaders must adapt to. Decision-making practices within Bahamian organisations also serve to illustrate this balance. For instance, whilst leaders ultimately have responsibility over final decision-making, they rarely do so without seeking input, listening to different perspectives, and encouraging participation before settling on a course of action (Gooden & Preziosi, 2004). Consequently, meetings often begin with informal conversation, an essential step in building trust and social cohesion—and decisions may take longer because multiple voices are welcomed into the process. Scholars describe this as a "clan" or participation-based approach, which is rooted in the Bahamas' close-knit social environment and extended family networks (Gooden & Preziosi, 2004; Jones, 2023). Interview insights further illustrate how Bahamian hierarchy operates in practice. According to Dr. Jason Styles, effective leaders must balance authority with approachability. As he noted: *"I am not here to be on top of you or micromanage. I am here to be the person by your side to make sure we get to where we need to be"* (Styles, 19 November 2025). This helps explain why public confrontation is rare, and feedback is typically offered privately to maintain harmony and interpersonal respect—an approach strongly reflected in the CCBS Survey (2025) results. Because organisations are often *"heterarchical,"* this means that influence flows through relationships and networks rather than strictly formal hierarchical lines (Styles, 19 November 2025; CCBS Survey, 2025). Leaders therefore need to combine traditional management skills such as decisiveness and organisational knowledge with the ability to read social dynamics and build consensus. Privileges associated with leadership, such as private offices, transportation, or status markers, vary widely across industries, underscoring that leadership expectations in the Bahamas depend as much on context as on formal rank. With respect to gender equality, it is progressing but remains a work in progress, with leaders slowly widening pathways for women in senior roles (Styles, 19 November 2025; Styles, Knowles, & Ebron, 2024). Overall, hierarchy in the Bahamas provides necessary organisational structure, but authority alone does not determine effective leadership there. Leaders who blend formal rank with relational skills, empathy, fairness, and accessibility hold the greatest influence. By maintaining respect, encouraging participation, and fostering trust, they help create an organisational culture that is both structured and collaborative. In short, Bahamian leadership blends authority with connection, reflecting national values of consensus, community, and mutual respect (Styles & Dean, 2024; Toby, 2025).

How Bahamians achieve leadership empathy

Empathy in Bahamian leadership is deeply shaped by the nation's communal and relationship-oriented culture (Styles, 19 November 2025). Close-knit communities, extended families, and shared moral values have long fostered a sense of care and attentiveness to others (Bethel, 2002). The collectivist orientation of Bahamian society places a profound emphasis on group cohesion and emotional awareness, traits that naturally support the development of leaders who are attuned to the feelings and needs of their teams (Saunders, 1992). Research into organisational culture shows that Bahamian leaders often adopt relational approaches, focusing on listening carefully, showing respect, and offering personalised support to those around them (Mujtaba, 2010). The CCBS Survey (2025) also provides clear evidence that Bahamian leaders actively prioritise the welfare of their teams. Dr. Jason Styles also emphasised the importance of this relational aspect in our interview with him: *"You cannot lead people you do not know... I respect each individual because you never know who is going to be your boss one day "*(19

November, 2025). This balance serves to illustrate how empathy in Bahamian leadership is not just a personal trait, but rather a deliberate approach that is deeply embedded in everyday practice. Communication in Bahamian workplaces also reflects this focus on empathy. For example, as aforementioned, the results of the CCBS Survey (2025) emphasise that the prevailing norm in Bahamian leadership is to deliver feedback privately to employees rather than publicly in meetings. Given the small-island context, leaders often know their employees outside work. Therefore, informal interactions, such as, for example, asking employees about their family or greeting colleagues personally, are part of how Bahamian leaders build trust within their organisations. Similarly, in our interview with them, Mendel G. Samuel noted that leaders often check in on employees' well-being personally, asking about family or personal matters in order to maintain trust and rapport (Samuel, 21 November 2025). As Lewis (2005) observes in relationship-centred cultures, *"trust precedes business,"* a principle that clearly guides Bahamian leadership practices. Inclusive decision-making is another important way through which empathy is expressed. Indeed. Dr. Styles informed us in our interview with him that inclusivity is central to the Bahamian leadership model. Styles emphasised that he involves staff in decision-making, creating opportunities for team engagement, and ensuring faculty across different islands feel recognised and valued (Styles, 19 November 2025). This is not just Styles' personal practice, however, Greenridge (2009) argued that respect is very important in the Bahamas, and one of the main ways through which leaders realise it is by inclusive decision-making, showing concern for workers' welfare, and engaging in polite, open communication—all attributes of the nation's relationship-oriented and collectivist culture (Greenidge, 2009). This demonstrates that empathetic leadership in the Bahamas combines attentiveness to people with the responsibility of guiding teams effectively. Flexibility and emotional awareness further define empathetic leadership in Bahamian contexts. Specifically, leaders must adjust their approach according to the situation, blending authority with friendliness to maintain the requisite harmony and support (Bowe, 2017; CCBS Survey, 2025). Styles illustrated this by describing his own leadership approach: *"I want to hear what people think because their perspectives matter, but sometimes I also need to make a decision. It is about being firm, yet fair"* (19 November, 2025). This illustrates that empathy in Bahamian leadership is both relational and practical: it shapes communication, decision-making, and team cohesion, reflecting a leadership style that is deeply attuned to the values and social networks of Bahamian culture.

Estonia

*Ghita Belhaj, Uma Bhattacharya, Nadine Blijham, Alejandro Hernández Arbizú,
Karmen Hiis & Su Kwan Jung*

Despite being one of the smallest countries in Europe, Estonia has become a
global exemplar of digital transformation, innovation, and adaptive governance
(Drechsler, 2018). This rapid modernisation has positioned the country far beyond
its geographic size. With a population of 1.37 million, Estonia's positioning
between Northern and Eastern Europe has left deep historical and cultural
imprints, which is expressed in both traditional and progressive mindsets and
reflected in the coexistence of native Estonians and Russians. Indeed, many
Russian speakers migrated to Tallinn and the industrial towns of North-East
Estonia during the Soviet era (Xu et al., 2025). After regaining its independence,
the country rapidly undertook reforms, including privatisation and flat-rate
taxation, which further separated it from Russian influence and led to its
integration into Western institutions (Lawrence, 2025), bringing sustained
economic growth in recent years (International Monetary Fund, 2021).

Today, the country has the highest number of start-ups and unicorns per capita in
Europe and is the home of internationally renowned businesses like Skype and
Bolt, which has led to both substantial foreign investment and pluralistic
organisational cultures. Whilst the Soviet legacy emphasised hierarchy and
systematic control, Nordic influences promote equality and organisational trust
within contemporary Estonian organisations (Kalmus, 2007). Specific values,
expressed via proverbs like *"Rääkimine hõbe, vaikimine kuld"* (Speech is silver,
silence is gold), which emphasises the value of silence, reflects a culturally
embedded preference for restrained, introspective, and calm communication
(Rannut, 2023). In light of the country's coexisting yet contrasting influences,
the following chapter aims to explore how business leadership is understood and
practiced in Estonia by drawing on academic research as well as original empirical
data from a cross-cultural survey and an interview with an Estonian leadership
scholar.

How Estonians characterise leaders?

Estonia's leadership culture is undergoing a profound shift that is strongly influenced by its culture and history. During the rule of the Soviet Union, leaders practiced their power in a directive and hierarchical manner, where authority was linked to control, bureaucracy, and political loyalty. Following the restoration of its independence in 1991, the country transitioned towards a liberal market economic system, a movement which helped to spearhead the introduction of new leadership approaches within Estonia as well as redefining economic structures, national ownership, and the organisation of labour in the country (Tuulik & Alas, 2010). Mullamaa (2024) posits that this historical backdrop goes some way to explaining why contemporary Estonian business leadership tends to favour trust and low hierarchical imbalance. This is because the collectivist ideology during the Soviet era created a national distrust of collective structures (Jaakson, personal communication, 17 November 2025). Consequently, Tuulik and Alas (2010) argue, contemporary Estonian leadership is characterised by shared responsibility and participation. These people-oriented traits are increasingly reflected through an emphasis on emotional awareness and recognition of individuals' skills within organisations. By setting clearly defined goals, leaders demonstrate confidence in their employees' ability to act independently (Tuulik & Alas, 2010; Tuulik et al., 2013). As this emerging leadership style becomes more entrenched within Estonian organisations, Estonian leaders are increasingly expected to align employees' tasks with their talent, whilst, simultaneously, cultivating an environment of open communication within teams (Tuulik & Alas, 2010; Tuulik et al., 2013). This was also corroborated by the results of the CCBS Survey (2025), insofar as the respondents emphasised how much more important employee competence is than formal positions, stating that *"leadership in Estonia is democratic,"* employee input is valued, and *"people from all ranks are invited to participate in decision-making".* Furthermore, the respondents described Estonia's organisational culture as *"very flat and [characterised by] informal relationships, based on respect,"* in which *"very direct and open speech is allowed from employees towards managers"* (CCBS Survey, 2025). The respondents also underscored that leaders should communicate in a *"Plain and direct manner"* and balance authority and independence by providing clarity without micromanaging those they lead, as evidenced by the following extract: *"[managers should] grant teams considerable autonomy"* (CCBS Survey, 2025). Because of this directness, the common approach amongst leaders is straightforward communication via clear and transparent speech and actions (CCBS Survey, 2025). Mullamaa's (2024) qualitative findings lend further support to our own survey findings by showing that Estonians value both competence and hierarchy in their leaders. At the same time, independence remains relevant, insofar as employees are addressed directly regarding their assigned tasks and often involved in more than one departmental role (Mullamaa, 2024). Indeed, as one respondent noted, *"leaders often believe that subordinates are self-driven and want to develop themselves"* (CCBS Survey, 2025). Compared to other leadership models, Estonian business leadership is distinguished by its ability to create environments that are structured and collaborative, which, in turn, allows for innovation to thrive alongside accountability, rather than relying solely on charisma or strict forms of authority (Tuulik & Alas, 2010). At the same time, it is important to stress that the survey results also underscored that there are some important differences across organisations in Estonia. For instance, several respondents noted that Estonian companies are "less hierarchical," describing them as "very flat, with a lot of bottom-up activity, which drives companies forward" (CCBS Survey, 2025). However, other results point towards variations, with some respondents stating that *"leadership styles are very different in companies. In smaller companies, a more autocratic style is common, whilst in bigger, more advanced, or successful companies, an inclusive leadership style prevails."* Another respondent yet still observed that Estonian leadership was defined by an *"old-fashioned leadership style, lack of modern thinking, and poor offboarding practices"* (CCBS Survey, 2025). Jaakson (2024) similarly pointed out that due to history, some leaders resist the implementation of EU directives, which can prevent organisations from becoming truly flat and equal workplaces (Jaakson, personal communication, 17 November 2025). Overall, Estonian business leadership is undergoing a period of transition in which directive and hierarchical models persist alongside more democratic, competent, and trust-based leadership styles. This persistent hybrid approach stems from Estonia's culture of independence and practicality, yet it also reflects a gradual shift towards more participatory and respectful workplace relationships.

Survey results and what local respondents say

In order to complement the academic literature with empirical evidence from local professionals with knowledge and expertise of Estonian business leadership, the CCBS Survey was administered to 60 senior and upper-middle managers in the country, including CEOs, founders, CTOs, managing directors, and functional heads. The most noteworthy findings emerging from the survey are discussed in turn below. The first significant finding is that leadership legitimacy in Estonia is predominantly grounded in professional competence rather than formal status, as evidenced by the fact that over 90% of the respondents identified organisational experience, market expertise, and technical competence as the main foundations of leader credibility, whereas age and appearance were rarely considered to be important (CCBS Survey, 2025), thus supporting meritocratic leadership theory (Bass & Bass, 2008). Next, there were divergent opinions with respect to the level of gender (in)equality within Estonian organisations. Whilst a clear majority (63.3%) of respondents agreed with the statement that men and women have equal access to senior leadership positions in the country, a notable minority (36.7%) were neutral on the subject or disagreed with the statement (CCBS Survey, 2025). This indicates that although equality is widely endorsed as a norm within the country, its realisation remains uneven across organisational contexts, which is consistent with Nordic–Baltic research on this issue (Eagly & Carli, 2007). The next key finding is that Estonian leadership is characterised by a remarkably low power distance. This is evidenced by the fact that all of the respondents reported that employees can address their leaders by their first name (CCBS Survey, 2025), thus indicating that formal titles play only a minor role in daily interaction and reinforcing other research findings that show Estonia's classification as a flat working culture (Hofstede, 2001; Mockaitis, 2007; Kooskora, 2008). In line with this, decision-making is perceived as relatively flexible, with more than half of the respondents disagreeing with the statement that managers are unlikely to reverse decisions once they have been made, reflecting a shift towards more adaptive, trust-based forms of leadership (Tuulik & Alas, 2010). Allied with this, communication was described as being highly direct yet largely non-confrontational, with the open-ended responses emphasising "clarity, low personal ego, informality, and efficiency" (CCBS Survey, 2025; Lewis, 2005; Rannut, 2023). At the same time, attitudes towards personal distance remain mixed, thus suggesting that respect and authority are often maintained through professional boundaries rather than emotional closeness (CCBS Survey, 2025). Finally, only 22% of the respondents reported that competition within teams is encouraged, which suggests that although performance is valued, organisations are not strongly driven by internal competitiveness. Having said that, strong moral expectations are placed on leaders to care for their people, insofar as 61% of the respondents either agreed or strongly agreed with the statement that managers should actively spend time ensuring employee well-being, whilst 22% of the respondents were somewhat supportive of this practice (CCBS Survey, 2025). Overall, the results of the CCBS Survey (2025) portray Estonian leadership as meritocratic, low in power distance, communicatively direct, and grounded in both professional competence and social responsibility.

Local leadership analysis

Krista Jaakson: an Estonian leadership scholar

Krista Jaakson is an Estonian PhD graduate in Management, Industrial Relations, and Organisational Behaviour, with almost two decades of experience as an Associate Management Professor at the University of Tartu. She teaches master's students about business strategy, negotiation, and responsible leadership, and leads an Estonian Science Foundation research grant focused on ethical organisational culture. Her research in Culture, Society, and Economics, alongside her contributions at Eesti Pank (Bank of Estonia), the Delta Management School, and the Baltic Family Firm Institute, testify to her extensive knowledge and expertise in Estonian business leadership. At the start of the interview, Jaakson (17 November, 2025) described today's Estonian leadership environment as largely risk avoidant and rigid, underscoring a cultural preference for stability and local orientation. She elaborated on this by explaining that Estonians are *"... straightforward and direct. ... like Dutchies in that sense."* (17 November, 2025), which is reflected in regular short meetings and fast, efficient communication. Once known for its openness and adaptability, Jaakson informed us that Estonia's level of wealth has made material success become a dominant measure of status that many managers fear losing. Because this change happened quite rapidly, its effects appear stronger than to comparable Western countries. This comfort with engaging in riskless activities contributes to a lack of ambition amongst leaders. As she put it: *"There are so few of the entrepreneurs who dare to say that we want to conquer the world. I mean, maybe a few companies"* (Jaakson, 17 November 2025). Jaakson continued to explain that generational differences further shape Estonia's business leadership culture. Whilst older workers are used to greater complexity and workloads, younger employees prioritise mental well-being, sometimes at the cost of productivity. Jaakson's research supports this shift, insofar as she told us that *"80% of the leaders we surveyed recently, say that the number one motivating factor for their employees is a friendly atmosphere (...) nice colleagues and social fabric."* (17 November 2025). Additional motivational factors are the company's reputation, success and pay. According to Jaakson, the most successful Estonian leaders acknowledge that employee motivation remains most important for attracting and retaining the best talent. Furthermore, she noted that responsible leadership plays a role as well: *"Almost 50%, so almost every second leader, thinks that social contribution and charity are quite important as a motivating aspect."* (Jaakson, 17 November 2025). This movement towards a more humanising leadership form is reinforced by Estonia's history. Jaakson elaborated on the fact that the Soviet influence still shapes managerial behaviour to this day, contributing to a widespread distrust of collective representation,

42

trade unions, and work councils. This perspective extends to external regulations, where many Estonian leaders resist EU directives: *"(...) I think what also comes from the previous sort of legacy is that we do not welcome these norms and directives from the European Union, which are aimed at actually promoting workplaces and making them more equal"* (17 November 2025). Approaches such as gender quotas or transparent salary ranges are often perceived as irrelevant measures in organisational practice.

Looking forward, Jaakson expects further and bigger integration of AI into systems and decision-making. However, she also stressed the rise of *"heart skills"* over *"hard skills"* amongst Northern countries, which involves asking questions like, *"How to stay in touch as a human being with your employees? How to be empathetic? How to add value beyond what AI can do?"* (Jaakson, 17 November 2025). Whilst both developments seem contradictory, together they highlight that as technology advances, the human aspect of leadership becomes ever-more important.

Estonian Social Media Review

Online discourse portrays Estonian leaders as results-driven, integrity-focused, and collaborative - a blend of traditional and modern expectations. From a more traditional perspective, Taavi Veskimägi, former CEO of Elering, links personal integrity, and accountability to effective Estonian leadership. In his column *"Hea juhtimine,"* he emphasises the importance of consistency between a leader's words, decisions, and daily behaviours, arguing that what truly matters is how a leader acts *"siis, kui keegi ei näe"* (when nobody is watching) (Veskimägi, 2022). In a later interview, he explains that one of his most significant leadership lessons in Estonia has been *"minna laskma õppimine,"* which refers to learning to let go of control, trusting others, and focusing on strategic decisions instead of micromanaging (Sarapik, 2023). Leadership coach Raimo Ülavere extends this conversation by questioning the criteria used to evaluate leaders. In both his articles and LinkedIn posts, he criticises the tendency to assess Estonian leaders primarily by visibility or image, arguing that qualities such as introspection, emotional self-control, and *"julgus ausalt rääkida"* (the courage to speak truthfully) are often overlooked despite being essential for modern leadership (Ülavere, 2022, 2025). From a more developmental angle, Ruti Einpalu (2023) stresses the importance of high-quality dialogue in leadership conversations. She argues that discussions about individual growth should be frequent, substantive, and genuinely developmental, rather than reduced to formal checklists or one-sided *"evaluation talks"* (Roots, 2023). Self-awareness and inner work are particularly central in Ivar Raav's approach to leadership in Estonia. In an interview-based article, Uusen (2025) conveys Raav's nine practical recommendations for leaders, including recognising bodily signals as meaningful information and clarifying one's personal values. In his own article, Raav (2025) further develops these ideas by introducing the concept of the *"nähtamatu vari"* (invisible shadow) within organisations, referring to the unwritten rules, unofficial power structures, and emotional climate that often shape behaviour more strongly than formal frameworks. From a contemporary, team-focused perspective, coach Jaanika Rannula portrays Estonian leaders as coaches and facilitators rather than someone who relies solely on top-down directives. Her work shows how team coaching can support organisational change by strengthening mental health, shared accountability, and collective problem-solving amongst employees (Rannula, 2021). Together with Aili Nurmeots, she describes *"coach'iv juhtimine"* as a human-centred approach that balances space for individuality with clear results. However, Rannula and Nurmeots (2024) warn that "coach-style leadership" risks becoming a mere buzzword if leaders adopt its language without changing their everyday practices of inquiry, feedback, and self-reflection. Because Estonian leaders are increasingly held accountable not only for performance but also for employee engagement and well-being, organisations place growing value on leaders' ability to mentor, engage in meaningful dialogue, and consciously shape the deeper culture of their organisations. Together, these perspectives suggest that Estonian leadership culture is evolving towards a more reflective, values-driven, and people-centred model.

In-country leadership bestseller
One of the best-selling books about Estonian leadership, called "Kuidas olla juht, keda sinu inimesed päriselt vajavad?" (How to Be the Leader Your People Really Need) was written by Jaanika Rannula and Aili Nurmeots, and functions as a comprehensive compass for various management styles and coaching practices in the country. The two co-authors are experienced coaches and trainers within Estonian organisational cultures, with their book serving as a blueprint for how to adapt management to people's needs by focusing on people-centred leadership. Their extensive research with top Estonian leaders, coaches and trainers revealed how coach-style leadership is applied and experienced within the country's organisational environment. The goal of the books is to support leaders in discovering and adjusting their inner resources, rather than describing a specific type of leadership. The authors argue that Estonian leaders stand between a traditional, control-oriented management style and a more modern, coaching approach that focuses on employees' well-being (Rannula & Nurmeots, 2023). Many leaders in Estonia continue to uphold a strong emphasis on processes and efficiency due to earlier more directive traditions. This outcome-oriented mindset

can result in excessive power imbalances, low trust, and poor communication, particularly as employees want more involvement, autonomy, and genuine recognition. Their survey data reveals that only around one-quarter of Estonian employees feel engaged at work, which is significantly lower than engagement levels in high-performing global companies. To bridge this misalignment between leaders and their teams, they promote "coach-style leadership". In this leadership style, instead of primarily giving instructions, leaders ask questions and listen actively to create shared responsibility for outcomes. Whilst coach-style leadership requires setting clear goals and maintaining accountability, it also creates trust-based relationships that acknowledge individual strengths and encourage employees to contribute to solutions. The book emphasises that in the future, Estonian leadership should combine the country's traditional strengths, such as discipline, practicality, and efficiency, with a greater emphasis on engagement and psychological needs. Leaders who embrace this approach rather than merely giving commands can ensure workplaces where employees feel genuinely valued and trusted, improving organisational performance and strengthen national competitiveness (Rannula & Nurmeots, 2023).

Local leadership book		
Title	Kuidas olla juht, keda sinu inimesed päriselt vajavad?	
Subtitle	Coach'iv juhtimine kompass	
Author	Jaanika Rannula & Aili Nurmeots	
Publisher	Äripäev	
Year	2023	
ISBN	9789916750179	

45

Estonian YouTube Review

Modern Estonian business leadership effectively combines authenticity, contextual awareness, and strong personal values, as illustrated in two YouTube interviews with Estonian leaders that will be summarised here in this section. One notable interview features Peeter Raudsepp, Director of the Estonian Institute of Economic Research, who speaks with leadership coach Toomas Soosaar during the Empowerment online seminar titled *"Juhtimine kiirete muutuste ajastul"* (Leadership in Times of Rapid Change). In this video, Raudsepp emphasises that Estonian leaders should "be themselves" instead of trying to imitate trendy role models, since there are no universal management formulae. He proceeds to discuss that each period in Estonian history and each organisation requires a different strategy for effective leadership (Raudsepp, 2025, 6:02). He goes onto describe a good Estonian leader as a true "eestvedaja" (front-runner) who genuinely believes in the organisation's goals. Such leaders can convincingly communicate these goals, inspire their colleagues, and foster joy in shared accomplishments and strong working relationships (Raudsepp, 2025, 7:50). Moreover, Estonian leaders must make decisions under time constraints and with limited information, whilst simultaneously, demonstrating that their choices are based on the best available data (Raudsepp, 2025, 10:05). Next, in an interview on the YouTube channel Framgångspodden, Alexander Pärleros speaks with Markus Villig, the Estonian founder and CEO of Bolt. Villig provides a unique perspective on leadership in Estonia, emphasising a modest and frugal style that keeps him close to his team. He highlights the importance of personally embodying Bolt's core values; for example, he still travels in economy class and expects his managers to handle company funds with the same care as they would their own (Pärleros, 2024, 3:12). When it comes to hiring, Villig prioritises diligence, intelligence and honesty, and he prefers individuals who can learn quickly. Within the small, rapidly expanding teams one sees in Estonia, having ethical workers is vital for fostering a trustworthy and co-operative environment (Pärleros, 2024, 38:42; 40:32). Furthermore, Villig asserts that for a business to be sustainable, a leader's personal motivation, whether it be for impact, status, or money. must be clearly aligned with the organisation's long-term mission (Pärleros, 2024, 41:08; 42:42). Combined, these interviews paint a picture that contemporary Estonian business leaders are expected to act as true eestvedajad (pioneers), adapt their approach based on the situation, uphold their moral principles and build ethical, productive teams.

Understanding hierarchy in Estonia

Estonian perceptions of hierarchy have been strongly influenced by the country's rapid shift from a socialist system to a liberal market economy. After the country gained its independence, foreign firms entered the market with their own management practices, whilst domestic companies tended to rely on inherited structures (Tuulik & Alas, 2010). According to Kooskora (2008), this resulted in two parallel hierarchical logics that still coexist in contemporary Estonian organisations, shaping the organisation of authority, ownership, and responsibility. Most domestically owned firms follow what Kooskora (2008) describes as a personalised, owner-centric model. Within this hierarchical structure, decision-making is highly centralised: the owner retains most authority, and managers act as directive leaders. Moreover, Tafel-Viia and Alas (2007) purport that communication in such organisations typically flows in a unidirectional manner - from top to bottom - with employees expected to support rather than influence decisions. Since development opportunities and strategic information are concentrated at the upper echelons of the organisation, professional growth is ordinarily limited to senior management, leaving lower-level employees with fewer chances to impact upon the organisation (Alas et al., 2018). Whilst this model can generate profits and enable quick decisions, research has shown that it restricts agility, innovation, and employee empowerment (Kooskora, 2008). In contradistinction to this, many foreign-owned firms in Estonia operate with a more institutional hierarchy. Whilst still top-down in nature, the structures within these particular types of organisations are characterised by clearer organisational layers, making it easier to delegate authority and responsibility from higher to lower levels (Kooskora, 2008). Jaakson connects this development to broader cultural resistance in the country towards strict authority following the Soviet era, which is epitomised by the sentiment: *"no more nomenklatura, we decide ourselves."* (personal communication, 17 November 2025). In practice, this has led Estonian leaders to blend formal structures with a work culture that values independence, competence, and shared responsibility (Mullamaa, 2024). Over time, both domestic and foreign-owned firms have increasingly adopted flatter, Western-style hierarchies. Within these organisations, there are fewer layers between employees and top management, and stakeholders are more often included in decision-making (Kooskora, 2008). The CCBS Survey (2025) strongly supports this perspective, insofar as the respondents reported that employees may address leaders by their first name, whilst almost all of the respondents disagreed with the statement that subordinates should use formal titles when speaking to managers. This suggests that, even when formal hierarchy exists, daily interactions remain informal. Within such settings, leaders are expected to motivate employees, listen to their views, and act as supporters rather than commanders (Tafel-Viia & Alas, 2007), thus representing a clear contrast to the traditional owner-centric model. Ownership structures are intricately linked to performance outcomes. Jones et al. (2005) found that shifts towards foreign or managerial ownership in Estonia are associated with higher productivity, faster growth, and stronger profitability. Foreign-owned firms outperform traditional owner-managed companies, whilst employee-owned firms may achieve short-term profitability but exhibit lower productivity and tend to contract over time. Overall, these findings suggest that Estonia's gradual shift towards institutional, manager-led, and more participatory hierarchies is fostering a more efficient and competitive economy, despite the persistence of the old owner-centric model.

How Estonians achieve leadership empathy

In Estonia, empathetic leadership extends beyond ethics and mere compliance, to instead encompass emotional understanding and inclusiveness by valuing employees' individuality, talents, and well-being (Mullamaa, 2024). The degree of empathy shown by leaders is closely tied to their cultural background (Mockaitis, 2007), which is why Mullamaa (2024) refers to *"empathetic and culture-competent leading"* (p. 12). Typically speaking, Estonian business leaders demonstrate empathy towards those that they lead through personal recognition, respect, and trust, and viewing their employees as capable individuals who deserve autonomy rather than close supervision and forms of micromanagement (Mockaitis, 2007; Mullamaa, 2024). This characterisation of Estonian business leadership was corroborated by our interviewee, Krista Jaakson, an Estonian leadership scholar, who informed us that, *"80% of the leaders we surveyed recently, say that the number one motivating factor for their employees [younger employees] is a friendly atmosphere (...) nice colleagues and social fabric"* (17 November, 2025). Similarly, in Bilgin et al.'s (2016) research, which involved interviews with Estonian leaders, two of their interviewees reported, *"I lead people by feeling them,"* whilst another noted, *"I try to consciously emphasise positive feedback, reward and recognition"* (p. 12).

Recent findings from the Eesti juhtimisvaldkonna uuring (Vadi et al., 2022) reinforce the importance of empathic leadership within Estonian organisations, insofar as the research demonstrated that Estonian leaders prioritise transparent communication, individual development, and employee welfare as core elements of effective leadership. This was also corroborated by the results of the CCBS

Survey (2025), which indicated that most of the respondents who participated believe that Estonian managers should devote time to ensuring their team members' personal well-being. Similarly, Krista Jaakson highlighted that younger employees increasingly value mental health and well-being – albeit sometimes at the cost of productivity (17 November ,2025). This is important because other research has shown that leaders who foster trust and support individuality report higher levels of team engagement and satisfaction (Vadi et al., 2022). It is important to stress here that Estonian empathy is typically calm and measured in nature, rather than being, say, emotionally expressive. In this regard, the results of the CCBS Survey (2025) point towards genuinely mixed attitudes towards personal distance between leaders and employees: whilst around two-fifths of leaders preferred to maintain professional space from their employees to preserve respect, a similar proportion disagreed with this notion (CCBS Survey, 2025). One explanation for this is that, as Lewis (2005) purports, Estonian communication is pragmatic and reserved in nature, which means that leaders ordinarily *"contact only those directly involved in a task"* and value competence over formal rank. Here, empathy is expressed less through overt emotional displays and more through culturally sensitive behaviours: respecting privacy, providing clarity and efficiency, and adapting to employees' comfort levels (Mullamaa, 2024). In conclusion, then, Estonian leaders empathise with those that they lead primarily through showing trust, being fair to them, and communicating in a considerate manner, rather than through constant visibility or emotional intensity.

Finland

*Tiia Kallio, Kevin Boom, Serkan Dural, Claudi Elberse, Mariam Jvarsheishvili,
Kristina Kovshova & Artem Nozhenko.*

Suomi (Finland), or as it is commonly referred to, *"Tuhansien järvien maa"* (the
Land of a Thousand Lakes), is situated in Northern Europe, and shares its borders
with Sweden, Norway, and Russia. The country is distinguished by its remarkable
landscapes, including approximately 188,000 lakes and extensive forests that span
much of its territory (Tikkanen, 2002). Besides its striking natural endowments,
Finland's economy is underpinned by strong constitutions, prudent fiscal policy,
and a highly skilled workforce. This combination increases the country's
competitiveness by leveraging sustained investments in research and innovation,
which, in turn, fosters digital transformation by supporting a strategic transition
towards sustainable and green growth (OECD, 2017). Although the country
underwent urbanisation and industrialisation later than its Scandinavian
neighbours, Finland has nevertheless developed an education system which is
consistently ranked amongst the best, as reflected in the PISA (2015) results and
evidenced by ongoing reforms, research and policy innovations aimed at meeting
global standards (Ahtiainen et al., 2023). A core principle of the Finnish education
model is its commitment to equality and universal access, which has been shown
to foster long-term societal trust, social cohesion, and strong civic values
(Sahlberg, 2011). These broader societal commitments are also strongly reflected
in Finnish workplace culture, which prioritises reliability, honesty, and directness
(Lämsä, 2010). Finnish business leadership is distinguished by a characteristically
low hierarchical distance, trust-based managerial relations, and preference for
direct yet respectful forms of communication (Lewis, 2006). Leaders are expected
to justify decisions transparently, facilitate collaborative problem-solving, and
cultivate psychologically safe environments rather than rely on their positional
authority alone. These features form the conceptual foundation for examining
how Finnish organisations understand and enact effective leadership (Saari et al.,
2018). With this in mind, the subsequent chapter provides a comprehensive
understanding of business leadership and organisational practices in Finland by
combining insights from academic literature, survey data, and local perspectives.

How the Finns characterise leaders?

Managers in Finland prioritise open communication within teams and collaborative decision-making over directives from above, which is commonly characterised as a consensus-oriented leadership style (Lämsä, 2010). This approach is reflective of a deeply embedded cultural ideal of equality in which leaders should use open communication rather than authority to justify decisions and employees expect their ideas to be heard (Lämsä, 2010). Finland's direct, honest, and performance-oriented leadership style prioritises problem-solving over unproductive small talk, which is grounded in respect for both efficiency and other people's time (Ström et al., 2024). In Finland, trust is seen as essential to good leadership and inter-organisational cooperation, and leaders are expected to foster transparency, integrity, and dependability. For example, Finnish leaders often implement transparent decision-making process, such as openly sharing strategic plans and financial information with employees, which allows teams to understand the rationale behind major business moves (Hakanen & Häkkinen, 2015). This is also reflected in the results of the CCBS Survey (2025) where the respondents emphasised low hierarchy, active listening, and transparency as defining features of Finnish leadership. Mr Esa Lehtinen, CEO and Business Coach from Hämeenlinna, underscored that effective Finnish leadership leans on "*low hierarchy and equal treatment of employees*" (CCBS Survey, 2025). Another respondent, a CEO and Head of Learning and Development in Training and Coaching Services, reinforced this by describing Finnish leadership as "*striving for human-centeredness and low hierarchy, away from bridges and towards transparent information sharing and decision-making*" (CCBS Survey, 2025). According to an OECD study (2021), Finland's high level of institutional trust is reinforced by public ideals of participation and transparency, which reflects Finland's expectations for responsible decision-making. Leaders frequently worry about managing communication and feedback, assisting subordinates, and resolving organisational problems, which are deemed to be essential to good leadership (Pirttilä et al., 2019). Feedback is ordinarily given in a private, constructive manner, which also reflects the country's preference for modesty and respect for one's own privacy (Petkova, 2015). Indeed, the CCBS Survey (2025) confirms this insofar as most of the respondents indicated that leaders should give criticism privately rather than during staff meetings. Moreover, Finnish executives tend to view themselves as part of the group rather than authoritative figures, encouraging autonomy and cooperation within relatively flat organisational structures (Hofstede et al., 2010). Hence, Finland's leadership style leans towards participative and consensus-oriented behaviour rather than autocratic or democratic approaches. The CCBS Survey (2025) results also support this insofar as the majority of the respondents agreed that managers should *"actively spend time ensuring the personal well-being of their team members"*. At the same time, the respondents showed support for encouraging competition within teams to improve results, thus suggesting that Finnish leadership balances consensus with performance-driven expectations, integrating supportive team culture with goal-oriented practices (CCBS Survey, 2024). Brandt et al. (2016) also argue that Finnish CEOs frequently demonstrate emotional intelligence, self-control, and civility, contributing to effective multicultural leadership. Lämsä (2010) adds that Finnish leaders often take responsibility for their decisions and balance authority with approachability, expressing decisiveness without unnecessary formality. Similarly, Ström et al. (2024) add that moral courage and self-reflection are central to Finnish leadership, insofar as leaders rely on inner ethical judgment rather than formal authority. Authentic leadership in Finland is thus respected only when it aligns with moral integrity and humility, reflecting a dedication to collective well-being (Takala & Kemppainen, 2007). Companies like KONE and Supercell are useful examples of how these traits play out in practice within Finnish organisations. In these companies, managers foster transparency, admit mistakes, involve employees in problem-solving, and use flat hierarchies to delegate responsibility (Ryky et al., 2025). Further evidence for this comes from the interview with the CEO and leadership trainer, Elina Aaltoainen, who explained that Finnish leaders often view the use of explicit authority as a personal failure, noting that if a leader must resort to *"I tell you what to do"*, then it is commonly interpreted within organisations as a sign of a lack of trust (9 November, 2025). She added that effective leadership in Finland is instead grounded in creating connection through dialogue, where influence is achieved by involving employees rather than directing them (Aaltoainen, 9 November, 2025). To summarise, Finnish leadership is characterised by a combination of fairness, transparency, and adaptability, grounded in trust-based relationships, dialogue-driven influence, and equality.

Survey results and what local respondents say

The CCBS Survey (2017–2025) gathered insights from 130 professionals in Finland, providing a robust picture of the country's leadership culture. An analysis of the most recent 2025 data, supported by a larger 2015–2020 dataset, confirms that Finnish leadership is people focused and relatively egalitarian in its approach. Finnish leaders are widely seen as supportive and approachable. For example, in the 2025 survey, 80% of the respondents agreed that managers should *"actively spend time ensuring the personal well-being of their team members"*. This preference aligns with the 2015–2020 data, where 87% of the 100 respondents shared the same view (CCBS Survey, 2015–2020). Similarly, a majority of leaders indicated that they do not prefer to *"retain personal distance"* from employees, with 57% in 2025 and 78% in the 2015-2020 survey expressing this opinion on Finnish leadership. This finding correlates with research by Ström et al. (2024), who found that Finnish leaders commonly demonstrate human-centred and relational leadership styles, emphasising approachability and interpersonal connection. This also finds support from one of the respondents from the 2025 survey, who described Finnish leadership as "[having a] *low hierarchy"*, reflecting a broader emphasis on equality in manager-employee relations. Regarding decision-making, the 2025 survey suggests a tension between group input and decisiveness. Whilst a strong majority (70%) of the respondents indicated that once a decision is made, they are *"not likely to change it easily"*, thus reflecting the *"decisive"* quality mentioned by Dr. Salin in our interview with them (10 November, 2025), this is nuanced by other responses in the survey. For instance, Tuomas Parnoen, an IT leader, noted in the 2017 survey: *"I feel it is usually easier to revise the decision made here compared to other countries."* suggesting that decisiveness can coexist with flexibility. Finally, vision and competence emerged as central to Finnish leadership. In 2025, *"visionary thinker"* was the top ranked expectation of leaders, whilst organisational skills and experience were most often cited by employees as reasons to admire their leaders. As CEO Esa Lehtinen put it, a key Finnish trait is *"kirkas suunta"* (*"a clear direction"*) which underlines how crucial a shared, understandable vision is for followers. With regards to gender equality, the 2025 data indicated that many respondents agree men and women have equal opportunities to attain senior roles, but a sizeable proportion remained neutral on this question. This appears to suggest that whilst some progress has been made, the issue of gender equality in Finnish leadership is an evolving one. Taken together, the CCBS Survey findings indicate a stable pattern of people-focused, low-hierarchy leadership in Finland. Respondents consistently emphasised equality, trust, and transparent communication - results that closely align with aforementioned academic research from Lämsä (2010), Lewis (2006) and Viljanen (2022), who describe Finnish leadership as cooperative and non-authoritarian in nature. The survey also reinforced expectations of approachability, shared decision-making, and respectful private feedback, mirroring long-standing cultural preferences in the country. Overall, the data suggests that whilst Finnish workplaces continue to evolve, their core leadership values remain notably consistent (CCBS Survey, 2025; CCBS Survey, 2015-2020).

Local leadership analysis

Lotta Salin: a Finnish leadership scholar

Lotta Salin is a postdoctoral researcher at the University of Eastern Finland, who began her academic career in 2021 and specialises in electronic leadership. Her focus is on how leaders guide remotely working employees as well as virtual and hybrid teams in the post-pandemic era in which leadership went through a fundamental shift, resulting in high demand for competent e-leaders and new skills such as maintaining genuine human connection through technology. In the interview, Dr. Salin began by describing a typical Finnish leader as down-to-earth, approachable, and honest, reflecting Finland's low power distance (10 November, 2025). She proceeded to emphasise that leaders are usually addressed by their first names and are expected to interact without formality, both online and in-person. As the interview progressed, she explained how Finnish leadership has evolved over recent decades. Whilst, historically, leaders held higher status and employees looked for approval from authority figures, today hierarchies have flattened, and leadership has shifted towards a more inclusive, human-centred approach (Salin, 10 November, 2025). Leaders act as team members, promoting collaboration and dialogue instead of one-sided decision-making. Dr. Salin explained that many Finnish leaders deliberately avoid micromanagement, operating on the *"baseline assumption that the employees are worthy of trust and everybody wants to do their best and succeed in their job"* (10 November, 2025). Equality has become a core value with a greater emphasis on consensus, empathy, and transparency (Salin, 10 November 2025). Distinctive cultural traits include low hierarchy, strong work-life balance, and respect for boundaries. In Dr. Salin's words, Finnish employees *"truly have the eight-hour working day"* and are not expected to be constantly available in the evenings, because *"work is not the whole*" of their lives (10 November, 2025). When asked about cross-cultural differences, she noted that compared to other Scandinavian counties, Finnish leaders tend to be a bit more straightforward and decisive, preferring efficient decisions once all perspectives have been heard (Salin, 10 November, 2025). Later in the interview, Dr. Salin proceeded to discuss the topic of authority. In Finland, authority is subtle - leaders do not command or control but rather guide their teams, remove obstacles, and ensure that their decisions are justified (Salin, 10 November 2025). In cases of conflict, Dr. Salin notes, Finnish leaders aim to handle them *"sensitively and with respect"* (10 November, 2025). All involved parties are invited to share their perspectives, and decisions are made through negotiation and compromise. Her research also underscores that empathy and trust are essential components of effective leadership, especially within remote work settings. Although Finland still lacks extensive academic peer-reviewed research on these topics, both leaders and employees consistently identify them as being vital (Salin, 10 November, 2025). To build credibility whilst maintaining human connection, Dr. Salin recommends that leaders approach employees with sincere care, treat them as individuals, and keep their promises. The interview concluded with differing generational expectations. Dr. Salin noted that younger employees, especially millennials and Gen Z, expect leaders to prove their competence through their actions, valuing soft skills such as empathy, social support, and active listening more than positional power (10 November, 2025). Conversely, for her own generation, she added, the expectation is *"having the respect and politeness for everybody, no matter of their title"* (Salin, 10 November, 2025). Effective leaders, Dr. Salin concludes, *"stand with the team"* - showing care, reliability, and understanding when challenges arise (10 November, 2025). These qualities, grounded in Finland's individualistic yet human-oriented culture, form a leadership style defined by trust, equality, and genuine care for people.

Elina Aaltolainen: a Finnish cross-cultural trainer

Elina Aaltolainen is a professional coach and CEO from Finland who has worked with management and leadership teams for over twenty years. She is trained in educational psychology and education, with additional certifications in a variety of fields, including four years of therapy studies. Aaltolainen described a typical Finnish business leader as someone who emphasises logic, integrity, honesty, and approachability. As she put it: "*So they say what they mean, and they mean what they say. They have quite often, let us say rational idea of human beings*" (Aaltolainen, 9 November 2025). She also points out that many leaders now actively research human behaviour, trust-building, and individual differences with the goal of acting as influencers and trust-builders who grant authority and believe professionals will bear responsibility (Aaltolainen, 9 November 2025). She proceeded to add that Finnish organisations generally show respect for people and have a high value for human beings through their policies (Aaltolainen, 9 November, 2025). Importantly, she noted that there has been a wider cultural shift "*from authoritarian leadership to trust-based leadership,*" in which workers are viewed as peers and equals with skill, creativity, and the capacity to learn; the leader's job is to trust, grant authority, and set an example (Aaltolainen, 9 November 2025). Finland's hierarchy is "*really flat,*" according to Aaltolainen. Along with delegated authority, Finnish leaders place a strong focus on having specific goals and boundaries so that people are aware of what is expected of them and the boundaries of their actions (Aaltolainen, 9 November, 2025). Aaltolainen was very clear about authority and how employees view it: "*most of the good leaders... if they end up using their authority, they feel that they have failed*" (Aaltolainen, 9 November 2025). As she noted: "*People want clear goals and defined boundaries, so they know what is expected and where they have room to act. That is positive authority - it creates clarity and trust. Micromanagement, however, is a negative form of authority; it signals a lack of trust in the employee's ability to organise their own work. If a leader ends up micromanaging, most Finnish leaders would see it as a failure rather than a strength*" (Aaltolainen, personal communication, 18 November 2025). She also defined a "*human concept*" failure as a common mistake made by foreign managers in Finland, which involves, amongst other things, treating people like tools or evaluating their worth (Aaltolainen, 9 November 2025). As Aaltolainen writes: "*It often occurs when a manager does not recognise a person's inherent worth. In the Nordic and especially Finnish leadership tradition, every individual is considered valuable in themselves. Respect is shown by listening, involving people, and leading inclusively. Managers coming from cultures where worth must be constantly earned, rather than recognised, may therefore face conflicts in the Finnish context*" (Aaltolainen, personal communication, 18 November, 2025). In conclusion, it is critical to remember to treat people as human beings rather than as lines in an Excel file when working in Finland (Aaltolainen, 9 November 2025). According to Aaltolainen, it all begins with a "*need to challenge the view of how we see human beings*" (Aaltolainen, 9 November 2025).

In-country leadership bestseller

The book *All about Management and Leadership - A Finnish Perspective* is written by three leading Finnish experts in management and organisational development. Timo Raikaslehto is a strategy specialist with over twenty years of experience advising executives and boards. Seppo Mansukoski has a long career in leadership training and public-sector management development, complemented by several national and international roles in professional training organisations. Professor Lasse Mitronen brings extensive academic and industry experience, having worked in senior positions in Finnish retail and later in university research on strategic and service management. Together, the authors bring broad experience in Finnish leadership practice and research, combining executive consulting, leadership training, and academic expertise to provide authoritative insight into national leadership behaviours. Their book posits that leadership in Finland is not merely a function of hierarchical authority but rather a nuanced experience in balancing decisiveness with empathy, strategic foresight, and operational rigour with human-centred sensibilities. Through detailed interviews, case studies, and examples conducted by the authors from Finnish organisations such as KONE and Supercell, the book demonstrates how Finnish leadership achieves a delicate balance between egalitarian collaboration and strategic decisiveness. It reveals that Finnish leaders actively cultivate flat hierarchies, employee autonomy, and inclusive decision making, whilst simultaneously managing complex areas in corporate governance, ICT strategy, and responsible leadership. The book further explores how Finnish leaders navigate the tension between tradition and change, integrating foundational principles with adaptive practices to respond to a rapidly evolving business environment. By fostering ethical accountability, psychological safety, and rational transparency, the book illustrates that organisational success in Finland is achieved not merely through formal authority or procedural competence, but through human-centred, participative, and resilient leadership behaviours that align strategic objectives with employee well-being. The book was chosen for its rigorous integration of theory and practice, combining the author's extensive perspective on Finnish leadership, making it an invaluable resource for studying contemporary leadership in dynamic organisations.

Local leadership book	
Title	*All About Management and Leadership*
Subtitle	a Finnish Perspective
Author	Timo Raikaslehto, Seppo Mansukoski, Lasse Mitronen
Publisher	Professional Publishing Finland OY
Year	2024
ISBN	978-952-7401-17-0

TIMO RAIKASLEHTO · SEPPO MANSUKOSKI · LASSE MITRONEN

ALL ABOUT MANAGEMENT AND LEADERSHIP
– a Finnish perspective

Professional Publishing Finland Oy

Finnish leadership YouTube review

Henkka Hyppönen, a Finnish author, television broadcaster, and leadership specialist, explores the essence of successful management in Finland's business environment in his YouTube presentation *Mitä on hyvä johtajuus?* ("What is Good Leadership?"). He believes that *"The modern management model is significantly closer to the Finnish model"* which has a flat hierarchy (Speakersforum, 2018, 1:00). According to Hyppönen, leadership is about empowering others rather than exerting control or authority; this is a reflection of Finland's progressive workplace culture, which emphasises mental health and shared responsibility. In another video, Riitta Viitala, Professor Emeritus at the University of Vaasa, discusses people-oriented leadership in TET Talks - *Jakso 3: Ihmisläheinen johtajuus*. Viitala (2024) emphasises that empathy and human connection are essential for sustainable leadership in Finland: *"I do not see how anyone can succeed as a leader without empathy"* (10:57). She criticises leaders who prioritise short-term financial gains over people, warning that when CEOs *"are not interested in leadership development,"* organisational results decline (22:15). Within such environments, talented employees often *"jump overboard"* to preserve their well-being (24:12). She concludes that Finnish leadership excellence exists only when employees *"feel seen, heard, and taken into consideration with appreciation"* (33:23). Frank Martela, Assistant Professor at Aalto University, develops this idea further in his talk on Nordic minimalist leadership. He argues that a leader's role is not to control every decision, but to *"minimise their own power in order to maximise the shared impact"* (Martela, 2023, 2:03). To illustrate this, he refers to several Finnish companies, including Supercell, where CEO Ilkka Paananen describes his ambition to be the *"world's least powerful CEO"* by giving teams autonomy and trusting their judgment (Martela, 2023, 2:44, 11:10). Similar principles can be seen at firms like Nokia and Wolt, where leadership is built around a clear sense of direction combined with responsibility pushed down to teams (Martela, 2023, 0:33, 9:19). Martela breaks this this down into fur elements, Direction, Ownership, Boundaries, and Trust, which together reflect a broader Finnish belief that people perform best when they are trusted rather than tightly controlled (Martela, 2023, 5:32).

Understanding hierarchy in Finland

Although Finland is widely regarded as an egalitarian society, hierarchical structures remain a defining feature of its organisational landscape. Formal authority within organisations is manifested through decision-making power, reporting lines, and resource control. These are concentrated amongst senior management, whilst lower employees often have limited influence over strategic outcomes (Soininvaara, 2020). Importantly, this hierarchy is not merely a procedural or structural artefact; rather, it is operated in tandem with culturally embedded norms that shape perceptions of legitimacy and authority within professional contexts. Finnish cultural values, particularly the emphasis on competence, achievement and recognition, underpin these organisational hierarchies (Sequeira et al., 2024). From early socialisation, individuals internalise the importance of merit and prestige, which subsequently informs workplace behaviours and expectations regarding leadership and decision making. Consequently, employees may defer to formal authority not simply because of institutional mandates but because organisational roles are interpreted through culturally mediated understanding of expertise and status (Sequeira et al., 2024). The emphasis placed on expertise was supported by the results of the CCBS Survey (2025), insofar as the respondents highlighted organisational experience and clear decision-making as defining expectations of Finnish leaders, suggesting that hierarchical legitimacy is rooted primarily in demonstrated competence rather than positional dominance. Indeed, as Senior Content Strategist, Tiia Konttinen, stated: *"Finnish leadership is characterised by a high level of trust and a strong sense of autonomy. The leader does not emphasise himself but rather creates a space where experts can use their own abilities. This creates ownership, independence, and efficiency in organisations without unnecessary showing-off"* (CCBS Survey, 2025). This dynamic produces a distinctive hybrid organisational hierarchy that is formally codified yet culturally reinforced, allowing egalitarian ideals to coexist with structural authority. Our interview data further illustrates this hybrid arrangement: CEO Elina Aaltolainen noted that Finnish organisations maintain some hierarchy mainly to *"make clarity around boundaries,"* yet leaders are expected to be approachable, *"sit in the same rooms where everyone else sits"*, and avoid emphasising their status (Aaltolainen, 9 November 2025). Within professional environments, this hierarchy manifests in both gender and role stratification. According to the Finnish Ministry of Social Affairs and Health (n.d.), women continue to face persistent vertical segregation, slower promotion pathways, and underrepresentation in senior and top-level management. Men advance more quickly and reach higher earnings earlier, demonstrating entrenched structural barriers that limit women's leadership progression. Several of the survey respondents also pointed out cultural expectations surrounding fairness and equal treatment, yet their mixed perceptions suggest that gender equality in leadership is acknowledged as improving but not fully realised, aligning with reports on vertical segregation (CCBS Survey, 2025). Finland's corporate hierarchy, in contrast, operates within a context of low power distance, with a score of 33, reflecting a culture rooted in meritocracy, ethical leadership and participative management. Power is decentralised, communication is direct, and managers act as accessible, coaching leaders who empower their teams (Devatstablee, 2022). This view aligns closely with Aaltolainen's interview insights, where she emphasised that Finnish leaders *"very seldom talk about this kind of commanding way,"* relying instead on dialogue, shared problem-solving, and trust-building as the primary mechanisms of influence (9 November, 2025). Moreover, public-sector HR Manager Sari Soivio Käki noted a gradual shift *"from directive leadership towards servant leadership and increasing community self-direction,"* thus signalling continued movement towards involved, trust-based authority (CCBS Survey, 2025). This structure allows hierarchy to coexist with egalitarian principles, creating professional environments where influence is earned and power is exercised responsibly. This ethos, grounded in equality, transparency, and shared responsibility, reflects a historical shift from rigid top-down practices towards the Nordic model of participatory governance. Reforms in the 2010s strengthened local autonomy and collaboration, shaping leaders who value initiative and inclusiveness (Alava et al., 2024). Therefore, the hybrid blend of formal authority and cultural egalitarianism allows hierarchy and participatory practices to coexist effectively.

How Finns achieve leadership empathy

In Finland, leadership empathy develops within a context of high societal trust and low hierarchical distance, where cooperation and fairness guide organisational behaviour. According to the OECD (2021), Finland ranked amongst the highest-trust countries in the EU, with 64 per cent of Finns reporting confidence in public institutions, compared with an OECD average of 45 per cent. This trust forms the foundation for transparent and people-centred leadership. Leaders are expected to act with moral awareness and emotional balance, recognising that credibility depends on listening and responding rather than commanding. Empathy in Finnish organisations is not expressed through unconcealed emotion but rather through consistent, trust-based interaction (Hakanen & Häkkinen, 2015). As Elina Aaltoainen explained in our interview with them, Finnish empathy begins with the leader's own self-reflection: *"It starts from understanding myself, the self-awareness, and then it leads usually to seeing also those things in others"* (9 November, 2025). She emphasised that genuine understanding of others becomes possible only when leaders move beyond surface-level facts and opinions and instead reflect on their own experiences - such as moments of doubt, frustration, or searching for meaning – which makes them more capable of seeing employees as individuals with similar human needs (Aaltoainen, 9 November 2025). Moreover, Hakanen and Häkkinen (2015) observed that effective Finnish managers rely on openness, procedural fairness, and constructive dialogue, noting that these qualities strengthen interpersonal trust and reduce power asymmetries within teams. A practical example of this is the shift away in recent years from the private-office culture that was common a decade ago. According to Aaltolainen (9 November 2025), many contemporary leaders *"do not want to make a number of themselves"* and instead choose to sit with employees during lunch and work in the same shared spaces. Such everyday practices illustrate Finnish leaders' commitment to openness and help foster an environment in which information is shared transparently, and employees feel encouraged to ask questions or challenge decisions in team discussions. Conversations are usually calm and focused on finding shared agreement, with managers listening carefully before offering their perspective, ensuring that all voices are heard. Such practices make employees feel that their opinions genuinely influence outcomes, reinforcing both mutual trust and a sense of collective responsibility (Lämsä, 2010). Similarly, Fonsén et al. (2022) noted that educational leaders in Finland value self-reflection and employee well-being as central components of professional competence, linking empathy directly to sustainable leadership formation in society and overall performance. Similarly, Brandt et al. (2016) found that transformational leadership, particularly individualised consideration, and intellectual co-work stimulated by shared responsibility, has a positive effect on profitability within Finnish firms, suggesting that empathy contributes to both motivation and productivity. Comparable findings in public-sector leadership show that feedback, fairness, and human presence are perceived as essential for motivation and engagement (Pirttilä et al., 2019). This cultural foundation resonates with Aaltoainen, who noted that Finnish organisations have undergone a *"strong cultural shift from authoritarian to trust-based leadership,"* where leaders view employees as *"peers and equals"* and build commitment through honesty, integrity, and leading by example rather than through control (9 November, 2025). These practices align with Finland's broader cultural model, where authority is legitimised by competence and mutual respect rather than positional power (Lämsä, 2010). Aaltoainen also underscored that foreign managers occasionally struggle in Finland when they approach leadership from a non-human-centred perspective (9 November, 2025). She described a case in which a manager *"valued some people more than others"* and treated employees as tools rather than individuals, triggering organisational crisis and even declining financial results (Aaltoainen, 9 November 2025). Empathy is therefore achieved through dialogue, self-regulation, and trust, allowing Finnish leaders to maintain efficiency whilst protecting psychological safety. Within this system, understanding others is not separate from management effectiveness; it is the mechanism that turns equality and professionalism into lasting organisational performance (Salmi et al., 2020).

Greenland

Guido Boogaard, Hanna Hunya, Marit van de Kamp, Georgina Kasteleijn,
Sharnelle Power & Mina Zakian

Greenland, or *Kalaallit Nunaat* as it is otherwise known, is above all a vast, icy island distinguished by glaciers, silence, and dramatic coastal landscapes (Nuttall, 2012). Although it is the world's largest island, its population is smaller than that of many European towns, which, in turn, creates a society that is geographically expansive yet socially close-knit (Hansen et al., 2020). Everyday life across its dispersed settlements is defined by harsh weather conditions, tight community networks, and cultural traditions that continue to anchor Greenlandic identity to the present day (Nuttall, 2012). The Greenlandic language (*Kalaallisut*), an Inuit-Aleut language, remains paramount to the country's identity and contributes towards strong social cohesion despite ongoing modernisation and the long-standing Danish influence on the island (Mønsted, 2025). Today, Greenland faces major issues that affects its future, including, amongst other things, climate change, resource development, and shifting geopolitical interests that are reshaping the Arctic region (Jungsberg et al., 2025). These pressures not only influence its economy and environment but also how institutions and communities organise themselves. As Greenland increasingly navigates global partnerships and local expectations, its leadership practices have evolved accordingly (Hansen et al., 2012). Contemporary Greenlandic leadership reflects a hybrid style that combines traditional values of trust, reciprocity, and communal responsibility with the demands of modern governance and international cooperation (Hansen et al., 2012). Legitimacy is rooted not in formal authority but rather in relationships, cultural balance, and acceptance by the community, which is deeply connected to Inuit leadership traditions, such as those observed in Tiniteqilâq, where respect and practical skill guide influence rather than rank (Rasmussen, 2020). Together, these characteristics underscore Greenland's unique social and organisational landscape, making it a compelling subject for examination. The following chapter examines business leadership in more depth by drawing on academic literature, survey data from local C-level managers, and interviews with experts on Greenlandic leadership.

How Greenlanders characterise leaders?

Since the introduction of the Self-Government Act in 2009, questions over what constitutes effective leadership have become central to organisational life in Greenland. Leadership is characterised by relational legitimacy, participation, and community embeddedness rather than by hierarchy or individual authority (Hansen et al., 2012). According to Rasmussen (2020), leadership in Greenland operates through *"territories of interaction,"* where legitimacy is earned by negotiating relationships and maintaining mutual respect within close-knit communities. Within these small societies, professional and personal relations often overlap, which means that leaders must continuously balance formal decision-making with informal social obligations. Rasmussen (2021) further observes that leadership in Greenlandic organisations is deeply contextual and adaptive in nature, emerging through interaction rather than command. That is to say, effective leaders engage in ongoing dialogue, attentive listening, and collective sense-making to maintain harmony in small organisational settings. This participatory practice aligns with Inuit and Nordic cultural traditions of collective harmony and non-confrontation (Nooter, 1976; Rasmussen, 2021). Hansen et al. (2018) similarly found that Greenlandic managers perceive leadership as a shared process rather than an individual trait, emphasising collaboration and mutual accountability. These findings illustrate a broader concept of *"territories of interaction,"* which reflects an Inuit-derived relational logic (Rasmussen 2020) where leadership legitimacy emerges from maintaining harmony (*ataqatigiinneq*) and mutual support (*inuussutissarsiorneq*) within the community. Historically, Inuit communities relied on consensus-building and shared responsibility for their survival, and these principles continue to shape modern Greenlandic organisations. Consequently, leaders are expected to guide their employees through dialogue and demonstrations rather than directive forms of authority. This dynamic is also evident in Greenland's industrial contexts. Rasmussen (2023), in her empirical study, *"When the boat comes in,"* demonstrates that leadership at fish factories emerges out of the practical coordination of daily tasks rather than, say, from formal titles; leaders guide by example and earn legitimacy through participation in collective work. Samuelsen's (2010) analysis in *Grønlandsk Ledelseskultur* also underscores that Greenlandic leaders tend to value humility, presence and balance over authority or charisma. Humility, in this context, reflects the cultural expectation that leaders remain approachable and self-aware, avoiding any display of superiority within a society that emphasises equality and cooperation. This perspective aligns closely with the results of the CCB Survey (2025), insofar as the majority of the respondents indicated that, as leaders, they prefer to maintain a certain professional distance from employees in order to uphold mutual respect, whilst, simultaneously, recognising the importance of dedicating time to the personal well-being of their team members. The respondents also identified several key qualities they believe Greenlandic leaders should possess, which included being visionary thinkers, good listeners, consensus seekers, and decisive in their actions (CCBS Survey, 2025). When viewed together, these qualities illustrate how leadership legitimacy in Greenland arises from relational integrity rather than personal dominance. Smeds et al. (2016) reinforces this perspective, arguing that sustainable leadership in Arctic contexts depends on community embeddedness and ethical responsibility towards individuals and the environment. Collectively, these studies underscore that Greenlandic leadership intertwines with social, environmental, and moral accountability during everyday organisational practices. Leadership ideals also overlap with entrepreneurial values. Studies on mining and entrepreneurship (Kadenic 2017; Wennecke et al. 2019) show that Greenlandic leaders prioritise cooperation and long-term community benefit over short-term profit. This expanded notion of stewardship with leadership being exercised both *with* and *for* the community reflects the societal expectation that authority should be transparent, participatory, and rooted in local context. Finally, Greenlandic leadership is characterised by legitimacy that comes from long-standing relationships and everyday community interaction. As one of our interviewees, a leadership consultant, explained, Greenland has a *"small… village feel, everybody knows everybody,"* which means leaders often work with people with whom they already share *"a different relation or a different history"* (20 November, 2025). They proceeded to inform us that decision-making tends to be collaborative and rooted in social responsibility, partly because actions have lasting visibility: leaders know they may *"meet them again next week in a social setting"* (20 November, 2025). Rather than relying heavily on hierarchy, Greenlandic leaders act as facilitators who maintain trust, inclusion, and shared values, often moving fluidly between professional and personal spheres. Social life and leadership overlap naturally; as our interviewee put it, at community gatherings *"you do not come as a boss or an employee… just hosts and guests."* (20 November, 2025).

Survey results and what local respondents say

To explore leadership tendencies and organisational practices in Greenland, this study draws on data from the CCBS Survey (2025), which was administered to a small group of senior managers and C-level executives with extensive leadership experience in Greenland. Whilst the respondent group is limited in size, their insights nevertheless offer meaningful insights into the leadership culture within Greenlandic organisations. By analysing the survey responses alongside the open-ended comments, this section identifies several key patterns that illuminate how leadership is both understood and practised in the Greenlandic context. First, the survey results reveal that managerial decisions in Greenland tend to remain unchanged once they have been taken, which suggests a steady and consistent leadership style. Notably, however, this decisiveness is balanced by a clear reluctance to confront subordinates directly in staff meetings. Indeed, according to the respondents, Greenlandic leaders prefer non-confrontational communication and aim to maintain harmony within workplace interactions (CCBS Survey, 2025). In fact, this emphasis on relational balance emerged as a recurring theme in the dataset. A further salient finding concerns the strong prioritisation of employee well-being amongst Finnish leaders. All the respondents agreed that effective leadership requires spending time supporting the personal welfare of employees, thus underscoring both the community-oriented and relational character of Greenlandic organisational life (CCBS Survey, 2025). One respondent offered a particularly illuminating comment, explaining that: *"Collective decisions are made here in Greenland. But if I as a leader express my attitude too quickly, then the others will adapt this – and then I really do not get their honest opinion about a problem"* (CCBS Survey, 2025). This statement underscores the cultural significance of consensus and illustrates how leaders navigate the risk of unintentionally shaping group opinions. Another respondent identified *"Kultur"* (culture) as the defining characteristic of Greenlandic leadership, which reinforces the notion that leadership practices are deeply embedded in local norms of togetherness, humility, and collective responsibility. Next, competition within teams was generally avoided, with collaboration and consensus preferred over rivalry, further reflecting a cultural preference for cohesion rather than internal competition (CCBS Survey, 2025). Preferences for receiving criticism varied amongst the respondents, thus suggesting flexible communication norms rather than a strict adherence to a single preferred style. Similarly, views on whether office space or transportation function as symbols of status differed across the respondents, implying that material markers of hierarchy are not uniformly emphasised (CCBS Survey, 2025). Overall, the survey results protray Greenlandic leadership as collaborative, people-centred, non-confrontational, and grounded in shared community values. The findings shed light upon a leadership culture that seeks harmony, prioritises well-being, and emphasises collective decision-making, which are all features that distinguish Greenlandic organisational life from more competitive or individualistic models.

Local leadership analysis

Verena Huppert Karlsson: a Greenlandic leadership scholar

To gain first-hand insight into Greenlandic leadership styles and organisational culture, we conducted an interview with leadership consultant Verena Huppert Karlsson. She has eight years of professional experience in Greenland, where she carried out research on the Greenlandic labour market and later served as HR Manager for the national shipping company Royal Arctic Line. Today, she continues to work closely with Greenlandic organisations whilst based in Copenhagen (28 November, 2025). In our interview with her, Huppert Karlsson described Greenlandic organisational culture as being deeply shaped by the social dynamics of small communities. She proceeded to explain that because many towns are tightly interconnected and people often know one another outside of work, the workplace becomes an important social space where relationships are maintained. As she put it, colleagues frequently behave as if they are part of an extended household, and daily routines such as taking shared breaks, talking informally, or simply *"being together"* are essential to employee well-being. This expectation for warmth and informality underlines how Greenlandic employees rely on emotional proximity and familiarity as the basis of effective collaboration (28 November, 2025). Verena Huppert Karlsson moved onto underscore how this cultural pattern extends naturally to leadership. Leaders are expected not only to manage operations but to participate in the community-like atmosphere of their teams. She observed that it is entirely normal for a leader to adjust to employees' personal needs and to show visible understanding of everyday challenges they are facing. One of her examples illustrated this vividly: if a manager has no childcare available, then bringing their child to the office is seen as reasonable and fully acceptable. Such actions do not undermine someone's authority; rather, they reinforce an understanding that professional and private life often coexist in practical ways in Greenland (28 November, 2025). This level of integration also reinforces the expectation that leaders must show genuine, personal interest in their employees, taking time to listen, check in, and maintain regular informal dialogue. At the same time, Verena Huppert Karlsson pointed to several organisational challenges that complicate leadership development in the country. One of the structural limitations she emphasised is the absence of Greenlandic-language leadership education. *"There is no leadership education… in Greenlandic"* she noted. This means that many current leaders have either learned through experience or taken courses abroad, most commonly in Denmark or the UK (28 November, 2025). This creates a gap in leadership knowledge which, in turn, creates a reliance on imported models that do not always fit Greenlandic cultural realities. She also described the difficulties faced by foreign leaders entering Greenlandic organisations for the first time, who often assume that workplaces operate similarly to those in Denmark, and thus fail to anticipate differences, such as the preference for flat hierarchies, subtle communication styles, and an aversion to open confrontation. According to Verena Huppert Karlsson, disagreement is rarely expressed directly instead employees may comply outwardly whilst internally questioning decisions, which requires leaders to actively create opportunities for discussion to avoid misunderstandings. This dynamic means that leadership in Greenland relies heavily on proactive communication and the ability to read social cues rather than expecting explicit verbal feedback (28 November, 2025). Overall, Verena Huppert Karlsson underscored that successful leadership in Greenland demands cultural sensitivity, interpersonal awareness, and an understanding of how social closeness shapes expectations within organisations. Leaders must navigate a work environment where professional authority is balanced with personal accessibility, and where maintaining harmonious relationships is essential for organisational stability.

Anonymous: a Greenland cross-cultural trainer

We explored leadership dynamics in Greenland further by conducting an interview with a senior legal manager and leadership consultant who has worked across public and private organisations in both Denmark and Greenland for more than fifteen years, but who wished to be anonymous (20 November, 2025). Their extensive professional experience offers valuable insight into how leadership is shaped by the country's uniquely small and interconnected context (20 November, 2025). According to the interviewee, most Greenlandic organisations are small to medium-sized, often owner-led, and characterised by minimal hierarchical layers (20 November, 2025). This creates a setting in which leaders and employees frequently know one another personally, and as they explained, *"it all comes down to the small pond,"* which means that everyday leadership decisions have long-term social consequences (20 November, 2025). Leaders must therefore adopt a relationship-oriented approach, as *"you will meet your employees again and again,"* whether socially or professionally (20 November, 2025). Such conditions demand a form of leadership that is careful, consistent, and attuned to community relationships (20 November, 2025). The interviewee proceeded to draw a clear distinction between Scandinavian leadership norms and those found in Greenland. In Denmark, they noted, leadership feels flatter, with employees informally granting legitimacy to their managers; however, *"in Greenland, the power distance is longer,"* and leaders are viewed more as formal authority figures (20 November, 2025). Employees often seek direction and reassurance, based on the fact that many *"do not want to do something they have not been allowed to do,"* preferring confirmation before making decisions (20 November, 2025). He further explained that Greenlandic workers will *"rather do less and stay within the lines"* which makes leadership more directive and hands-on compared with Denmark (20 November, 2025). This is one reason why foreign leaders often struggle when entering the Greenlandic labour market, because many of them expect high autonomy and replaceability within the workforce, yet the interviewee stressed that *"you need to work with what you have,"* because firing an employee rarely means a suitable replacement is available (20 November, 2025). Furthermore, leaders must handle conflict sensitively, as *"you will meet them again next week in the store,"* making dismissals socially demanding in ways unfamiliar to outsiders (20 November, 2025). He went on to explain that leaders who arrive with aggressive or highly efficiency-driven styles often fail to integrate: *"if they do not adjust, they usually move out again,"* thus emphasising the importance of cultural adaptation (20 November, 2025). Leadership in Greenland is strongly influenced by relational networks. Professional identity is often tied to family connections, with the interviewee noting that introductions typically begin by explaining *"who you are connected to,"* rather than referencing one's job title (20 November, 2025). This deeply relational culture also shapes workplace interactions; leaders and employees frequently socialise outside work, and as they recalled, *"I have been to many of my colleagues' birthdays,"* which contrasts sharply with Danish norms (20 November, 2025). Such closeness reduces professional distance, shaping leadership into a more personal and trust-dependent role (20 November, 2025). Later, they discussed how younger employees increasingly expect modern leadership practices, including frequent dialogue and continuous development opportunities (20 November, 2025). In this respect, they observed that this new generation *"wants more for themselves"* and values quicker progression, though at times they may *"want the benefits without delivering the work,"* which can create generational tensions (20 November, 2025). This is why they argued that age now shapes leadership preferences more strongly than cultural background, demonstrating a shift in Greenlandic workplace dynamics (20 November, 2025). Finally, they opined that leadership in Greenland is defined by community size, cultural expectations, and long-standing social relationships (20 November, 2025). Effective leaders must balance higher power distance with relational closeness, lead with sensitivity in a limited labour market, and navigate a work environment where social and professional spheres frequently overlap (20 November, 2025). Those who adapt their leadership approach to these realities contribute to sustainable, culturally aligned leadership within Greenland's distinct context (20 November, 2025).

In-country leadership bestseller

Ledelse i Grønland (Leadership in Greenland) is a 2019 research publication by Mette Apollo Rasmussen and Poul Bitsch Olsen from *Ilisimatusarfik* (the University of Greenland) and Roskilde University. It offers one of the first in-depth studies of how leadership is practiced in Greenlandic organisations. The authors explore how leaders operate in a society that combines strong local traditions with modern business demands. Whilst some challenges are uniquely Greenlandic, rooted in language, geography, and community ties, most leadership issues are universal. Rasmussen and Olsen present Greenlandic leadership as a collective activity, created through cooperation, dialogue, and shared understanding rather than through individual authority. Drawing on interviews with leaders from major companies like Royal Greenland, Air Greenland, TELE-POST, and Pisiffik, the study identifies four key themes in Greenlandic business leadership: mutual dependence within networks, leadership dilemmas, professional competence, and the need for academic education. Networks are essential for collaboration, but they can also limit innovation when they reinforce familiar perspectives. Therefore, effective leadership in Greenland, so the authors conclude, requires courage to face dilemmas, skill in building relationships, and the competence to handle uncertainty. More specifically, it is about finding the best decisions together rather than simply making them alone. Hence, the book ultimately portrays leadership in Greenland as a living, relational process, which is both deeply connected to community values whilst striving toward modern professionalism.

Local leadership book	
Title	*Ledelse i Grønland*
Subtitle	Kaffi aassaviuk?
Author	Mette Apollo Rasmussen, Poul Bitsch Olsen
Publisher	Ilisimatusarfik Press
Year	2019
ISBN	978-87-7975-160-3

Greenland Leadership YouTube review

The lecture *Kolonialisme i Grønland: tradition, ledelse og arv* from Aarhus University (2023), presented by Søren Rud, Associate Professor at the University of

Copenhagen and specialist in Greenlandic colonial governance, explains how colonial Danish administration historically embedded hierarchy and authority within Greenlandic organisations. However, the speaker shows that leadership in modern Greenland has gradually shifted towards *fællesskab* (community) and *tillid* (trust) as key coordination mechanisms for leaders on the island (Aarhus University, 2023, 3:20; 8:42). He describes how decision-making takes place in small, interconnected communities, where leaders balance personal and professional roles—*"you lead people you know"*—which illustrates how close social relations shape leadership in Greenland (Aarhus University, 2023, 14:12; 31:05). Within both local organisations and municipalities, decisions are often made collectively after extensive dialogue so that everyone feels heard. This slower, inclusion-oriented process strengthens *fællesskab* and *tillid*, and serves to illustrate how Greenlandic leadership prioritises relationships over hierarchy (Aarhus University, 2023, 23:00–26:00). The second video, *Fremtidens ledelse: Hvordan ser den ud og hvordan gør du dig klar?* (The leadership of the future: What does it look like and how do you prepare for it?), published by Feedwork (2023), features Jonas, a leadership consultant at the Danish organisational development firm Feedwork, which specialises in psychological safety, hybrid work, and leadership development. The speaker explains how leadership in Greenland is changing from control to trust, purpose, and empathy, which is reflective of a more human-centered mindset. As he states in the video: *"The modern leader leads through trust, not supervision"* (DR, 2023, 4:50). This is visible in modern hybrid Greenlandic organisations where managers rely on trust and autonomy rather than close supervision. Another key insight is that *"We should not just understand people — we should feel them"* (DR, 2023, 10:50), ehich illustrates how empathy and emotional awareness are becoming essential leadership skills in Greenland. Finally, the video argues that future leaders in Greenland must be authentic, responsible, and value-driven, balancing social, ethical, and environmental goals — *"Leadership of the future is about responsibility — for people, the planet and profit"* (DR, 2023, 8:20). When viewed together, these videos shed light on how Greenlandic leadership is evolving from hierarchical authority to relational responsibility. Leaders are not distant figures but rather part of the communities they guide, relying on trust, empathy, and moral accountability. This hybrid model, combining Inuit values and modern organisational principles, represents a culturally sustainable and authentic form of leadership rooted in community rather than hierarchy (Aarhus University, 2023; DR, 2023).

Understanding hierarchy in Greenland

Hierarchy in Greenlandic society is strongly shaped by Indigenous Inuit roots, the historical ties to Denmark, and the country's small, community-based social structure (Rasmussen, 2023). In contrast to countries where hierarchy is overtly institutionalised or status-driven, Greenland reflects a subtle and relational form of hierarchy grounded in trust, respect, and collective responsibility. Leadership tends to be horizontal in tone; however, the authority of elders, managers, and community leaders who demonstrate competence, care, and relational awareness are also recognised (Rasmussen, 2023). According to Hofstede's cultural dimensions, Greenland does not have extensive national data due to its size and autonomy within the Danish realm. Nevertheless, qualitative research suggests that the power distance and degree to which "less powerful" individuals accept unequal power distribution is moderate to low, especially when directly comparing Greenland to many non-Nordic societies (Hofstede Insights, 2024). This aligns closely with the results from the CCBS Survey (2025), which indicate that academic titles, formal address, and visible markers of rank are generally unimportant in Greenlandic workplaces. Indeed, many of the respondents articulated that leaders are ordinarily addressed by their first names, thus reinforcing the egalitarian values inherited from Inuit culture (Nooter, 1976; Hastrup, 2022). The survey also indicated that employees respect leaders primarily based on their organisational experience and technical competence rather than age, appearance, or family background (CCBS Survey, 2025). Hence, in Greenlandic organisations, hierarchy is generally soft, negotiated, and embedded in community relations. Leaders rely on shared understanding, dialogue, and previously received feedback rather than formal rank to support their decisions (Muhr et al., 2022; Ilisimatusarfik, 2022). These practices mirror the findings of the CCBS Survey (2025) where Greenlandic leadership culture was framed as collaborative and community oriented. The "small society" context means that excessive formality can damage legitimacy; instead, leaders cultivate respect through *ataatsimoorneq* (togetherness) and *inaarut* (a sense of moral responsibility), both of which frame leadership as a collective process of maintaining balance and integrity (Rasmussen, 2020). Moreover, Rasmussen (2020) observes that Greenlandic leadership practices intertwine professional responsibility with community belonging, making relational accountability more important than positional authority. At the same time, the Danish administrative influence introduced more formal organisational structures into Greenlandic institutions, such as government, education, and business, which creates what some scholars describe as a "hybrid hierarchy", where formal roles and accountability exist but are negotiated through personal relationships and dialogue (Hansen et al., 2020; Rasmussen & Olsen, 2022). Leaders are thus expected to maintain harmony within teams, by acting as a representative, and avoiding direct confrontation, which is consistent with a collectivist and high-context communication style (Muhr et al., 2022). These expectations regarding approachable and competence-based leadership are supported by the CCBS Survey (2025), which similarly reports that formal rank holds less significance than relational qualities. One respondent, Taitsianguaq Olsen, underscored the cultural foundation of these expectations, noting simply *"Kultur"* as the guiding force behind leadership behaviour (CCBS Survey, 2025). Olsen also emphasised that leaders are expected to be "visionary thinkers" and "good listeners," and that leadership credibility rests primarily on organisational experience and technical competence rather than age or status markers. Their responses also pointed to the value placed on resourcefulness and strong political connections, further underscoring that legitimacy in Greenlandic organisations is earned through demonstrated capability, cultural responsiveness, and the maintenance of reciprocal relationships (CCBS Survey, 2025). Whilst hierarchical differences do exist, employees expect leaders to remain accessible and human, reflecting the cultural emphasis on equality and mutual respect, or *inustiaq* (being a good and respectful person). This aligns with Hofstede's (2024) observation that in lower power-distance cultures, leadership is participative rather than autocratic, and subordinates feel comfortable voicing opinions respectfully. As Rasmussen (2023) notes, Greenlandic leadership practices continue to evolve as leaders navigate local expectations of equality whilst engaging with global partners and state institutions. In short, hierarchy in Greenland is best understood as relational rather than positional: leaders hold authority through their ability to maintain trust and balance collective interests. Whilst formal structures exist, the Greenlandic approach to hierarchy remains rooted in cultural continuity, community, respect, and reciprocity, illustrating a nuanced adaptation of Hofstede's framework to an Arctic Indigenous context.

How Greenlanders achieve leadership empathy

Leadership empathy in Greenland is deeply shaped by the island's unique social, cultural, and environmental context, where governance operates across vast distances and within close knit communities (Norden, 2023). As an autonomous territory of Denmark with limited economic independence, Greenlandic leaders must balance practical realities with cultural sensitivity, demonstrating empathy as both a relational and structural necessity (Reuters, 2025). Empathy in this context extends beyond emotional awareness, rather, it functions as a mode of governance that acknowledges the interdependence between traditional Inuit values, local livelihoods, and national policy priorities. Whilst these broader contextual dynamics influence leadership at a societal level, studies of organisational life in Greenland show that empathy is most visible in everyday workplace interactions. As our interviewee, Verena Huppert Karlsson explained, Greenlandic workplaces operate as *"a kind of family because it is a small society… there is no big difference between home and work"* (28 November, 2025). Leadership is therefore practiced in small, tightly interconnected communities where relational expectations, shared cultural norms, and collective responsibilities shape how leaders communicate and make decisions. In this context, empathy becomes a practical organisational tool. Leaders are expected to *"make space"* for employees' personal circumstances because this flexibility is embedded in workplace culture. Karlsson illustrates this by citing the example of a top leader bringing their children to work if childcare falls through (28 November, 2025), which would be viewed as normal and acceptable rather than unprofessional. Karlsson's personal research highlights three decisive factors that determine whether employees stay or leave a workplace in Greenland: social belonging, communication, and leadership quality (28 November, 2025). Empathy directly contributes to all three of these factors. Moreover, in a context in which employees avoid open confrontation, leaders rely on empathetic dialogue and involvement to surface concerns that would otherwise remain unspoken (DR, 2023). Ultimately, empathy enables leaders to navigate the boundaries between professional roles and community relationships, making it not only a cultural expectation but a critical business capability for sustaining workforce stability and to ensure organisational effectiveness in *the land of the people*. Greenlandic organisations demonstrate that leaders are expected to listen attentively, avoid direct confrontation, and engage in communication that preserves harmony within the group (DR, 2023. Rasmussen's empirical work in fish factories, for example, shows how leadership emerges through ongoing relational exchanges in which managers demonstrate respect for workers based on their situated knowledge, respond sensitively to everyday concerns, and encourage collaboration rather than directive control (Rasmussen, 2023). Such practices illustrate a culturally grounded form of empathetic leadership where authority is negotiated through care, presence, and relational attentiveness rather than formal hierarchy. Rasmussen and Olsen (2022) further emphasise that leadership in Greenland is closely tied to *ilinniartumik suleqatigiinneq which means* working together in a manner that prioritises balance, mutual respect, and community well-being. In this view, empathy is not merely an interpersonal skill but rather a foundation for legitimate leadership, shaping how decisions are made and how leaders are perceived by their teams (Rasmussen & Olsem, 2022). The findings from the CCBS Survey (2025) reinforce this emphasis on relational care and harmony-oriented communication, insofar as the respondents reported indirect feedback, consensus-building, and support for employee well-being as central elements of empathetic leadership, reflecting a strong cultural preference for maintaining cohesion and avoiding interpersonal conflict. Listening skills and cooperative decision-making were also consistently identified as core expectations for leaders. As one respondent, a CEO in the mining sector, explained: *"one prefers collective decision-making here in Greenland. But if I, as a leader, express my opinion too quickly, others will adapt to it, so I do not get their honest view on the problem"* (CCBS Survey, 2025). The same respondent emphasised that effective leaders in Greenland are expected to be *"good listeners"* and *"consensus seekers,"* and that employees evaluate leaders based on organisational experience, market expertise, and technical competence, rather than formality or authority alone (CCBS Survey, 2025). These insights further demonstrate that empathetic leadership in Greenland is expressed through restraint, dialogue, and the creation of psychological space for others to speak, an approach designed to preserve relational harmony and ensure genuine participation in organizational decisions. In this way, empathy plays a central role in sustaining organisational functioning in Greenland. It enables leaders to bridge diverse perspectives, respect local knowledge, and cultivate trust within workplaces shaped by close relationships and strong cultural continuity. This echoes what Northouse (2022) describes as transformational empathy with leadership that strengthens inclusion, fosters mutual understanding, and contributes to collective resilience within complex social environments.

Kenya

Senne Bakker, Benjamin Abd El-Malek, Nadia Appia-Kubi, Maureen van der Greft,
Bibi van Ooien & Isa Veldhuis

Kenya, formally the Republic of Kenya, is a strategically placed nation in East Africa bordering the equator, with a population of over 51.4 million people in 2018, according to the Global Policy Unit (2019). Its capital, Nairobi, is a major financial hub and hosts the United Nations' largest headquarters outside of New York, underscoring Kenya's regional and global influence. The country is renowned for its cultural and geographical diversity, (Sobania, 2003), as evidenced by the fact that it is home to 40 ethnic groups, each of which have unique traditions, languages, and practices that shape social and organisational life (Kilonzi et al., 2023). Whilst English and Swahili are the official languages, Swahili's historical role as a trade language continues to influence communication via its proverbs and expressions, such as the saying *"Haraka haraka haina baraka"* ("hurry, hurry has no blessings"), which reflects the value placed on patience and pragmatism in daily life ("Swahili Proverbs: Methali za Kiswahili", n.d.). Economically, Kenya is one of Africa's fastest-growing markets, driven by the agricultural and service sectors, and increasingly, the technological sector. The country is also a continental leader in renewable energy, with geothermal power from the Rift Valley accounting for much of its electricity supply (International Energy Agency, 2024). Tourism is also vital economically, with safaris and wildlife reserves attracting over 1.5 million visitors in 2022, underlining the sector's role in economic growth and global reputation. Nevertheless, challenges such as income inequality and climate vulnerability remain. The national motto, *Harambee* ("pulling together"), embodies Kenya's collective spirit of resilience and ambition. This spirit also shapes Kenyan business leadership, which is deeply influenced by community ties, kinship networks, and consensus-building traditions, where oratory and public persuasion play pivotal roles (Sobania, 2003). These cultural elements blend with modern governance and business practices, creating a leadership style that balances formality with warmth and inclusiveness (Oino, 2023). The following chapter explores Kenyan leadership styles in greater depth, drawing on academic literature, surveys, and interviews with local experts and professionals.

How Kenyans characterise leaders?

Kenyan leaders are widely characterised as adaptive, pragmatic, and community-orientated, blending respect for hierarchy and cultural tradition with increasing openness and innovation. Kenya's tradition of collective problem-solving, embodied in *Harambee* ("pulling together"), continues to shape how employees and stakeholders expect leaders to behave. This philosophy fosters mutual support, community responsibility, and inclusive participation, influencing leadership attitudes towards collaboration, ethical engagement, and accountability in social and business contexts (Nicolaides & Ndlovu, 2023). This heritage continues to shape contemporary leadership expectations across various business settings, from multinational corporations to agile tech start-ups. A clear example of how *Harambee* influences expectations for business leaders in Kenya can be seen in the way businesses such as Java House and Kikopey engage with their employees. Both companies foster collaborative relationships through interactive campaigns and co-creation opportunities—managers actively seek out and incorporate feedback from staff, genuinely valuing their input in product development and community initiatives (DHL, 2024). Marcia Gillespie, a cross-cultural trainer, affirms that this aligns with a broader cultural shift in Kenya towards more collaborative leadership, where communication is less about giving orders and more about listening, observing, and involving others in decision-making (11 November, 2025). According to DHL (2024), such practices directly reflect the tradition of *Harambee*, where leaders are expected to encourage open communication, inclusivity, and shared responsibility, underpinning workplace accountability, and ethical engagement. This collaborative approach, rooted in Kenya's culture, helps leaders earn trust and loyalty, whilst, simultaneously, driving shared success and sustainable growth. Building on this foundation, Kenyan leadership is shaped by rapid economic growth, a youthful workforce, and connections to global markets, which demands adaptability and innovation (Kim, 2025). Public institutions are undergoing a shift from traditional, authoritarian approaches towards participative and transformational styles, which focus on employee motivation, involvement, and innovation and leads to better performance, albeit its adoption remains limited at this moment (Kibai & Awuor, 2024). The results of the CCBS Survey (2025) indicate that Kenyan leaders are expected to be good communicators, encourage feedback and combine hard work with inclusivity, which reflects the local *"harambee"* philosophy of community-centred decision-making. Whilst respect for seniority still holds influence in Kenyan organisations, leaders increasingly must balance authority with inclusiveness by fostering participation and consensus-building in decision-making.

This evolving style highlights visionary and transformational leadership, employee empowerment, and effective communication as vital to boosting organisational performance (Ng'ang'a et al., 2024). Kenyan leaders also exhibit pragmatism and goal orientation, promoting teamwork, social responsibility, and constructive feedback, whilst, simultaneously, upholding accountability and discipline. Communication skills, especially persuasive oratory and storytelling, are prized, reflecting cultural traditions that use public speaking to mobilise and unify groups. To cite an example, CEOs at Family Bank exhibit pragmatism and goal orientation by setting clear targets and inspiring employees through storytelling and motivational speeches. They actively promote teamwork, encourage constructive feedback, and emphasise accountability and discipline to ensure everyone understands their roles and responsibilities. (Gonnah & Ogollah, 2016). Gillespie also informed us that Kenyan leadership is shifting towards more collaborative styles in which leaders mentor teams, empower young talent, and cultivate innovation within organisational goals (11 November, 2025). Ethical behaviour is also vital, insofar as leaders serve as role models whose actions influence organisational culture and climate. These traits enhance trust and foster positive environments in Kenyan organisations (Maru et al., 2024). Vision and adaptability remain crucial to navigating Kenya's economic diversity from traditional agriculture to fast-evolving fintech. This is reinforced by the fact that Kenyan employees strongly expect leaders to be both visionary thinkers and powerful decision-makers (CCBS Survey, 2025). Strategic leadership, characterised by visionary and flexible management, helps organisations anticipate market trends and drive sustained growth and innovation (Ng'ang'a et al., 2024). These insights are supported by our interviewee, Marcia Gillespie, who notes that Kenyan leadership balances respect for hierarchy and cultural tradition with growing openness, collaboration, and humility. She underscores that effective leaders use persuasive communication and active listening, adapting to context while building trust. Additionally, she points out that female leaders often face initial challenges gaining acceptance but earn strong loyalty once credibility is established (Gillespie, 11 November 2025). These nuanced experiences illustrate the evolving nature of Kenyan leadership, complementing the traditional *Harambee* ethos with modern demands for inclusiveness and ethical governance.

Survey results and what local respondents say

In order to examine leadership dynamics in Kenya, a comprehensive survey was administered to local executives and highly educated professionals with knowledge and expertise of the country's organisational culture and leadership landscape. The results of the CCBS Survey (2025) reveal a wide-ranging set of perspectives on leadership styles and practices amongst Kenyan managers, highlighting both consistent tendencies and notable areas of divergence. The following section discusses the most noteworthy findings from the administered survey in turn. The first significant finding is that leaders are generally perceived as firm decision-makers who are unlikely to reverse their choices once made, whilst most consider not meeting deadlines to being equivalent to failure itself, thus reflecting a strong result-driven orientation (CCBS Survey, 2025). The respondents were divided with respect to whether Kenyan leaders typically confront subordinates during staff meetings, which suggests that assertiveness in group settings varies considerably across individuals. In contrast, a clear majority of the respondents reported identifying closely with the statement that leaders should invest time and effort in the personal well-being of their team members, thus underscoring the continued importance of people-centred leadership in Kenya (CCBS Survey, 2025). The next notable finding from the survey is that competition within teams is widely supported as a means of improving outcomes, whereas there were differing perspectives over whether leaders should maintain personal distance from their employees and whether criticism should be delivered indirectly (CCBS Survey, 2025). The open-ended responses from the survey do shed light on uniquely Kenyan leadership traits; for example, an accountant manager from Nairobi stated that Kenyan leaders have a tendency to begin with solutions and then work backwards from there (CCBS Survey, 2025). In addition, a solutions consultant in Nairobi reported the following: *"Kenyan leadership styles reflect a balance of traditional values with an openness to modern, inclusive practices. The unique blend of a community-centred approach driven by Harambee, a Swahili term meaning 'pull together'"* (CCBS Survey, 2025). In addition, Daniel Nyamera, a COO of Synergy Company Limited, stated the following: *"In Kenya, the CEO tends to have the final authority on decisions. People are employed mostly based on who they know, especially inside the organisation"* (CCBS Survey, 2025). The respondents also identified several notable Kenyan leadership books, such as *"Uongozi wa Kike,"* Patrick Lumumba's works, *"The Future Leaders,"* and Millie Odhiambo-Mabona's *"Rig or Be Rigged,"* reflecting a diverse intellectual landscape. Although academic titles are not seen as essential, many leaders still view them as somewhat beneficial. Next, whilst opinions were mixed about whether subordinates should address leaders by their titles, most leaders expressed feeling comfortable about being addressed by their first name (CCBS Survey, 2025).

Local leadership analysis

Marcia Gillespie: a Kenyan cross-cultural trainer

Marcia Gillespie works as a cross-cultural trainer for the United Nations (UN) in Kenya and as a witness protection trainer for the International Criminal Court (ICC) in The Hague. She has worked several times in Kenya and has spent a year living and working there. Besides Kenya, she has worked in Ethiopia, Central Africa, Ivory Coast and the Seychelles. At th ebeginning of our interview, Marcia characterised the country's leadership environment as distinct and powerful (11 November, 2025). She placed Kenya, alongside South Africa, *''at the forefront''* of progressive development on the continent. She opined that their leadership is *''stronger and more proactive''* than in regions such as the Seychelles. Fore xample, she informed us, in the Seychelles, a director might still be viewed as *''my friend''* and *''on a similar level''*, whereas in Kenya, however, it is *''quite a hierarchical type of leadership''*. It is not only defined by someone's position but also by the *''extra layer of tribal influence''* (Gillespie, 11 November 2025). She proceeded to explain how depending on the individual's position within their tribe and *''how your tribe is seen by other tribes''*, Kenya has a system that is simultaneously *''positional and tribal''* (Gillespie, 11 November, 2025). This strong cultural identity in the Kenyan hierarchy led Marcia to voice a long-term concern, which is that Kenya *''might lose themselves''*. This is because due to the high volume of international organisations, local citizens are *''more likely to adapt''* to foreign cultures rather than the Western world adapting to them. In this regard, Marcia specifically encouraged groups such as the Maasai, who are moving into Nairobi for work, that *''it is okay to still wear your robes if you are going to be working in Nairobi. Do not change to fit in''* (11 November 2025). Another challenge in Kenya is faced by female leaders, who are *''unfortunately still perceived differently''*. Although, Marcia informed us, female leaders are highly respected once they are established, they must first *''prove themselves''* to gain the group's trust. This testing phase, which involves subordinates carefully examining the leader's capability, can be severe. Marcia recalled speaking to a woman who felt she was *''almost set up to fail''*. *''It is almost like setting traps''* and they will *''pose this problem and see how you sort it out''*. Only when a woman demonstrates that she *''knows what she is talking about''* does she achieve acceptance and loyalty. Luckily, she does see improvements happening in this area but very *''polepole''* (slowly) (Gillespie, 11 November 2025). In response to a question about generational differences, Marcia told us that driven by *''Western influence''* and *''digitalisation''*, the younger generation is *''more challenging in terms of questioning''* and is *''not just accepting what they are being told''* (11 November,

2025). In Kenya, this shift is moving towards a *''more collaborative''* style, where instead of *''this is what you will do''* , the conversation is shifting to *''let us sit around and talk about it''*. Marcia did go on to caution that this shift must be done *''respectfully''* for Kenya to maintain its cultural footing. To succeed in the Kenyan environment, Marcia emphasised that leaders must *''research the styles that are current in that country''* and *''look at your own and kind of try to meet halfway''*. She added that leaders need to be more *''open''* and that *''You get things done by listening, by observing, by sometimes being a bit humble''* and definitely *''do not assume''*. A leader should be open by *''being vulnerable''* and not being afraid to say that they do not know the answer because that makes them human, and humans make mistakes (Gillespie, 11 November 2025). When we asked Marcia about the influence Kenya has had on her, she mentioned that it has made her *''more open''*. *''Whilst people say it is a small world, the world is a big place with different cultures, but there are so many good things, and there are so many things you can learn from others''* (Gillespie, 11 November 2025).

Kenyan Social Media Review
Alongside academic research and survey and interview data, another useful resource foe finding out empirical insights about Kenyan business leadership is social media platforms. In this respect, Kenyan social media reveals a picture of Kenyan business leadership that is ambitious, ethical, service-oriented, and strongly relational in nature (Kavashe, 2025; Nduati, 2025). More specifically, business leadership in Kenya is portrayed less as individual acts of heroism on the behalf of leaders and more as a demanding service that requires continuous checking in, clearly understanding each person's role, and putting people in the right positions so the organisation stays aligned (Nduati, 2025). In an interview, corporate leader Rita Kavashe stresses that Kenyan business leaders must prove they can deliver results *"in an ethical manner,"* which serves to demonstrate one way in which trust in Kenyan leadership is increasingly tied to integrity and performance rather than foreign oversight, whilst, simultaneously, noting that female leaders continue to encounter strong gender bias when attempting to advance into senior roles within Kenyan organisations (Kavashe, 2025). Another central theme in online discourse on Kenyan business leadership is initiative and lifelong learning. Specifically, Kavashe describes pushing her own Kenyan company into new government tenders, seeking better deals from overseas partners, and entering a technical environment *"knowing that I have to learn,"* which frames good Kenyan leadership as being grounded in being proactive, curious, and resilient (Kavashe, 2025). Kenyan online commentary on business leadership further stresses the importance of collaborative and caring leadership, which is

exemplified by Kavashe bringing together dealers, sales staff, and banks during a financial crisis to co-create solutions in a *Harambee*-style process (Kavashe, 2025), whilst businessman William Kabogo argues that a leader should succeed "*amongst your peers*" by working with others and finding mutual opportunity rather than, say, undermining one's colleagues (Kabogo, 2025). Airline executive Allan Kilavuka adds a personal dimension to these discussions by reminding Kenyan leaders that "*you are taking care of 4,500 people but who is taking care of you,*" thus emphasising self-care as part of responsible leadership, which complements Nduati's view of leadership as a kind of "*war*" that demands stamina and constant adaptation (Kilavuka, 2025; Nduati, 2025). Viewed together, these Kenyan voices depict business leadership as being characterised by ethical performance, shared effort, and care for both followers and self, in addition to being grounded in local social and cultural realities (Kavashe, 2025; Kabogo, 2025; Kilavuka, 2025; Nduati, 2025).

In-country leadership bestseller

One of Kenya's bestselling books on leadership is '*Growing a Business Empire: How to Effectively Manage Leadership Succession for Organisational Growth,*' which was written by Dr. Mary Mugo in 2019. Dr. Mary Mugo is an innovative academic scholar from Kenya who has worked in senior management positions in both the public and private sectors. She has helped organisations achieve sustainable growth, which testifies to her leadership abilities and management skills. Dr Mary Mugo has written multiple books on various topics within management and about building effective organisations (Mary Mugo, 2024). In this particular book she argues that ineffective planning and leadership transitions are the reason why many Kenyan businesses, mostly family businesses, are unable to take advantage of the international market. Simply put, many Kenyan leaders know the importance of successful planning but do not seem to plan for it. This is because, according to Mugo et al. (2015, p. 4), "*many family companies in Kenya seem to suffer from the founders' syndrome*". As a founder, they have a huge passion, which helps with organisational growth but over time this can also limit the company's opportunities for expansion. The Kenyan founders who suffer from this issue make decisions on their own, without considering input from others in their organisation. In many Kenyan family organisations, meetings are held to get status reports and not for strategic reasons, whilst the senior staff are usually friends of the founder, which makes the board underqualified and vastly intimidated by the founder. Therefore, she emphasises the importance of effective leadership transition management in Kenya in order to ensure both continuity and long-term organisational growth. To this end, Mugo advises that a good Kenyan leader must plan well for their exit and coach the right person to take their position when it is the right time in order to ensure minimal interruption in the day-to-day running of the organisation. As she puts it, *"And as they say, failure to plan is planning to fail"* (Mugo, 2022, p. 7). An example that Mugo cites in her book is the Kenyan family business Chandaria, which has grown over several generations due to both good management succession plans and adapting various growth strategies, such as merging, exporting and product development (Mugo et al., 2015). The book also provides a practical guide on how to implement effective planning, timing, and management strategies to ensure business continuity and growth in Kenyan organisations (Mugo, 2024).

Local leadership book	
Title	*Growing a Business Empire*
Subtitle	How to Effectively Manage Leadership Succession for Organizational Growth
Author	Dr. Mary Mugo
Publisher	Zionpearl Publishers
Year	2019
ISBN	9966821422

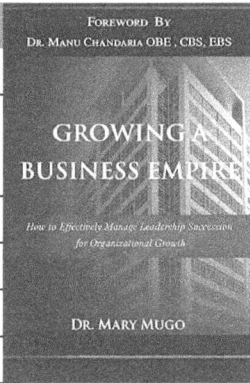

Kenya leadership YouTube review

What Kenya needs from its leaders is the topic of debate on Citizen TV. Kenya's Day Break: four contributors with a leadership background in business discuss how *"Leaders are being called upon to go an extra mile … to coach, listen and empower their teams"* (YouTube, Day Break | Leadership: What Kenya Needs, 2025, 04:00–04:30), emphasising a shift towards transformational leadership in the country. Another contributor goes on to say, *"What Kenya needs is not just management of the workforce but true leadership that inspires and guides"* (06:10), thus suggesting that effective Kenyan leaders inspire rather than manage. Another speaker notes that the country should give youth a chance: *"youth must be given a seat at decision tables; Kenya cannot ignore young leaders anymore"* (11:30). The discussion then moves onto the topic of how moral leadership and accountability are now the core expectations for Kenyan business leaders. Overall, Day Break sends out a message that Kenya's leadership model is shifting from positional authority to relational influence: valuing empathy, inclusion, and mentorship. In the next video to be summarised here in this section, Michael Joseph, the former CEO of Safaricom, provides insight into the business perspective of leading in Kenya. He says in his YouTube interview, Michael Joseph on Leadership in Kenya, that: *"Leadership here is not about rank or title; it is stepping up when things are tough"* (KTN Entertainment, 2024: 02:15). He insists on resilience and responsibility being key traits for Kenyan leaders to embody. Furthermore, he explains: *"In Kenya's corporate world, you have to build trust fast, for resources move and only relationships last"* (KTN Entertainment, 2024: 04:00), alluding to *Imani*, or trust, as being what matters above all for lasting success. Joseph also states in the video that: *"Empowerment means giving people decisions; you cannot micro-manage everything if you want growth"* (KTN Entertainment, 2024: 06:40), which cements *kuaminiana*, or mutual trust, and decentralisation as a Kenyan corporate value. Moreover, Joseph points out that successful leadership in Kenya requires an understanding of the culture and adaptability since leaders have to deal with diverse teams and changing market realities. His observations show that Kenyan corporate leadership is increasingly people-centred, anchored in collaboration, trust, and long-term relationship building rather than hierarchy. The mindset of Kenyan leadership in a business perspective is strongly forward-looking, and innovation driven (KTN Entertainment, 2024). This can be evinced from the various ideas discussed by Prof. Bitange Ndemo, a well-known Kenyan entrepreneurship scholar. He insists on self-reliant development and affirms that *"aid has never developed any country"*, an approach indicative of strong and independent institutional leadership (Accelerate TV, 2022, 02.30). Ndemo goes on to emphasise that technological transformation is vital: *"Africa could take advantage of growing talent, urbanisation and infrastructure to lead in the fourth industrial revolution"* (Accelerate TV, 2022, 04.55). He believes in innovation coupled with social impact: *"an advocate of development strategies leveraging emergent technologies and social enterprise"* (Accelerate TV, 2022, 06:55). These statements present the Kenyan leadership style as pragmatic, orientated toward the future, and anchored around sustainable, locally driven development.

Understanding Hierarchy in Kenya

Hierarchy is a defining feature of social and organisational life in Kenya, shaping how authority, respect, and leadership are expressed. Hofstede's (2010) concept of power distance, defined as the extent to which the less powerful members of organisations and institutions accept and expect that power is distributed unequally, offers valuable insight into how Kenyans perceive leadership and authority within their workplaces and communities. At the societal level, authority in Kenya is closely linked to markers such as age, educational attainment, and socio-economic status. In fact, employees look up to their leaders based on organisational experience, market experience, and technical competence (CCBS Survey, 2025). Job titles also command a lot of respect in organisations, and it is important for subordinates to address leaders by their titles or positions when communicating, according to the results of the CCBS Survey (2025). Academic research also demonstrates that individuals who occupy higher-status categories, particularly older, more highly educated, or professionally senior individuals, tend to be perceived as more legitimate decision-makers. For example, Munene (2002) demonstrates that these demographic role-structure characteristics significantly influence both how authority is distributed and how expectations around leadership are formed within Kenyan institutions. As a result, younger or lower-ranking individuals are more likely to defer to those with seniority, which, in turn, reinforces hierarchical norms. These dynamics sustain a cultural environment in which unequal power relations are widely accepted and embedded in everyday organisational practice (Munene, 2002). In business settings, hierarchy is reinforced through seniority and respect for authority. Kenyan organisations are typically hierarchical, and older individuals or those in senior positions are often deferred to and treated with considerable respect. Decision-making is generally centralised, with senior managers retaining final authority. This was also confirmed by our interviewee, Marcia Gillespie, who informed us that the leadership landscape in Kenya is *"quite a hierarchical type of leadership"* (11 November, 2025). Lower-level employees are rarely involved in strategic decisions, and because approval typically moves through multiple hierarchical levels, organisational processes can become slow and inefficient. This strong hierarchy is maintained by formal distance, as evidenced by the fact that most of our survey respondents reported that leaders prefer to retain a personal distance from their employees to maintain respect (CCBS Survey, 2025). Similarly, Muriithi (2020) shows that Kenya's strong hierarchical cultural norms shape how leadership is interpreted and enacted, insofar as employees tend to expect clear direction and authoritative guidance from their superiors rather than relying on autonomous decision-making. Consequently, leadership in Kenya often takes on a paternalistic or directive form: superiors are viewed as knowledgeable and experienced, whilst subordinates demonstrate loyalty and deference. This aligns with Hofstede's (2010) assertion that in high-power-distance cultures, ideal leaders act as *"benevolent autocrats"*. Yet, as Kenyan organisations become more globalised, a generational shift is emerging. Younger professionals, particularly within Nairobi's private sector, show a growing preference for participatory leadership practices that emphasise open dialogue, collaborative problem-solving, and innovation (Kamau & Kamau, 2019). Marcia Gillespie affirmed this by saying that she sees subtle changes in the newer generation driven by western influences and digitalisation. She says this generation is more challenging in terms of questioning and is not just accepting what they are being told (Gillespie, 11 November 2025). Successful Kenyan leaders therefore need to blend respect for traditional hierarchy with consultative management, maintaining formal authority whilst fostering open communication and trust. In conclusion, hierarchy in Kenya is not merely a structural formality but a deeply rooted cultural reality. It shapes how decisions are made, how authority is perceived, and how leaders maintain order and respect within their organisations. Understanding Kenya's power distance and its cultural nuances is essential for effective leadership, teamwork, and cross-cultural collaboration in this dynamic and rapidly modernising society.

How Kenyans Achieve Leadership Empathy

Within the Kenyan context, empathy has emerged as a particularly vital leadership attribute, which is deeply interwoven with cultural traditions and contemporary governance practices (Luchivisi et al., 2025). Kenyan business leadership is characterised by a strong empathetic approach that values collective well-being alongside individual achievement (CCBS Survey, 2025). Empathy is embedded within Kenyan culture through the philosophy of *Ubuntu*, which is rooted in many African traditions. *Ubuntu*, which is commonly translated as "*humanity towards others*" or "*I am because we are*", embodies the principle that personhood is realised through relationships with others. Within Kenyan workplaces and community settings, *Ubuntu* is not just theoretical; rather, it shapes how leaders encourage collaboration, compassion, and mutual support by engaging in practical behaviours such as communal living, shared responsibilities, and collective child-rearing, all of which reflect the philosophy's values of empathy and interconnectedness (Meda Foundation, 2024). This philosophy manifests in Kenyan leadership through an emphasis on social harmony and collective responsibility in national development initiatives (Odari, 2020). Beyond its cultural foundations, empathy is reflected in diverse Kenyan leadership practices that prioritise active listening, inclusion, and community engagement. Leaders inspired by *Ubuntu* actively engage their communities, listen to diverse perspectives, and make decisions that value cultural sensitivity and fairness. Our interviewee, Marcia Gillespie confirmed this by saying that as a leader in Kenya *"you get things done by listening, by observing, by sometimes being a bit humble"* (11 November, 2025). This collaborative spirit also extends to conflict resolution, where leaders strive for dignity and inclusivity, crucial for fostering peace in multi-ethnic contexts (Zivkovic, 2025). The concept of *Harambee* ("*pulling together*") further reinforces empathic leadership by encouraging collective action and mutual support. Gillespie informed us that especially the younger generation in Kenya prefers a *"more collaborative"* style where leaders *"sit around the table and talk"* rather than issuing top-down orders (11 November, 2025). Originally mobilised for community development projects, *Harambee* principles have permeated various sectors, including health initiatives, education, and business enterprises (Mbithi, 1977). Kenyan leaders demonstrate a strong work ethic and entrepreneurial spirit, ensuring that tasks are completed effectively whilst, simultaneously, maintaining their commitment to empathetic engagement. Gillespie emphasises that Kenyans are extremely diligent people who pursue their goals whilst maintaining a friendly and cooperative approach to teamwork (11 November, 2025). Empathy-driven leaders become role models, building trust and providing moral guidance for their communities (Zivkovic, 2025). This combination of determination and empathy creates a leadership style that is both results-orientated and people-centred. Contemporary Kenyan leaders increasingly adopt consensus-driven and servant-leadership approaches, emphasising dialogue and shared responsibility over traditional top-down authority structures, as evidenced by the results of the CCBS Survey (2025). These approaches—especially the use of *Ubuntu's* human-centred focus for ethical decision-making—are particularly significant given Kenya's ethnic diversity (Meda Foundation, 2024). By incorporating *Ubuntu* principles, leaders are better able to maintain social cohesion and advance collective development initiatives beyond traditional top-down approaches (Luchivisi et al., 2025). Furthermore, Kenyan leaders are notably accommodating of other cultures and inclusive in their decision-making processes, recognising that diverse perspectives strengthen outcomes and foster unity (Odari, 2020). Gillespie also emphasised that Kenyan leaders should respect cultural identity and urge employees to embrace and retain their cultural heritage rather than adhere to foreign standards (11 November, 2025). Overall, then, within the Kenyan context, empathy transcends being merely a cultural value; rather, it serves as a practical leadership tool that enables leaders to comprehend diverse community viewpoints and foster collective belonging (Odari, 2020). This integration of traditional values with modern leadership practices, combined with a hard-working, entrepreneurial mindset and cultural inclusivity, positions empathy as both a cultural inheritance and a strategic necessity for effective governance in Kenyan businesses.

Kosovo

Kaan Birinci, Kimon Bletsis, Raoul van Dort, Dennis Grimme,
Luuk Hagoort & Pim Warmerdam.

Kosovo's leadership story is best captured through the language of hospitality and obligation. The Kanun Albania's historic customary law that continues to resonate amongst Kosovar Albanians enshrines the duty to honour one's guest with *"bukë, kripë e zemër"* (bread, salt, and heart), and is a norm that has long shaped expectations of stewardship, care and moral standing in public life (Yamamoto, 2000; Latifi, 2018). Kosovo sits at the crossroads of the Western Balkans and is characterised by a young population, a sizeable diaspora that shapes daily life through remittances and transnational ties, and institutions that are still in the process of consolidating after the country's independence (Latifi Sadrija, 13 November 2025; World Bank, n.d.). In light of this, it is perhaps unsurprising that research indicates that interpersonal trust often exceeds trust in formal bodies (UNDP, 2019). These aforementioned social relations are ordinarily organised around kinship and reciprocity, whilst the moral vocabulary of *besa* (pledged word), *mikpritja* (attentive hospitality) and *nder* (honour) remain salient, both within public and private spheres (Latifi, 2018; Hamiti, 2024). Against this backdrop, leadership is framed through a lens of credibility and care (Lokaj & Latifi Sadrija, 2020). Kosovo's organisational culture blends entrepreneurial energy with practical constraints inherited from the period of transition, which means leaders are forced to routinely balance relationship-building with disciplined execution. Indeed, in public organisations and private firms alike, leaders' credibility grows when they can communicate their purpose clearly, explain decisions, and broker cooperation amongst those that they lead (Latifi, 2018). Ultimately, these dynamics determine how authority is gained, how decisions are accepted and how change takes root (World Bank Group, 2020). When viewed together, Kosovo offers a vivid case for examining how culturally endorsed leadership prototypes intersect with legitimacy, informality and organisational change. The following chapter explores what effective leadership looks like in Prishtinë/Priština Kosovo today, by drawing upon academic research (House et al., 2004) and interview and survey data with local professionals and experts in the field of Kosovar business leadership.

How the Kosovar characterise leaders?

Kosovo's expectations of leaders are shaped by its post-conflict, institution-building setting, strong kinship ties, and a sizeable diaspora that continues to influence economic and social life (Lokaj & Latifi Sadrija, 2020). Studies on social cohesion show that interpersonal trust often outpaces trust in public institutions, which means that legitimacy tends to take centre stage when it comes to how authority figures are judged in the country. Related to this aforementioned point, a first, enduring expectation of Kosovar leaders is integrity in the form of promise-keeping, which is neatly captured in the Albanian concept of *besa* (trust), that is, a pledge of honour that obliges that leaders follow-through and protect those that they lead (Yamamoto, 2000). Indeed. scholarly work on the *Kanun* (customary law) and Albanian oral tradition treats besa (*trust*) as a cornerstone of social order in Kosovo. When applied to the organisational context, this translates into the expectation that business leaders will keep their word, safeguard their teams, and act consistently in the face of pressure (Fox, 1989/1992; Tarifa, 2008). Closely related to this is the concept of *mikpritja* (hospitality), which with respect to business leadership specifically means that leaders must exhibit visible care for both their clients and teams, and be responsive and respectful (Tarifa, 2008). Moreover, managers are expected to cultivate a safe environment in meetings, resolve issues promptly, and invest in mentoring, which is consistent with GLOBE's humane orientation (Hamiti, 2024; House et al., 2004). When considered in conjunction with one another, *besa* and *mikpritja* foster a prototype of the Kosovar leader as a trustworthy guardian, who is decisive, yet relational, which goes some way to explain why Kosovar leaders are seen as being more legitimate when they act in visionary and inclusive ways, an approach which is consistent with a transformational approach (Mexhuani & Mexhuani, 2023). In Kosovo there is typically a reciprocal relationship between leadership styles and organisational culture, which has clear implications for employees' readiness for change: leaders who model clarity of purpose and fairness can shift the organisational norms and increase employees' openness towards new practices (Lokaj & Latifi Sadrija, 2020). This framing of Kosovar leadership finds support in the results of the CCBS Survey (2025), where local leadership was described as being *"dominated by relationship-building and trust,"* with one respondent noting that a Kosovar leader *"relies much more on trust, loyalty, and personal credibility"* than rigid formalism, which makes clarity and follow-through decisive in practice (CCBS Survey, 2025). Moreover, another respondents also underscored the gap between imported models and local credibility cues, speaking of *"different contradictions between leaders in Kosovo and literature abroad"* (CCBS Survey, 2025). Similarly, one executive reported that there is simply a *"different mentality,"* which means change gains acceptance when leaders protect relationships, make expectations explicit and deliver on promises (CCBS Survey, 2025). These findings resonate with Implicit Leadership Theory (ILT) and GLOBE: people use shared schemas to judge who "fits" as a leader, and in Kosovo those schemas reward integrity, in-group protection and community-minded achievement. In practice, leaders signal their integrity by making decisions auditable and fair. For example, publishing tenders and awards through the national e-procurement system and conducting public tender openings, by separating ownership and management and adopting basic board rules in family firms, and by applying merit-based recruitment and codes of conduct in the civil service (Public Procurement Regulatory Commission, Finally, ethnographic research documents how kinship networks permeate both private and public spheres in Kosovo, shaping flows of information, trust, and obligation (Latifi, 2018). Effective leaders are therefore expected to cultivate *nder* (honour) in their dealings, whilst, simultaneously, building bridges across family, municipal and professional networks; in practice this routinely means combining formal procedures with credible relational brokerage (Latifi, 2018; Fox, 1989/1992; UNDP, 2019). Transparent communication in Kosovo's firms means managers explaining the rationale and trade-offs behind decisions, stating timelines, owners and next steps, and issuing brief written recaps. They proactively disclose constraints and mitigation plans, apply clear criteria for allocations and promotions to avoid perceptions of favouritism, and invite questions through open Q&A or designated channels behaviours that bolster credibility and perceived legitimacy (Mexhuani & Mexhuani, 2023). This is confirmed by our survey respondents who emphasised that credibility in Kosovo is earned less through formal procedure than through transparent communication and dependable promises, with leaders expected to explain trade-offs and timelines, and then deliver as agreed (CCBS Survey, 2025). In summary, Kosovars tend to characterise effective leaders as those who are trustworthy and keep their promises. Whilst these expectations align with global theories that emphasise culturally shared prototypes, they are locally inflected by kinship, diaspora-driven opportunity structures, and the practical constraints firms navigate (Lord et al., 2020; Lokaj & Latifi Sadrija, 2020).

Survey results and what local respondents say

The CCBS Survey was conducted in order to gather local insight into business leadership styles and practices in Kosovo. Participating in the survey allowed C-level executives and other highly qualified professionals in the country with an in-depth understanding of Kosovar business leadership practices to share their knowledge and expertise with us. To enhance the validity and credibility of the findings, we combinated data from multiple periods of data collection. The most significant findings emerging from the survey are discussed in turn below. Overall, the responses portray a decisive form of leadership that is paired with respectful candour. Firstly, with respect to decision-making processes and confronting performance issues in their teams, many of the respondents endorsed leaders who hold their position once a decision has been made, and who are also willing to address problems with employees' work promptly in team settings (CCBS Survey, 2022-2025). The next significant finding is that one senior respondent spoke of a recurring theme in the dataset, namely the distance between imported management models and local credibility cues. As they put it: *"there are different contradictions between leaders in Kosovo and literature abroad"* (CCBS Survey, 2025). Next, there were divergent opinions expressed with respect to the importance placed on addressing leaders by their titles, as many of the respondents reported that it was acceptable to refer to leaders by their first-names, whereas others disgareed with this statement (CCBS Survey, 2022–2025). One explanation for this, as one one healthcare CEO from Pristina put it, is that there is a "different mentality" in Kosovo, which posits that leaders' legitimacy is earned through engagining in predictable conduct rather than ceremonial markers (CCBS Survey, 2025). The next interesting finding is that most of the respondents agreed with the statement that leaders should actively check in on their employees' workload and health; however, it is also important to stress that several respondents expressed the value of keeping professional boundaries intact. The composite picture here is therefore not one of permissive leniency but rather structured care: leaders are expected to be available, to notice strain early, and to act on it without blurring professional roles and boundaries (CCBS Survey, 2025). In response to questions about what constitutes the basis of leaders' credibility, the respondents pointed to competence over pedigree. Moreover, in response to a question about what Kosovar employees admire in leaders, the most frequently cited qualities were organisational experience, market expertise and technical competence, with age or family background less frequently cited (CCBS Survey, 2022-2025). With regards to the respondents' expectations of leaders, the most frequently cited traits were resourcefulness, the right professional networks and cognitive strength, with charisma present but not decisive (CCBS Survey, 2022–2025). Recica, a general manager explained why this configuration was preferred in Kosovo: *''in a small economy with strong community ties and the legacies of post-war rebuilding, leadership relies much more on trust, loyalty, and personal credibility, and leaders are expected to be competent and highly approachable, visible, and personally connected to their teams and communities"* (CCBS Survey, 2025). This is in line with the sentiment expressed by Indira Kartallozi, who stated in our interview with her that *"new leaders in Kosovo must be open-hearted"* (14 November, 2025).

Local leadership analysis

Indira Kartallozi: an Kosovar sustainability and leadership specialist.

Indira Kartallozi is a sustainability leadership specialist whose work spans across business, civil society, and education in Kosovo. She draws on a broad portfolio that includes co-directing the UK-based Kaleidoscope Futures Lab, founding and directing Sustainability Leadership Kosovo, and contributing to executive progammes at the University of Cambridge Institute for Sustainability Leadership. In our interview with her, she offered a nuanced account of how leadership is shaped by Kosovo's political, social and institutional context. At the beginning of the interview, Kartallozi described Kosovo's leadership landscape as being constrained by *"hierachies that are still very strong"* and a political environment in which *"corruption has become normalised"* (14 November ,2025). She argued that these sytemic issues contribute towards widespread distrust, particularly amongst young people, many of whom view international organisations as ineffective. As she proceeded to note, externally driven reforms are often *"copy-paste models that do not speak to Kosovo's lived experience"* (Kartallozi, 14 November 2025). Central to Kartallozi's approach is the belief that leadership is defined by behaviour rather than formal authority. She emphasised in our interview that *"leadership is not the title, it is the ability to challenge systems and ask difficult questions"*, a principle she integrates into progammes that teach sytems thinking to executives, youth and community leaders (Kartallozi, 14 November 2025). Her environmental activism illustrates the resistance faced by those who expose governance failures: *"The moment you expose corruption, doors start closing and you suddenly do not get the licenses, you do not get the funding"* (Kartallozi, 14 November 2025). Later in the interview, Kartallozi also shed light on ethical dilemmas pertaining to diversity and inclusion in Kosovo. Specifically, she informed us that many leaders in the country are hesitatant over employing minority or LGBTQ+ individuals out of fear of public backlash. As she put it, *"They worry that doing the right thing will hurt their business,"* thus underscoring the tension between ethics and social pressure in the country (Kartallozi, 14 November 2025). Despite these obstacles, she identified signs of progess in the Kosovar context, especially amongst the younger generation who *"are not afraid to speak up, not even to the president,"* and who often ask the most challenging questions in leadership sessions (Kartallozi, 14 November 2025). Towards the conclusion of the interview, Kartallozi advised foreign leaders entering Kosovo to adopt humility and curiosity in their leadership approach. As she opined: *"You cannot arrive here assuming you know better. Kosovo does not need rescuing, it needs partners who are willing to understand the context"* (Kartallozi, 14 November 2025). In conclusion, Kartallozi's reflections potray leadership in Kosovo as deeply relational and evolving, shaped by systemic constraints yet driven forward by the younger generation who are commited to transparency, inclusion, and structural change.

Thelleza Latifi Sadrija: a Kosovar scholar

Thelleza Latifi Sadrija is an Associate Professor, who is currently based at the University "Haxhi Zeka" in Kosovo, and specialises in leadership, organisational culture and management practices. Her research examines how leadership in Kosovo is shaped by cultural values, historical legacies and evolving expectations within businesses (Latifi Sadrija, 13 November 2025). In our interview with her, she explained that "good leadership" in Kosovo's private sector is often defined in pragmatic terms: a good leader is someone who keeps the business stable, ensures salaries are paid, secures clients and responds quickly to problems. Yet employees increasingly value relational qualities, such as respect, fairness, clear communication and recognition, which do not always align with current practices (Latifi Sadrija, 13 November 2025). Latifi Sadrija proceeded to explain that leadership in Kosovo resonates strongly with the transactional–transformational framework. Transactional leadership remains dominant, rooted in reward-based motivation, whilst transformational elements are mostly espied in either younger or internationally educated managers who articulate their vision and support employee development (13 November, 2025). In response to a question about cultural frameworks like Hofstede and GLOBE, she noted that whilst these help to explain tendencies such as high power distance and personalised authority, they do not fully capture the impact of post-conflict reconstruction, migration and diasporaric influences (Latifi Sadrija, 13 November 2025). She emphasised that leadership in Kosovo has distinctly local dimensions. Many firms are family-owned, and leaders often combine managerial authority with a moral or protective role. Loyalty, personal trust and direct access to leaders therefore often weigh as heavily as formal procedures. At the same time, Kosovo's diaspora plays a major role: returning entrepreneurs introduce more structured and strategic management practices, creating hybrid leadership models that integrate relational traditions with elements of modern professionalism. Historical and institutional context continues to shape how leaders act. The legacy of Yugoslav socialism entrenched certain expectations of hierarchy, whilst post-war reconstruction forced many entrepreneurs to develop leadership skills through experience rather than formal training (Latifi Sadrija, 13 November 2025). Weak or changing institutions further encourage reliance on trusted networks and flexible problem-solving. As a result, ethical dilemmas frequently involve navigating between professional standards and social or familial obligations especially within SMEs (Latifi Sadrija, 13 November 2025). Cultural values such as respect for authority, strong in-group orientation and the desire to avoid loss of face shape communication styles and conflict management. In multi-ethnic or multilingual environments, inclusive communication and equal treatment are crucial for maintaining team cohesion. International and foreign-owned firms also exert significant influence by introducing formal HR structures and clearer performance and feedback mechanisms; employees often transfer these expectations back into local companies, gradually reshaping norms. Latifi Sadrija also noted that there are clear differences between sectors. Family-run SMEs rely on centralised and flexible leadership, whereas large companies employ more systematic and hierarchical processes, NGOs favour participatory values, and the public sector remains constrained by bureaucratic and political structures. Gender and generational shifts are slowly changing the landscape as more women and internationally exposed young professionals enter leadership roles, bringing a stronger emphasis on collaboration, communication and professional development (Latifi Sadrija, 13 November 2025). Looking ahead, she anticipates that Kosovo will continue developing a blended leadership style. Traditional strengths such as trust, personal relationships and adaptability will remain important, but organisations will increasingly need transparent procedures, strategic thinking and inclusive management practices to meet European standards and the expectations of younger talent. For foreign leaders entering Kosovo, Latifi Sadrija advises investing in personal trust, understanding local realities and avoiding the assumption that Western models can be applied unchanged. Effective leadership, she stressed, requires learning alongside local teams and adapting methods to the specific cultural and institutional context (Latifi Sadrija, 13 November 2025).

In-country leadership bestseller

The locally authored handbook *Suksesi i menaxhimit në shitje* (*Sales management success*) sets out what it takes to build and lead effective sales organisations in Kosovo and the wider Balkans. Written by Prof. Dr. Sc. Shpëtim Memishi, a Prishtina-based lecturer at AAB College and doctoral economist whose work focuses on sales management and managerial practice in Kosovo, his 2021 monograph *Suksesi i menaxhimit në shitje Kosovë* – Ballkan systematises sales-leadership processes for Kosovar and Balkan firms. He publishes and presents on Kosovo-centred management and economic topics in regional conferences, underscoring his practitioner–scholar focus on how leaders organise sales and performance in local firms. The core message of this book is that leadership is a managerial discipline, not a personality trait. In Kosovo's SME-heavy, relationship-dense market, this means managers must translate targets into weekly behaviours (client visits, follow-ups, proposals), keep a visible, simple pipeline, coach after key meetings and document next steps. Because informality and infrastructure reliability can disrupt plans, credibility grows when Kosovar leaders explain trade-offs, time-box recovery actions, assign clear owners and then deliver exactly what was promised to their teams and customers. Read this way, Memishi's emphasis on role clarity, pipeline discipline, consistent coaching and data-informed decisions fits how Kosovo's firms win trust and repeat business through punctual execution and dependable follow-through. Practically, the book fits with how many Kosovar businesses already work with diasporaric and regional partners. It provides clear guidance on territory planning, account prioritisation and transparent target-setting. A typical use case in Kosovo does more than keep the process on track; rather, it signals the traits people prefer in leaders. When a manager runs a 20-minute review, surfaces three pipeline risks, reallocates a senior to unblock an account and sends a concise written recap with owners and deadlines, they enact transparency, decisiveness and dependable follow-through. In a context in which interpersonal trust often exceeds institutional trust and commerce moves through dense networks, these behaviours are read as both promises kept (*besa*), and work-centred attentive coordination and respectful hosting, which is why teams and clients judge such leaders as being legitimate and reliable (UNDP, 2019; Latifi, 2018; World Bank Group, 2020). The tone of the book is candid and courteous; performance is paired with consistent support. As Memishi puts it, "*Sales are highly correlated with trust*", a line that resonates in Kosovo's relationship-dense market where credibility is earned through clear intent, fair tasking and dependable follow-through (Memishi, 2021, p.13). Because the text gives managers a shared Albanian-language vocabulary for coaching, inspection and visible delivery, it lowers the adoption barrier across mixed-experience teams. Its local cases and regional focus also narrow the translation gap found in imported management books, increasing the odds that these routines will stick in fast-moving Kosovar firms.

Local leadership book	
Title	*Suksesi i menaxhimit në shitje*
Subtitle	-
Author	Sphëtim Memishi
Publisher	Ura
Year	2021
ISBN	9789951784085

Kosovo leadership YouTube review

The RTV AlbSe programme is a recurring Albanian-language talk show on leadership and innovation produced by RTV AlbSe, a broadcaster serving the Albanian diaspora in Sweden and beyond; the show is explicitly promoted as educational, motivational and innovation-focused, with guest experts discussing topics such as "leadership in business", and episodes are streamed via the channel's Facebook and YouTube pages. In the reviewed episode, the host pushes beyond charisma to concrete managerial routines in Kosovo. Specifically, they explain the "why" behind targets, *"convert goals into weekly actions, and pair decisiveness with respectful communication in reviews"* (RTV AlbSe Official, 2022). The emphasis is on predictable structure, short check-ins, clear task ownership and tight feedback loops, so teams know what happens next and who is accountable. In this particular video, Dr. Fadil Citaku speaks directly about Kosovo's SME-heavy, relationship-dense market, stating that *"Managers earn credibility by making decisions, explaining trade-offs and keeping follow-through visible action"* (RTV AlbSe Official, 2022). With respect to management practice, the episode is explicit about how Kosovoar leaders should talk and act when pressure rises. Managers are urged to explain trade-offs when plans change, to publish brief written recaps that list what was decided, who owns which action and by when, and to recognise effort publicly whilst addressing bottlenecks in private (RTV AlbSe Official, 2022). Innovation is treated as disciplined iteration rather than slogans: leaders set a small experiment, define a short timebox and a single success metric, then close the loop with a brief lessons-learned before scaling. Tight feedback loops also hedge against execution risks that managers routinely report, including market informality and infrastructure reliability, so clear timeboxes, named owners and written next steps become practical safeguards for coordination and accountability (World Bank Group, 2020). The next video to be summarised is Labirinth on Radio Dukagjini, where consultant Suzana Lutolli discusses how Kosovar managers operationalise trust, a coaching stance and emotional intelligence in their day-to-day routines. More specifically, Lutolli treats business leadership in Kosovo as a repeatable operating system. She foregrounds three anchors for managers *"Trust is the foundation," "Don't manage, inspire,"* and emotional intelligence as a *"leader's secret weapon"* then maps them to everyday routines: make expectations explicit at the start of a cycle, translate goals into weekly actions, run short fixed check-ins, and keep follow-through visible so teams and clients know what happens next (Radio Dukagjini, 2024). The segment stresses the importance of clear ownership and respectful coaching when plans shift, with Kosovar leaders explaining trade-offs, assigning accountable owners and documenting next steps to prevent ambiguity. It also highlights habits that resonate in Kosovo's relationship-dense market, such as protecting client-facing time, recognising effort in public and addressing bottlenecks in private to preserve dignity whilst sustaining pace. Taken together, Lutolli's guidance frames credibility as something leaders build through predictable routines rather than charisma, and it is presented as practical advice for SME managers working across local networks and regional partners (Radio Dukagjini, 2024). For managers in Kosovo, the practical value of those videos is clear: the videos translates leadership in Kosovo into short, repeatable routines that earn credibility and sustain performance.

Understanding hierarchy in Kosovo

In Kosovo, hierarchy is interpreted through a dual lens: a young, still-consolidating institutional setting and dense interpersonal networks. As aforementioned, interpersonal trust often outpaces trust in state institutions, which means that legitimacy and respectful role boundaries are of paramount importance to how authority is judged in organisations (UNDP, 2019). Similarly, ethnographic research shows how kinship and relatedness structure obligations and influence, in such a way that formal rank is often read through relationships and reputation (Latifi, 2018). In Kosovar organisations, hierarchy is visible in how decisions are taken and escalated: choices are typically made a level or two above the team, and issues move up through the immediate manager rather than across units. Within public institutions this often means written memos, signature chains and director sign-off before changes proceed, which slows transformation when day-to-day routines do not match reform goals (Tahiraj & Krek, 2022; Halili & Kukovič, 2022). This framing of hierarchin Kosovar organisations is confirmed by the results of the CCBS Survey (2025). Insofar as most of the respondents endorsed the statement that once a decision is made it is not easily changed. Moreover, many of the respondents also agreed that it is typical for leaders in Kosovo to confront staff about performance issues in staff meetings (CCBS Survey, 2025). With respect to whether employees should refer to their leaders by their titles, interestingly the respondents were relatively divided, whereas the majority of the respondents reported that it was acceptable for employees to call leaders by their first names (CCBS Survey, 2025). The open-ended survey responses help to proivde additional nuance to why such structure is preferred. As Berat Recica notes, leadership in Kosovo *"relies much more on trust, loyalty, and personal credibility"* than on rigid formalised processes, so predictability within recognised channels is read as fair and credible (CCBS Survey, 2025). In firms, managers use short check-ins and written decision recaps to keep coordination tight and reduce ambiguity, a practical response to operating constraints such as market informality and infrastructure reliability reported by businesses in Kosovo (World Bank Group, 2020). Because interpersonal trust frequently outweighs trust in formal bodies, credibility rests on predictable, fair conduct rather than distance, so effective leaders make clear who decides what, explain trade-offs and document next steps (UNDP, 2019; Latifi, 2018). This pattern helps explain why employees often expect clear decision rights, defined lines of escalation and visible coordination from leaders. At the same time, exposure to the diaspora and international partners brings more participative routines in outward-facing firms, especially around project reviews and feedback. Effective hierarchical leadership in Kosovo looks practical and explicit: managers make and explain decisions, set timelines, name owners and next steps, and keep role boundaries clear whilst remaining accessible for clarifying questions an emphasis consistent with public-sector analyses that call for clearer organisational and procedural arrangements to improve coordination (Halili & Kukovič, 2022). Studies of large Kosovar organisations describe closed, hierarchical communication patterns and the performance benefits when information sharing and involvement are formalised (Abrashi, 2023; Hyseni et al., 2023). Status tends to be read through reliability and fairness more than distance, which mirrors civil service survey evidence on the importance of impartial management practices for integrity and performance in Kosovo's administration (Meyer-Sahling, et al. 2018). Analyses of Kosovo's administrative modernisation highlight fragmented coordination and the need for clearer organisational and structural approaches, reinforcing the premium leaders place on role clarity and procedure in day-to-day management (Halili & Kukovič, 2022). Taken together, hierarchy in Kosovo is widely read as responsible stewardship rather than social distance. Leaders who decide, explain and coordinate effectively, whilst creating predictable channels for participation, are best positioned to earn trust and sustain performance.

How the Kosovar achieve leadership empathy

In Kosovo, leadership empathy is judged less by displays of warmth in the abstract than by whether managers tangibly protect people's work conditions and dignity whilst keeping performance on track. Cultural anchors such as *mikpritja* (attentive hospitality) and *besa* (trust) translate into business expectations that leaders must listen carefully, follow through reliably and create room for employees to speak without fear of penalty (Hamiti, 2024; Fox, 1989/1992). Empathy is thus operational rather than ornamental: managers put it into practice by scheduling regular one-to-one meetings, using perspective-taking to spot workload strain early, and adapting tasking whilst explaining unavoidable constraints (Skakon, et al. 2010; Leiter & Maslach, 2014). These routines support psychological safety and learning within teams (Edmondson, 1999) and, in Kosovo's relationship-dense workplaces, help leaders convert authority into credibility through visible care and follow-through (Latifi, 2018; Lokaj & Latifi Sadrija, 2020). These practices are in alignment with the GLOBE construct of humane orientation as well as with evidence that empathic, other-focused leadership enhances employees' willingness to contribute beyond formal roles (House et al., 2004; Ilies et al., 2007). In Kosovo's relationship-dense workplaces, empathic conduct sustains high-quality leader–member exchange by signalling respect and predictability, which, in turn, supports commitment and cooperation (Graen & Uhl-Bien, 1995). This is confirmed by the results of the CCBS Survey (2022-2025), insofar as most of the respondents endorsed active, routine check-ins by managers, as evidenced by the fact that they agreed with the statement that leaders should actively spend time ensuring the well-being of team members. However, many of the respondents also indicated that it is common for leaders to retain distance from their employees to preserve the requisite respect (CCBS Survey, 2022–2025). When viewed together, this describes a norm of respectful proximity rather than either detachment or over-familiarity. As one general manager put it, in Kosovo leadership *"relies much more on trust, loyalty, and personal credibility,"* and leaders are expected to be *"competent, highly approachable, visible, and personally connected"* to their teams, which explains why empathic routines that pair availability with clear boundaries are judged crediblly (CCBS Survey, 2025). In outward-facing Kosovar firms, this empathy is enacted as a form of disciplined reliability: managers state issues plainly, set short corrective time frames, assign accountable owners and close the loop in writing so that care and coordination move in step with one another. International and diaspora exposure also nudges teams towards these predictable routines, whilst operating constraints reported by firms make transparent tasking and visible follow-through efficient and credibility-enhancing. Such practices strengthen leader–member exchange and discretionary effort, and they support psychological safety by acknowledging uncertainty whilst clarifying the next steps (Edmondson, 1999; Graen & Uhl-Bien, 1995). For example, after a client delay, a project lead in a Kosovo tech SME would summarise the cause, time-box the fix, name owners and circulate a brief recap, pairing decisiveness with respectful coaching, which is consistent with local evidence linking clarity and fairness to change readiness (Lokaj & Latifi Sadrija, 2020). Local scholarship helps to situate these behaviours. Ethnographic work documents how kinship and relatedness shape obligations and reputation, which means credibility rests on visible fairness and follow-through, not mere status (Latifi, 2018). In short, Kosovars tend to view empathic leaders as those who listen, explain and act: they protect people, whilst, simultaneously, delivering results, using consistent communication and dependable promises to convert formal authority into durable trust.

Macedonia, North

Sander Schroevers,
with: Diederick van Walsem, Jordy van der Tak, Kaan Kara, Raymond van den Bos and Wester Klerk

Република Северна Македонија (Republika Severna Makedonija) is a land-locked state within the heart of the Balkans. The country of Macedonia's national identity is intimately bound with its positioning at a regional crossroads. With a population of just under 1.9 million people, the country is comparable in size to Sicily. Wherever one looks there is a mountain; with eighty percent of North Macedonia being covered by vast ranges, such as, for example, Šar, Bistra and Baba. Although to outsiders the national banner may be reminiscent of Japan's war flag, its design is actually rooted in an emblem of ancient Macedon. More specifically, North Macedonia's red flag with an eight-ray yellow sun is actually a reworking of an earlier sixteen ray *Sun of Vergina* design, which was abandoned after disputes with Greece. Lake Ohrid, one of Europe's deepest lakes, is a World Heritage site that blends exceptional aquatic biodiversity with a beautiful lakeside town that is often described as the *Pearl of the Balkans* (Dimitrova & Vesevska, 2020). Interestingly, *Ohrid* once hosted 365 churches, which is one for every day of the year. In contrast to other Yugoslav republics, North Macedonia achieved its sovereignty in 1991 through a referendum, which mean that its departure from the federation took place without any armed conflict. Contemporary census data portrays a multiethnic society in which Macedonians form the largest group, alongside sizeable Albanian, Turkish, Roma, Serb and Vlach communities, each with their own linguistic and religious traditions (Државен завод за статистика, 2022). Studies of Macedonian schoolchildren indicate that ethnic belonging is formed from an early age (Tomovska Misoska et al., 2020), whilst recent cross cultural business leadership research identifies meaningful differences between Skopje and the rest of the country with respect to the prevailing leaderships behaviours and values, which suggests that expectations of authority, informality and participation vary along urban regional lines and are gradually changing (Tomovska Misoska et al., 2024). In the following chapter we build upon these insights and, through primary and secondary research, explore how Macedonian business leaders and employees themselves describe effective leadership and organisational life within North Macedonia.

How do North Macedonians characterise leaders?

The organisational culture in North Macedonian reflects a landscape in which socialist legacies, Balkan traditions and European institutional influences coexist. A common Macedonian saying is *Со работа и трпение, сѐ се постигнува* (With work and patience, everything is achieved), which serves to illustrate the persistent and pragmatic style that is often expected of local leaders. Research indicates that North Macedonians primarily characterise effective leaders as individuals who demonstrate a specific blend of transformational and transactional qualities, with a strong emphasis on trust-building, vision, and adaptability within hierarchical structures. This preference is particularly evident within sectors where organisations led by managers who foster employee development report stronger performance-based outcomes (Bojadjiev et al., 2019; Hristova & Handjiski, 2024). However, a comprehensive cross-cultural study examining Slavic nations demonstrated that North Macedonians also prefer leaders who can combine a participative decision-making approach with clear hierarchical structures, which is emblematic of the country's enduring collectivist cultural orientation (Kožo et al., 2024). Consequently, effective leaders in North Macedonia must navigate a delicate balance between, on the one hand, empowering employees and, on the other, maintaining clear lines of authority that are demanded by high power distance cultural norms. Indeed, studies of Macedonian manufacturing firms suggest that the national culture remains associated with a relatively high power distance, which, in turn, keeps decision-making concentrated in the upper echelons of the hierarchy even in instances in which group loyalty and solidarity are valued (Sofijanova & Zabijakin-Chatleska, 2013). This suggests that whilst employees wish to be involved, they nevertheless continue to characterise a "strong" leader as someone who holds ultimate responsibility. Survey evidence from the North Macedonian subsample of the multi-year CCBS Survey (2023-2025) lends support to this characterisation of North Macedonian leadership. Specifically, when asked what they expect from their leaders, sixteen out of the nineteen respondents selected 'powerful decision maker'. In the qualitative component of the survey, one respondent, Dancho Dimkov, was explicit on this very issue: *"A typical Macedonian* [leader] *is* [all about] *micro-management. The boss is the highest person, and everyone needs to get approval from the boss."* This view was echoed by a CEO from Bitola, who noted that *"power and decision making [are] based on the leaders of the company"* (CCBS Survey, 2023-2025).

Trust and relationship-building also constitute key characteristics of leadership in North Macedonia. Research in the healthcare sector identified trust as a critical leadership dimension (Efremov & Dimitrievska, 2025). This emphasis on interpersonal connections is deeply rooted in the local culture and is encapsulated in the term мерак (merak), a word that describes a feeling of deep contentment derived from shared moments. One survey respondent, Ljubisav Lazarevic, noted: *"Business usually is settled outside of the office, in restaurants settings"* (CCBS Survey, 2023-2025). This serves to illustrate a leadership culture that values well-being and strong personal bonds alongside professional duties. As such, local leaders often focus their attention on *"being with the people,"* which is why approachability and shared experience are valued more highly than formal authority (Kostov, 2006). Comparative studies across Slavic countries position North Macedonia within a cluster that values humane-oriented leadership, characterised by compassion, generosity, and support for subordinates (Ljubica et al., 2024). The prevailing managerial style, shaped by the country's transitional economic standing, places strong emphasis on relationship management (Vasilić & Brković, 2017). Furthermore, the characterisation of leadership varies significantly by sector. Public institutions in North Macedonia exhibit distinct cultural profiles that favour leaders who can navigate bureaucratic structures whilst promoting innovation (Atanasova, 2023). Conversely, in the private sector, particularly within SMEs, leaders tend to drive organisational learning and enhance competitiveness via adaptive leadership styles (Krsteska et al., 2023). This distinction underscores that North Macedonians recognise context-specific leadership requirements, valuing flexibility and sector-appropriate behaviours (Stojkov et al., 2016). Nevertheless, empirical work reports that conservative organisational cultures with authoritarian leaders remain widespread, whilst more entrepreneurial cultures with participatory leadership exist but are less prevalent (Kostovski et al., 2015). Hence, Macedonian leaders must increasingly be hybrid figures, who must possess the *"Powerful decision maker"* status to navigate the system, whilst, simultaneously, maintaining the informality needed to build *"friendly and personal relationships with staff"* (CCBS Survey, 2023-2025). Recent research using the VOX Organizationis model indicates that some firms are slowly starting to place more emphasis on alignment, innovation, and environmental responsibility (Mileva et al., 2020). Ultimately, the ideal North Macedonian leader is someone who balances clear authority with genuine concern for employee well-being, integrating progressive practices with deeply embedded expectations of loyalty and hierarchy (Tomovska Misoska et al., 2024).

Survey results and what local respondents say

The CCBS Survey (2023-2025) was administered to nineteen senior professionals, including CEOs, founders, and executive assistants, working in North Macedonia in order to examine the prevailing business leadership skills and practices and organisational culture in the country. The most significant patterns in the dataset are discussed in turn below. The first recurring theme in the survey data is the prevalence of traditional, hierarchical leadership styles in North Macedonia. According to the findings, North Macedonian professionals characterise effective leaders through a distinctive lens of *"accessible authority"* (CCBS Survey, 2023-2025). Whilst academic literature emphasises a blend of transformational qualities, the respondents starkly underscored the necessity of social capital. When asked what employees expect their leaders to have, a resounding majority of the surveyed executives, from CEOs in Skopje to managers in Bitola, selected *"Access to the right work networks"* and *"Good political connections"* as being absolute prerequisites (CCBS Survey, 2025). This suggests that within the tight-knit Macedonian business ecosystem, leaders are characterised not only by their internal vision, but rather by their external ability to navigate complex political and social webs in order to secure resources. This characterisation is further complicated by a persistent dichotomy between *"modern"* and *"traditional"* leadership styles. One respondent, a CEO within the logistics sector, opined that *"Most of the so-called leaders are using the so-called Boss style leadership [approach]"*. Nevertheless, several respondents also reported there has been a gradual shift towards more participative and collaborative approaches in the country, particularly amongst younger professionals and within internationally oriented companies. Next, when local respondents were asked to identify what distinguishes Macedonian leadership from other countries, the answers revealed a business culture that is deeply rooted in social interaction. A final recurrent theme in the survey responses pertains to the gap between ideal leadership and the reality of leadership. One public health manager from Tetovo bluntly stated that *"in my country there are numerous managers that do not have the appropriate education and skills to be in such positions"* (CCBS Survey, 2024). This sentiment was echoed by a CEO, Jovanovski, who observed that *"leaders here do not understand the concept of servant leadership"* (CCBS Survey, 2025). These critical voices suggest a workforce that is becoming increasingly demanding, looking for leaders who offer more than just traditional authority. Overall, the insights from these respondents provide a nuanced picture of leadership within North Macedonia, shaped by both local customs and global influences.

Local leadership analysis

Dr Marjan Bojadjiev: a North Macedonian cross-cultural leadership scholar

Professor Marjan I. Bojadjiev is a Macedonian economist and leadership scholar with senior experience in both banking and higher education. After serving as CEO of major financial institutions in Skopje, he became Dean, then Rector and is now Provost and full professor of Leadership and Organisational Behaviour at University American College Skopje. He also lectures as a visiting professor at the University of Rome Tor Vergata and serves as Honorary Consul of Hungary for Southwest Macedonia, based in Ohrid.

According to Professor Bojadjiev, leadership in North Macedonia is embedded in a wider Eastern Orthodox and historically Byzantine tradition, which it shares with neighbouring Serbia and Bulgaria. He argued that this tradition is associated with a high acceptance of hierarchy and relatively collectivist values. Recent survey research on Slavic countries supports this view by reporting a very high score for North Macedonia on power distance and a continued expectation of strong leaders, even as more participative practices emerge (Kozo et al., 2024; Bojadjiev et al., 2015). During the interview, he described a clear generational contrast: his own Generation X was socialised into strict, formal hierarchies, whereas younger employees in international firms and IT companies are, as he put it, *"completely out of this scheme"*, preferring informal dialogue and joint decision-making (8 December 2025).

In terms of effective leadership, Professor Bojadjiev stressed that: *"Macedonian followers still expect their leaders to provide direction, but that authority needs to be grounded in moral credibility"*. Leaders should demonstrate honesty, integrity and consistency, communicate clear goals and then trust employees with sufficient autonomy to achieve them. He noted that foreign managers are usually welcomed warmly in North Macedonia, but may underestimate the informal "power structure games" that predate any formal reorganisation. For this reason, he advised that organisational change should be introduced gradually, with careful explanation and participation. As he concluded, followers will not trust a leader who does not first model trust, empathy and a genuine concern for their development (8 December 2025).

Social media review

Increasingly, a considerable number of citizens from North Macedonia articulate their perspectives on business leadership via a range of social media platforms, resulting in a rich tapestry of diverse opinions and viewpoints. The first perspective on North Macedonian leadership comes from Dzan Memed, who serves as the director of sales and digital banking at Halkbank AD Skopje, and appeared as a guest on the podcast Бизнис Лидер (S02E03). During the discussion, he asserts that contemporary Macedonian leadership is predicated upon *"trust and mentorship"* (Бизнис Лидер, 2023a), suggesting that young employees' development is dependent on experiencing a sense of value and support. In this respect, he outlines Halkbank's commitment to nurturing young talent through systematic training, emphasising that *"supporting young generations constitutes the cornerstone of authentic leadership."* Memed then proceeds to articulate that effective leaders in North Macedonia must engage in perpetual self-improvement, noting that *"success does not materialise instantaneously; those who exert effort will attain recognition."* The next perspective to be discussed here comes from Prof. Dr. Lazar Jovevski, a professor at the Faculty of Law *"Justinijan I"* at UKIM, who also acts as an advisor for labour and social policy to the Prime Minister. In the podcast Бизнис Лидер, Jovevski conceptualises leadership as an intrinsic aspect of existence, noting that leadership permeates every facet of life, including familial, professional, athletic, and political spheres. *"Anyone can emerge as a leader within their respective milieu"* (Бизнис Лидер, 2023b), he posits, elucidating that the journey commences with ongoing education and self-betterment. He stresses the necessity of cultivating positive habits, attitudes, and mindsets whilst advising against the tendency to attribute fault to others. He concludes his discourse with a poignant quote: *"Do not measure yourself against others; pursue your unique trajectory,"* underscoring that genuine leadership is initiated internally. Another North Macedonian who provides insight into leadership in the country is Entrepreneur Kosta Petrov, who has a substantial following on LinkedIn. He advocates for collaborative leadership as a pivotal element within the Macedonian business landscape, positing that leaders ought to both create an environment that is conducive to teamwork and harness diverse perspectives to facilitate positive outcomes (Petrov, K. n.d.). The final perspective to be considered here comes from the Former Minister of Education, Mila Carovska, who utilises her Instagram account to discuss two paramount leadership competencies within North Macedonia: empathy and trust. Effective communication also plays a significant role in exemplary leadership, insofar as it enables leaders to both discern the needs of the populace and mitigate against the likelihood of miscommunication (Carovska, M. n.d.). Ultimately, Carovska advocates for a leadership paradigm that prioritises collaboration amongst institutions and communities, which holds particular significance within the Macedonian public sector.

Local leadership book

One of the more practical leadership handbooks within the contemporary North Macedonian context is *Komuniciraj, pregovaraj, odlučuvaj - bidi lider* (*Communicate, Negotiate, Decide, Be a Leader*) by Sotir Kostov (2006). Published by the Macedonian Centre for International Cooperation (MCIC), it is not a commercial leadership title but rather was the core technical manual for the 2005–2010 decentralisation process and was widely distributed as the standard curriculum for newly empowered leaders. Within this framework, Kostov presents business leadership in North Macedonia as a cluster of interconnected roles, including, amongst other things, communicator, negotiator, decision maker and leader, upon which further roles such as policy maker, supervisor, institution builder, finance officer, facilitator and enabler are subsequently built. Drawing on detailed case material, he shows how active listening, transparent information sharing and regular contact reduce the perceived distance between leaders and those that they lead. The negotiation chapters adapt ideas from principled bargaining to Macedonian realities, encouraging leaders to search for "*wise*" agreements that reconcile competing interests, whereas the final section argues that effective leadership rests on vision, delegation and ethical influence and explicitly calls for the empowerment of women, minorities and economically marginalised groups. The handbook's status is reinforced by Kostov's public profile as a legally trained reform consultant and prominent television analyst, that helped shape the language of local management during this period. Together, these features make the book a localised reference point for how many Macedonians expect authority to be exercised within organisations today.

Local leadership book	
Title	*Комуницирај, преговарај, одлучувај – биди лидер [Communicate, Negotiate, Decide – Be a Leader]*
Subtitle	Kako do efektivna lokalna samouprava, KLS-manual no. 2
Author	Sotir Kostov
Publisher	MCIC, Skopje
Year	2006
ISBN	9989-102-23-6

Understanding hierarchy in North Macedonia

North Macedonia remains a deeply hierarchical society, which is discernible in both its extremely high score on Hofstede's Power Distance Index (PDI 90) and long-standing patterns of centralised control within organisations (Kozo et al., 2024). Under socialism, respect for authority and top-down decision making became institutionalised, and, indeed, many of these habits continue to shape everyday management practice within the country. A large-scale study by Bojadjiev et al. (2015) identified three predominant types of organisational culture within Macedonian companies, namely traditional, entrepreneurial and flexible. Within the traditional organisational culture, which is found in almost four out of ten companies in the country, decision making is centralised, communication flows mainly from top to bottom, and autocratic leadership is the prevailing approach. This pattern is particularly strong amongst older managers, with 63 per cent of leaders aged over 50 working within these traditional structures in contrast to 45 per cent of leaders aged 21 to 30 (Bojadjiev et al., 2015). At the same time, there is a clear trend towards more participative and democratic leadership styles within certain organisations in North Macedonia. For instance, in their research on Macedonian SMEs, Bojadjiev et al. (2019) demonstrate that many North Macedonian leaders now prefer democratic styles of leadership that involve employees within the decision making process. Amongst younger business leaders, more than half favour flexible and participatory cultures in which employees are valued for their expertise and abilities rather than for their position within the organisational hierarchy (Bojadjiev et al., 2015). Education is an important driver of this shift, especially study and work experience abroad, which, in turn, exposes Macedonian managers to more people-oriented forms of management (Doğar, 2021). This gradual softening of formality is also discernible in the results of the CCBS Survey (2023), insofar as many of the respondents reported that they address their managers by their first name, sometimes even using nicknames, within everyday communication. Despite this, hierarchy nonetheless remains an important organising principle within North Macedonian workplaces. Misoska et al. (2024) demonstrate that North Macedonian employees strongly value both consideration and initiation of structure within leaders, which suggests a preference for leaders who combine empathy and relational concern with clear guidance and role definition. Research into the preferred communication style amongst North Macedonian leaders appears to point in the same direction. Siljanovska (2022) reports that most employees see face-to-face meetings as a key responsibility of an effective leader and expect their managers to listen, inform and take decisions when needed. In practice, effective leaders in North Macedonia tend to balance traditional authority with approachability, so that respect for position coexists with trust, collaboration and room for employee initiative (Kozo et al., 2024).

How Macedonians achieve leadership empathy

In North Macedonia, leadership empathy is closely associated with both emotional intelligence and the cultivation and maintenance of trusting relationships with employees within the workplace. Indeed, studies show that managers who possess higher levels of emotional intelligence, especially empathy and social awareness, are more inclined towards transformational and affiliative styles of leadership, which, in turn, increases employees' motivation and levels of job satisfaction (Miklosh et al., 2024). Transformational leadership emerges as a highly valued characteristic amongst North Macedonian organisations, insofar as studies reveal that components influenced by emotional intelligence are strongly associated with effective leadership in the country (Drakulevski et al., 2017). Perceived organisational support is also a significant predictor of employee engagement in this regard, which suggests that leaders who provide visible forms of support help their employees feel valued and more willing to invest effort in their roles (Bozhinovska & Eftimov, 2024). Within the public sector specifically, individualised consideration, which is when leaders act as mentors and show concern for their employees' needs, has been found to be strongly associated with job satisfaction (Tasheva, 2016). When viewed in conjunction with one another, these findings indicate that empathy, expressed through support and recognition, is an important avenue through which to achieve effective leadership in North Macedonia. The cultural context further shapes how this empathy is expressed in practice within organisational life. As aforementioned, North Macedonia combines a relatively high level of power distance with a collectivist background and a marked orientation towards *"feminine"* values, such as, for example, caring, cooperation and concern for relationships (Kozo et al., 2024). Whilst, historically, leadership has often been rather autocratic in nature, reflecting centralised control and hierarchy, more recent research has underscored that there has been a gradual shift towards more participatory and people-oriented leadership styles, particularly amongst younger and better-educated leaders in the country (Doğar, 2021; Kozo et al., 2024). Similarly, leaders in Macedonian SMEs increasingly favour democratic leadership styles and strive to involve their employees in decision-making processes when possible (Bojadjiev et al., 2019). Survey-based research also indicates that employees attach strong importance to considerate and integrative leadership behaviours, which have been found to be positively related to cultural values that stress relational concern (Misoska et al., 2024). Similarly, communication studies show that employees expect successful leaders in North Macedonia to hold face-to-face meetings, share their emotions when appropriate to do so, and display keen interest in employees' motivation and work (Siljanovska, 2022). This depiction of North Macedonian leadership was also reinforced by the results of the CCBS Survey (2023), which showed that, in practice, many employees address their managers by their first name, which signals a certain closeness despite the persistence of formal hierarchies within North Macedonian organisations. In conclusion, then, empathic leadership in North Macedonia thus can be said to transpire when emotionally intelligent leaders listen carefully, communicate personally and create supportive relationships with their employees, whilst still operating within established organisational structures.

Morocco

*Sieb van der Laan, Iman Hossainpourian Taheri, Mahnaz Daneshgar,
Marwa Boujada, Sara El Fargoussi & Rosa Guenbour*

Founded in 788 AD with the establishment of the Idrisid dynasty, Morocco is one of the oldest continuously existing sovereign states in the world (Pennell, 2003). It occupies a strategic position at the crossroads of Europe, Africa, and the Middle East, which makes it a pivotal hub for trade, culture, and diplomacy. The country's official languages are Arabic and Amazigh, whilst French is widely used in business, government, and educational sectors, reflecting Morocco's colonial history under French and Spanish protectorates (Pennell, 2003). Moroccan culture is vividly expressed through its cuisine, such as couscous, the national dish, and tagine, which embody the nation's diverse regional flavours and communal traditions (Hoffman, 2019). Whilst tourism and agriculture are pillars of Morocco's economy, recent investments in green technology and solar power projects, such as the Noor Ouarzazate complex, underscore the country's ambition to position itself as a sustainable energy leader in Africa (International Energy Agency, 2022). The country's deep historical and cultural foundation informs Morocco's leadership practices and business ethics, insofar as honour, dignity, and relational harmony are of paramount importance (Moore & Hanson, 2017). The Moroccan concept of business ethics is closely tied to the cultural value of *tamaghrabit* (a sense of Moroccan identity). In professional settings, with ethical behaviour often being framed through l'*honneur* (honour) and l'*hchouma* (a moral sense of shame or propriety), which guide interpersonal conduct. Tuust and loyalty are also "*key elements of Moroccan business culture,*" forming the foundation of how leaders interact with employees and partners (Anonymous, 18 November 2025). Similarly, our other interviewee argued that Morocco's blend of collectivism, respect for tradition, and emphasis on relationship-building creates a uniquely Moroccan framework for responsible and community-centred business conduct (26 November, 2025). This will be further examined in the following chapter, which draws upon academic literature, survey data from local managers, and interviews with Moroccan leadership experts to gain deeper insight into leadership styles, hierarchical dynamics, and organisational practices within Morocco.

How Moroccans characterise leaders?

Leadership in Morocco is often linked to confident authority, calmness, and care for the team. This was illustrated by one of our interviewees, Mohamed Benboubker, a Moroccan entrepreneur and technologist, who informed that there is a cultural tendency in Morocco towards cooperation and politeness that business leaders must adhere to in order to effectively lead their teams (26 November, 2025). Moreover, academic research on preferred Moroccan leadership values show that effective leaders in the country are expected to give clear instructions to their employees (Forster, 2015). Not only must these instruction sbe clear, but as one of our interviewees expained, Moroccan leaders typically rely on indirect communication styles, which means that leaders expect their employees to understand nuances and unspoken expectations when providing instructions on what they want them to do (Anonymous, 18 November 2025). Interestingly, our other interviewee argues that this indirect communication style can create both trust and ambiguity, requiring leaders to navigate relationships carefully (26 November, 2025). Furthermore, it is important for leaders to take responsibility, and act as kind mentors towards those that they lead. In order to achieve this, they must combine authority with fairness and genuine concern for their employees, which is emblematic of a paternalistic leadership style in the Moroccan context (Ali & Wahabi, 1995; Forster, 2015). This fairness is often expressed through efforts to treat subordinates with respect and consistency, ensuring that rewards and discipline are applied justly rather than based on favouritism, whilst enuine concern, in turn, is exhibited through personal involvement in employees' wellbeing, such as, for example, leaders inquiring about family matters or offering support during personal difficulties (Moore & Hanson 2017). These traits are highly valued in Morocco's collectivist culture, where trust, loyalty, and social harmony are seen as essential to effective leadership. According to Benboubker, one of the ways in which leaders in Morocco maintain harmony is by being patient in their decision-making, which, in turn, ensures that all social expectations have been respected (26 November, 2025). Similarly, our other interviewee explained to us that it is vitally important for Moroccan leaders to be respectful and deeply committed to building trustworthy and loyal relationships with their employees. The main reason for this, she proceeded to inform us, is that trust and loyalty form the foundation of how leaders interact with their employees and partners (18 November, 2025). In this context, a leader's moral integrity and empathy carry more weight than charisma or self-promotion. However, more recent research shows that leadership styles in Morocco are slowly changing (Belrhiti, 2020). Younger managers who have international experience are becoming more open and supportive in their approach. They increasingly ask for employee input, coach their staff, and encourage innovation, whilst still making the final decisions themselves (Hassi, 2019; Lekchiria et al., 2018). One of our interviewees also argued that there has been a shift away from a traditionally authoritarian leadership style towards a more collaborative, open, and flexible approach (18 November 2025). This combination of traditional and modern leadership can be explained by Morocco's culture. As one of our interviewee explains, structure is necessary in Moroccan organisations to preserve order and clarity, but leaders must also seek to keep hierarchies moderate to maintain positive relationships with their employees (26 November, 2025). For instance, feedback is usually given privately and in a polite, relationship focused way, as trust and personal networks remain very important for getting work done (Balambo, 2014). More recent studies in Morocco indicate that transformational/"positive" leadership qualities—clear vision, individualised consideration, and ethical role-modelling—are increasingly valued across a range of sectors, not just in health and government. In public hospitals, for example, leaders who "adopt an appropriate mix of transactional, transformational and distributed leadership styles" are linked with higher motivation and commitment amongst staff (Belrhiti et al., 2020a, p. Abstract). Within multinational companies, transformational leadership is positively associated with greater organisational commitment (Palalić & Ait Sidi Mhamed, 2020). Within the educational sector, studies of Moroccan school principals also connect leadership attitudes and styles to higher levels of technology integration and improvement initiatives (Laouni, 2023). In summary, even though clear authority and respect for status are still important, Moroccan business leaders are now blending these traits with empathy, collaboration, delegation and shared responsibility (Benboubker, 26 November 2025).

Survey results and what local respondents say

In order to gain a more extensive and empirical understanding of leadership styles, practices, and business culture in Morocco, numerous C-level managers were invited to participate in the CCBS Survey (2017–2025). Drawing on several years of survey data collection enables us to provide a more reliable and comprehensive analysis of Moroccan business leadership skills and practices. The following section summarises the most noteworthy findings emerging out of both the 2017 version of the survey, which had over 50 respondents, and the 2025 version. The most significant findings emerging out of the surveys are summarised below in turn. Overall, the survey results underscore a culture that is hierarchical, relationship-oriented, and context-sensitive. The first noteworthy finding is that the respondents overwhelmingly reported that rules must be followed strictly and bending procedures without permission is discouraged within Moroccan organisations (CCBS Survey, 2017-2025). The importance of hierarchy is also reflected in the finding that the survey respondents consider titles, such as PDG (CEO), *Directeur*, *patron*, or *Moudir*, to be important, whilst referring to Moroccan leaders by their first name is generally considered to be disrespectful (CCBS Survey, 2017-2025). The importance of hierarchy was nicely illustrated by one of the survey respondents who opined: *"the hierarchical links within the company are stronger than leadership itself,"* thus reflecting the structural emphasis on authority in the country. Respect for formal positions was also found to be important in the most recent period of data collection, insofar as all of the respondents who participated identified failing to meet deadlines as being synonymous with failure (CCBS Survey, 2025). However, in accordance with one of our interviewees, who underscored that whilst structure is necessary in Moroccan organisations to preserve order and clarity, leaders must also seek to keep hierarchies moderate to maintain positive relationships with their employees (Benboubker, 26 November 2025), the results of the survey also showed that relational and supportive leadership is valued. For example, the CCBS Survey (2017) showed that the respondents viewed leaders spending time on employee well-being as being important, albeit a minority of respondents expressed concern that excessive empathy could reduce organisational efficiency. Similarly, in the most recent period of data collection, the respondents were unanimous that managers should actively ensure the personal well-being of their team members (CCBS Survey, 2025). The next key finding concerns the fact that whilst clarity is appreciated in leaders' communication, feedback and direction should be delivered privately rather than publicly, reflecting sensitivity to hierarchy and face-saving (CCBS Survey, 2017-2025). This finding is in accordance with previous research from Balambo (2014), which argued that feedback in Moroccan organisations is usually given privately and in a polite, relationship focused way, because trust and personal networks remain very important for getting work done in the country. With respect to what underpins leaders' legitimacy within Moroccan organisations, the results show that social networks, family background, and personal skills were the most commonly cited (CCBS Survey, 2017-2025). More specifically, with respect to the latter, the respondents highlighted attributes such as resourcefulness, eloquence, listening ability, and political connections as being of paramount importance. Overall, the data suggests that Moroccan leadership is hierarchical yet relational, combining accountability, authority, and situational considerations.

Local leadership analysis

An anonymous Moroccan cross-cultural trainer

Our first interviewee is a distinguished executive and leadership coach from Casablanca, Morocco, known for her extensive knowledge and expertise in organisational development, personal transformation, and leadership strategy. She is also a Moroccan executive coach who provides cross-cultural training. She supports professionals, migrants, and organisations in understanding cultural differences, managing integration challenges, and improving intercultural communication. With more than two decades of professional experience, she has built a career that merges technical knowledge, business leadership, and human development. During our interview, she highlighted several characteristics that define Moroccan leadership today and explained how these traits have evolved over time. When asked how she would describe a typical Moroccan business leader, they emphasised that Moroccan leaders are generally hardworking, respectful, and deeply committed to building trustworthy and loyal relationships. Trust and loyalty, she explained, are *"key elements of Moroccan business culture,"* forming the foundation of how leaders interact with employees and partners (18 November 2025). She proceeded to explain how Moroccan leadership has undergone a significant transformation over the past decade. Globalisation and technological innovation have played major roles in shifting leadership practices away from a traditionally authoritarian model towards a more balanced and modern approach. Whilst authority is still respected, leadership today integrates more collaboration, openness, and flexibility than before (18 November 2025). A distinctive feature of Moroccan leadership, she noted, is the combination of tradition and modernisation. That is to say, Moroccan leaders today must apply modern management practices, whilst, simultaneously, adhering to traditional values. In relation to the latter, she stressed that particularly personal relationships, loyalty, and mutual respect continue to hold strong influence within Moroccan workplaces. Indeed, this blend is one of the most striking aspects of leadership in Morocco (18 November 2025). The preferred communication style in Moroccan organisations also reflects this aforementioned cultural mix. According to them, Moroccan leaders typically rely on an indirect communication style, which contrasts with the direct style one finds within many Western cultures. This indirectness is intertwined with trust, insofar as leaders often expect their employees to understand nuances, intentions, and unspoken expectations (18 November 2025). In conclusion, she told us that another important aspect of Moroccan business life is structure, proceeding to discuss that approximately 90% of Moroccan companies are family businesses, with decision making tending to remain concentrated at the top. Hierarchy therefore continues to play a central role, even as leadership becomes more modernised and globally oriented (18 November 2025).

An anonymous Moroccan leadership expert

Our second interviewee is a Moroccan entrepreneur and technologist based in Casablanca. He co-founded the mobile software company MOBIBLANC in 2010, where he currently serves as the Managing Director, leading both strategic development and client partnerships. His academic background includes engineering studies at the École Mohammadia d'Ingénieurs in Rabat, where he specialised in computer networks, followed by a Master's degree in Air Transport Management from a university in Aix-Marseille. One of our interviewees provided an in-depth perspective on the characteristics of Moroccan leadership and the cultural forces that shape it (26 November, 2025). They began by emphasising that leadership in Morocco is deeply rooted in cultural norms. He explained that interpersonal warmth and the desire to maintain positive social relations strongly influence managerial behaviour. For example, he noted that saying "no" directly is uncommon because *"everybody is willing to help and to do business,"* which reflects a broader cultural tendency towards cooperation and politeness (Benboubker, 26 November, 2025). According to him, this indirect communication style can create both trust and ambiguity, insofar as it requires leaders to navigate relationships carefully. As the interview progressed, he described what he referred to as *"community leadership,"* distinguishing it from leadership models in more individualistic contexts. In Morocco, business networks tend to grow out of family, friends, and long-standing social circles. This form of leadership is often immaterial, prioritising loyalty, solidarity, and social responsibility over purely financial incentives. Our interviewee contrasted this approach with global models that focus primarily on efficiency and measurable outcomes (26 November 2025). Another defining characteristic of Moroccan leadership he noted is the value placed on patience. He proceeded to explain that compared to many European contexts, Moroccan leaders are less hurried and more willing to take time before making decisions. This slower pace is not perceived as inefficiency, but rather as a method through which to maintain harmony and ensure that all social expectations are respected (Benboubker, 26 November 2025). Simultaneously, hierarchy continues to play an important role in Moroccan organisations. One of our interviewees explained that structure is necessary to preserve order and clarity, yet leaders often seek to keep hierarchies moderate to maintain positive relationships with their employees (26 November, 2025). Turning to the practical realities of Moroccan leadership, he noted that leaders frequently depend on teams to advance projects and achieve goals, as independence is less common in the local business environment. Collaboration, delegation, and shared responsibility are therefore central to everyday leadership tasks. However, this teamwork is strongly influenced by relational dynamics, thus reinforcing the importance of interpersonal trust (Benboubker, 26 November 2025). When asked about cross-cultural comparisons, they underscored that Morocco's blend of collectivism, respect for tradition, and emphasis on relationship-building creates a leadership style that differs significantly from models in Western countries. Moroccan leaders are expected to be accessible, supportive, and socially aware, whilst, simultaneously, maintaining enough authority to guide their teams effectively. This balance between structure and relational warmth forms the core of modern Moroccan leadership. Through their insights, they portrayed a leadership model shaped by community bonds, patience, and cultural sensitivity in which trust, continuity, and social cohesion are valued just as highly as organisational performance. These qualities reflect the broader Moroccan culture, where leadership is not only about directing work but about sustaining meaningful human connections (Benboubker, 26 November 2025).

In-country leadership bestseller

One of the best-selling books about leadership was written by Fadoua Tahari in 2021 and is called *Les pratiques du leadership dans les entreprises privées marocaines* (Leadership Practices in Moroccan Private Companies Influence of National Culture). Fadoua Tahari is a Moroccan management scholar and Chartered Accountant with extensive experience in audit, consulting, and corporate governance. After beginning her career at PricewaterhouseCoopers, she later became Director of Consolidation and Compliance within a major Moroccan financial holding company. She holds a Doctorate in Business Administration as well as a PhD in Management Sciences from the University of Lyon. Her research focuses on leadership in Moroccan private companies, particularly the influence of national and cultural values on managerial practices.. The book *Les pratiques du leadership dans les entreprises privées marocaines* explores how leadership is shaped and experienced within Moroccan private companies. Tahari combines theoretical research with fieldwork in various enterprises to understand how cultural, social,and economic factors influence leadership styles. Specifically, she posits that leadership in Morocco is strongly influenced by a collectivist culture in which respect for hierarchy, family ties, and trust play a major role. Nevertheless, a hybrid leadership style is slowly emerging, blending traditional values such as loyalty and personal relationships with modern management practices focused on efficiency, participation, and innovation. A reader of this book would also learn how *moucharaka* (participatory decision-making) is increasingly used by Moroccan managers to involve employees in strategic discussions, whilst, simultaneously, still maintaining respect for senior authority. Another example is the growing emphasis on *qima zâida* (value creation), which is when business leaders combine relational trust with performance-driven practices, encouraging innovation, mentoring younger staff, and promoting socially responsible initiatives that strengthen both the organisation and the wider community. Tahari emphasizes that successful Moroccan leaders are often charismatic and relationship-oriented, and that they lead not only through formal authority but also through empathy, communication, and moral integrity. At the same time, she stresses the challenges in this context, such as limited employee autonomy and the tension between tradition and globalisation.

Local leadership book	
Title	*Les pratiques du leadership dans les entreprises privées marocaines*
Subtitle	Influence de la culture nationale
Author	Fadoua Tahari
Publisher	EMS Editions
Year	2021
ISBN	978-2-37687-517-8

Morocco leadership YouTube review

In his talk *"Entreprendre avec Vision, Valeurs et Impact,"* Moncef Belkhayat, Moroccan entrepreneur, former Minister of Youth and Sports, and founder of several national enterprises, presents a compelling reflection on the moral and social dimensions of business leadership in Morocco. Speaking in French to a Moroccan audience, Belkhayat emphasises that genuine Moroccan leadership begins with a sense of purpose, ethical integrity, and responsibility towards both employees and society at large. His message aligns with Moroccan cultural expectations that leaders act not only as decision-makers but also as moral guides who inspire trust and collective ambition (Ali & Wahabi, 1995; Forster & Fenwick, 2015). Belkhayat frames Moroccan leadership as a combination of vision, values, and impact. Vision, he argues, allows Moroccan leader to see beyond immediate profit and to imagine the broader contribution their organisation can make to national development. Values provide the ethical foundation that sustains credibility, which is particularly important within the Moroccan context where public trust and social respect are central to legitimacy (Benabdeljlil, 2007). Impact, meanwhile, refers to tangible results that improve people's lives; creating employment, supporting communities, and fostering pride in Moroccan innovation. This triad reflects the Moroccan tendency to blend entrepreneurial ambition with social responsibility, an approach which is consistent with recent research on transformational and ethical leadership in the country (Palalić & Ait Sidi Mhamed, 2020; Youssef & Benkirane, 2024). Throughout the presentation, Belkhayat's tone is both confident and compassionate. He stresses that authority without empathy fails to motivate, and that success in the Moroccan business sector depends on building relationships grounded in mutual respect. He encourages leaders to "listen with sincerity" and to "share the vision" so that employees feel included and valued. This echoes Morocco's collectivist orientation, where harmony, loyalty, and interpersonal warmth are essential to organisational cohesion (Smith & Boubker, 2014). His own manner of speaking, direct but courteous, also demonstrates the balance between authority and kindness that characterises Moroccan leadership communication styles. Belkhayat also highlights the importance of perseverance and optimism, traits that are deeply rooted in Moroccan cultural identity. He speaks about overcoming setbacks and maintaining composure in challenging environments, arguing that resilience strengthens both moral and managerial credibility. This attitude parallels the emphasis on calm determination and patience found in previous studies of Moroccan management culture (Akhlaffou, 2020). By combining moral conviction with practical optimism, Belkhayat illustrates how contemporary Moroccan leaders can inspire progress without abandoning traditional values of humility and solidarity. In summary, Moncef Belkhayat's talk offers an authentic representation of modern Moroccan leadership visionary that remains grounded in traditional ethical and cultural principles. His reflections show how empathy, fairness, and purpose are intertwined with authority in Morocco's evolving business environment. The video thus serves as both a motivational lesson and a case study in how Moroccan leaders integrate moral responsibility with entrepreneurial innovation, achieving influence through trust, care, and a shared sense of national purpose.

Understanding hierarchy in Morocco

In Moroccan businesses, particularly in the banking, telecommunications, and manufacturing sectors, organisational hierarchy remains a defining feature of management culture (Benabdeljlil, 2007). Research on Moroccan corporate governance and management practices shows that businesses typically maintain high power distance structures, where authority is centralised and decisions flow top-down from senior executives (Amine & Amine, 2010; Akhlaffou, 2020). For example, in many Moroccan firms, major strategic or financial decisions are made exclusively by senior managers, whilst lower-level employees are expected to follow instructions rather than challenge or question them, reflecting a cultural emphasis on respect for hierarchy and seniority (Ali & Wahabi, 1995; Mellahi & Wood, 2003). The results of the CCBS Survey (2017-2025) confirm this, insofar as the respondents overwhelmingly reported that rules must be followed strictly and bending procedures without permission is discouraged within Moroccan organisations. This is representative of enduring cultural values that emphasise respect for age, status, and seniority—principles that are deeply rooted in Moroccan social and religious traditions. Benabdeljlil (2007) found that in large Moroccan companies, managerial authority is not only functional but symbolic, which is to say that it signifies both competence and moral legitimacy. Consequently, decision-making tends to be concentrated in the upper echelons, with limited delegation. For instance, in many Moroccan banks and large industrial firms, strategic initiatives—such as the introduction of new technologies or marketing campaigns—are typically approved only after multiple layers of sign-off from senior directors, reflecting both respect for hierarchy and a preference for avoiding risk through collective endorsement (Benabdeljlil, 2007). Middle managers often act as intermediaries translating executive directives to operational teams rather than as autonomous decision-makers. This centralised pattern is reinforced by the bureaucratic legacies of state-owned enterprises and public administration, which still influence corporate practices (Benabdeljlil, 2007). Amine and Amine (2010) similarly argue that businesses in Morocco preserve strong vertical coordination mechanisms, where clarity of hierarchy ensures control and predictability. However, they also note emerging tensions between these traditional forms and contemporary management ideals that emphasise empowerment and participatory governance. This point was also noted by one of our interviewees, Benboubker, who stated that structure is necessary in Moroccan organisations to preserve order and clarity, but leaders must also seek to keep hierarchies moderate to maintain positive relationships with their employees (26 November, 2025). Many large firms have adopted formal participative tools— strategic committees, suggestion programs—but these mechanisms often remain consultative rather than truly decision-sharing. Leadership in Morocco is frequently paternalistic, combining authority with moral responsibility (Akhlaffou, 2020). Executives are expected to act as guardians of both performance and social harmony. Subordinates show deference not merely due to structural hierarchy but because authority is viewed as legitimate when coupled with fairness, care, and personal integrity (Akhlaffou, 2020). Forster and Fenwick (2015) observe that Islamic ethical norms—justice *(adl)*, *(ihtiram)*, and *(shura)* —shape leadership expectations. As a result, even when decision-making remains top-down, leaders are judged on how they protect their teams and uphold moral obligations. Whilst globalisation and professional management education have introduced new governance models into Moroccan businesses, the underlying hierarchical ethos persists. Akhlaffou (2020) shows that cultural traits such as collectivism and high power distance coexist with an increasing emphasis on performance metrics, corporate social responsibility, and agile management. This hybridisation produces organisations where symbolic respect for hierarchy remains vital, even as procedural autonomy expands in certain departments. Multinational subsidiaries in Morocco often adapt by localising management styles, maintaining clear authority lines whilst framing participatory initiatives within accepted norms of respect and consultation. Thus, effective management reform in Morocco requires acknowledging hierarchy as a culturally embedded coordination mechanism rather than an obstacle to modernisation (Benabdeljlil, 2007; Akhlaffou, 2020). In short, hierarchy in Moroccan businesses is best understood as a relational and moral order that sustains organisational stability and social harmony, whilst gradually adapting to global management norms.

How Moroccans achieve leadership empathy

Empathy in Moroccan leadership is rooted in a long-standing cultural emphasis on relationships, trust, respect, and collective harmony (Benboubker, 26 November 2025). In the Moroccan context, leadership empathy is not simply about emotional sensitivity but rather a moral and social expectation. That is to say, leaders are regarded as guardians of both professional and personal harmony within their teams. This is reflected in the results of the CCBS Survey 2017), insofar as the respondents viewed leaders spending time on employee well-being as being important. Similarly, in the CCBS Survey (2025), the respondents were unanimous that managers should actively ensure the personal well-being of their team members (CCBS Survey, 2025). Specifically, leaders are expected to understand employees' needs, provide guidance, and protect their dignity in the workplace (Forster & Fenwick, 2015). This empathetic orientation is often linked to the Islamic values of *rahma* (compassion) and *adl* (justice), which influence managerial behaviour across sectors (Akhlaffou, 2020). Consequently, a leader's capacity to show understanding and fairness is seen as being integral to their moral legitimacy and authority (Benabdeljlil, 2007). Moroccan leaders typically express empathy through personal involvement and attentive communication. As aforementioned, Moroccan leaders generally communicate in an indirect manner, which one of our interviewees argues helps to cultivate trust amongst their employees (26 November, 2025). Consequently, many managers invest time in maintaining close interpersonal relationships with their staff, frequently enquiring about family matters or showing flexibility during times of personal difficulty. Such gestures serve to reinforce loyalty and trust, which are highly valued in Morocco's collectivist culture (Ali & Wahabi, 1995; Smith & Boubker, 2014). Fairness is also demonstrated by applying consistent standards to all employees, avoiding public criticism, and giving feedback in private to preserve dignity. In this sense, empathy is practiced through actions that sustain social harmony rather than emotional expressiveness. This was corroborated by one of our interviewees, who also stated that interpersonal warmth and the desire to maintain positive social relations strongly influence managerial behaviour in Morocco (Benboubker, 26 November 2025). Similarly, Hoffman (2019) notes, Moroccan organisations often value discretion and restraint in communication, seeing these traits as signs of respect rather than detachment. The results of the CCBS Survey (2017-2025) also lend support to this, insofar as the respondents reported that feedback and direction should be delivered privately rather than publicly, reflecting sensitivity to hierarchy and face-saving. Empathy is also achieved through leadership models that integrate mentoring and moral example. Leaders are expected to guide their subordinates much like elder family members—offering advice, encouragement, and moral support. This approach reflects the enduring paternalistic leadership style found in many Moroccan organisations, where authority is combined with benevolence (Ali & Wahabi, 1995; Amine & Amine, 2010). However, recent studies show that such empathy-driven leadership is evolving. Younger managers, particularly those educated abroad or working in multinational environments, tend to adopt more participatory practices. They promote open dialogue, encourage employee input, and recognise individual achievements whilst maintaining clear hierarchical boundaries (Hassi, 2019; Palalić & Ait Sidi Mhamed, 2020). In public and non-profit sectors, research shows that empathetic leadership contributes to motivation and organisational commitment. For example, Belrhiti et al. (2020a) found that health-sector leaders who adopt an appropriate mix of transactional, transformational and distributed leadership styles foster stronger morale and engagement amongst hospital staff. Similarly, in Moroccan schools, empathetic and supportive principals are associated with higher levels of teacher collaboration and innovation (Laouni, 2023). In summary, Morocco achieves leadership empathy by combining cultural traditions of respect and moral responsibility with evolving practices of coaching and collaboration. Whilst authority and hierarchy remain central to organisational life, modern leaders increasingly express empathy through fairness, mentorship, and personal concern. By blending these approaches, Moroccan leaders manage to maintain social harmony whilst fostering engagement and trust—qualities that continue to define effective leadership in the country's changing business landscape. During our interview with the consultant, they also told us that she believes true leadership relies on empathy, emotional intelligence, and understanding others. She says leaders must value human connection, help people unlock their potential, and create supportive environments where individuals feel seen and motivated. For her, empathy is essential to meaningful, transformative leadership (18 November 2025).

New Zealand

Kyah Bedano, Julie Boiteux, Leonardo Ghelli, Iman Loonat,
Amicie de Montalembert & Ghislaine Rojer

New Zealand was one of the last great lands on Earth to be settled. Its first people, the Māori, did not just settle there; they pushed further east until eventually reaching the Chatham Islands, the final stop in humanity's long migration across the Pacific. This spirit of leading at the edge of the world continues to shape New Zealand leadership today (Sutton et al., 2007). The country's geographical position in the South Pacific has made it a vital gateway for trade, agriculture, and innovation. The Port of Tauranga, the largest in New Zealand, plays a significant role in export activity (New Zealand Trade and Enterprise, 2024). The nation has become a global leader in high-quality food exports, with world-class agricultural and horticultural industries producing dairy, meat, wine, and kiwifruit. Indeed, Zespri, a New Zealand based brand, is the largest kiwifruit supplier in the world, reflecting New Zealand's ability to combine innovation, sustainability, and global business acumen. Beyond agriculture, the economy has diversified into tourism, renewable energy, film and technology, sectors where entrepreneurial leadership and collaboration drive growth. The nation's environmental values, often captured in the *"clean, green New Zealand"* brand, reinforce its global reputation for sustainability, wellness, and quality. Tourism continues to thrive through both natural landscapes and the vibrant Māori culture that remains central to New Zealand's identity. Māori values such as *whanaungatanga* (kinship) and *kaitiakitanga* (guardianship of the land) inform contemporary business ethics and organisational leadership (Askarany & Lam, 2025). New Zealand's approach to business leadership is further shaped by its intellectual and cultural heritage. Sir Edmund Hillary's emphasis on resilience, humility, and vision reflects the country's broader leadership ethos, which balances individual initiative with collective responsibility. Together, Māori philosophy and European influences have created a distinct business leadership that values inclusivity, collaboration, and sustainability (Forsha, 2017). In this chapter, we will examine New Zealand's business leadership practices through both primary and secondary data from local professionals and experts.

How New Zealanders characterises leaders?

Leadership in New Zealand reflects a distinctive blend of cultural, social, and economic influences. The nation's British-inspired institutions have cultivated a collaborative, informal business environment, whilst the Māori worldview, which emphasises collective values, kinship, and relational accountability, adds a powerful layer of community-centred leadership to the mix (Forsha, 2017). These dual strands underpin what New Zealanders consider "good leadership." In the CCBS survey (2015-2020), most respondents chose "good listener," "consensus seeker," and "visionary thinker" as essential leadership qualities, with one executive noting that *"New Zealand is very driven by egalitarian ideas,"* adding that leaders are expected to remain *"humble... and approachable,"* which echoes the Māori principles of *whakaiti* (humility/modesty) and *manaakitanga* (hospitality/caring for others) (CCBS Survey, 2015-2020). Leaders take responsibility for mistakes, share credit, and model service rather than authority. Inspirational motivation refers to articulating a vision that energises others and connects with *whanaungatanga* which means a sense of belonging (Roche et al., 2015). This is reflected in additional survey responses like the following one: *"employees like to be consulted on many topics"* (CCBS Survey, 2015-2020). For instance, managers may align sustainability or community initiatives with shared social purpose. Intellectual stimulation involves encouraging innovation and critical thinking, which are highly valued traits in New Zealand's diverse, adaptive workplaces. Together, these qualities illustrate how transformational rather than transactional leadership dominates local practice (Pfeifer & Love, 2004). This was also corroborated by the results of the survey, where the respondents frequently described New Zealand workplaces as *"flat," "less formal,"* and *"based on soft skills-not status"* (CCBS Survey, 2015-2020). Murphy (2013) also found that effective New Zealand managers think laterally, foster learning, act as role models, and take responsibility for results. The effective leader is not a rule-enforcer but rather a trust-builder who empowers teams and promotes collaborative innovation. Similarly, Haar et al. (2018) identify five pillars of Māori leadership: *whakaiti* (humility), *manaakitanga* (care for others), *whanaungatanga* (relationships), *kaitiakitanga* (guardianship), and *tikanga Māori* (cultural authenticity), all of which translate directly into organisational leadership behaviours in Aotearoa. These values are reflected not only in theory but also in everyday workplace expectations, including expectations around collaboration, respect, and relational accountability. This connection was evident in the interview with Dr Meredith Marra, who noted that New Zealand organisations increasingly recognise and value Māori approaches to leadership, particularly the emphasis on collective responsibility, relational trust, and subtle expressions of authority (11 November, 2025). In practice, *whakaiti* is visible when leaders downplay their own status, redirect praise to the team, and remain approachable rather than relying on positional authority (Ruru, 2016). The importance of understanding diversity also emerged in the CCBS Survey (2015-2020), where one Māori respondent emphasised that *"understanding and managing cultural diversity [...] is essential to good business outcomes"*. *Manaakitanga,* which refers to showing care, hospitality, and support for others, is enacted in organisational settings when leaders invest time in staff wellbeing, welcome new employees like *whānau* (extended family), and offer flexibility for *whānau*-related commitments (Harris et al., 2016). Although *manaakitanga* was not explicitly referred to in the interviews, Dr Marra's observations align closely with this principle, insofar as they emphasised that effective New Zealand leaders demonstrate care through everyday relational practices, being present (11 November, 2025). These actions reflect the underlying spirit of *manaakitanga*, in which leadership is expressed through relational attentiveness and genuine concern for people rather than through transactional or authority-driven approaches. *Whanaungatanga* is visible when leaders prioritise relationship-building, for example, taking time for *kanohi ki te kanoh*i (face-to-face interaction) conversations and sharing kai (food) with staff (Haar & Brougham, 2013). *Kaitiakitanga* is demonstrated when leaders make decisions that protect environmental and community wellbeing over the long term, for example, adopting sustainable practices even when they reduce short-term financial gains (Harris et al., 2016). *Tikanga Māori* is enacted when leaders integrate Māori protocols and values into everyday organisational life, such as opening *hui* (meeting) with *karakia* (traditional Māori prayers or chants), recognising *mana whenua* (indigenous people who have historic and territorial rights over the land), and using collective, consultative decision-making that upholds *mana* for employees and stakeholders (Scarlatti, 2024). The University of Auckland Executive Education (2020) extends this philosophy through the concept of *mauri,* the life force that sustains wellbeing in organisations. Leaders who "care for the mauri" ensure positive energy, balance, and engagement. Practically, this means supporting work-life balance, inviting employee input, and fostering purpose-driven projects. Such actions keep workplaces inclusive, motivated, and resilient. Overall, New Zealand leadership is characterised by humility, authenticity, and empathy. Leaders act as facilitators who listen, consult, and guide collective progress rather than assert dominance. This approach, grounded in both Māori principles and egalitarian national values, explains why collaboration, trust and wellbeing remain central to the New Zealand understanding of effective leadership.

Survey results and what local respondents say

To gain a better understanding of business leadership skills and practices in New Zealand, we administered a survey to C-level executives with proven managerial experience in the country. In order to strengthen both the credibility and validity of the findings, we combined data from multiple periods of data collection (CCBS Survey, 2015-2025). The responses from the local professionals reveal a leadership style characterised by informality, egalitarian values, and a strong emphasis on competence over status. The most significant findings from the survey are summarised in turn below. First, one of the key features of the New Zealand leadership approach is flexibility in decision-making. This was evidenced by the fact that only 46.9% of respondents agreed with the statement that *"once a management decision has been made, it will not be changed very easily,"* whereas 53.1% reported that decisions can and should be reconsidered (CCBS Survey, 2015-2025). This was illustrated by one respondent, who noted: *"New Zealand is a very egalitarian culture and leadership is earned, not given by right of position."* The CCBS Survey (2025) respondents also confirmed this view by rejecting the idea that managerial decisions remain fixed, which shows a more pragmatic authoritarian leadership. The next significant finding is that informality is central to the New Zealand workplace, as illustrated by the fact that the respondents consistently noted that leaders do not maintain distance from employees in order to preserve respect. Several respondents claimed that it is acceptable for leaders to be called by their first name; indeed, one respondent noted that this is *"even the case for the Prime Minister"* (CCBS Survey, 2015-2020). Next, several respondents emphasised that effective leadership in New Zealand involves paying attention to the personal wellbeing of staff members. As described by one respondent *"a holistic approach [...] the growth of the business is wholly connected to the personal and professional growth of the employees."* (CCBS Survey, 2015-2020). The preference for cultivating close relationships was also confirmed by the responses about communication preferences in New Zealand organisations. Whilst the earlier respondents preferred indirect confrontation, which as one respondent noted stemmed from the fact that *"managers in New Zealand tend to avoid personal confrontation"* (CCBS Survey, 2015-2020), the more recent survey responses show that leaders are more open to receiving direct criticism (CCBS Survey, 2025). Regarding team dynamics, whilst collaboration and consensus-building remain core expectations, there is also recognition that competition can play a constructive role. This is reflected in the CCBS Survey (2015–2020) data, insofar as 55.6% of the respondents agreed (to varying degrees) that managers should encourage some competition within teams to achieve better outcomes.

This suggests that although cooperation is prioritised, a moderate level of healthy competition is considered beneficial. This perspective was also shared in the CCBS Survey (2025) responses, where several participants noted that competition can support organisational performance. Finally, in response to the question about which qualities are most admired in leaders in New Zealand, the most frequently cited responses were organisational experience, technical competence, and market knowledge (CCBS Survey, 2015-2025).

Local leadership analysis

Meredith Marra: a New Zealand scholar

Dr Meredith Marra is a Professor of Linguistics at Victoria University of Wellington and a leading expert in workplace discourse, intercultural pragmatics, and leadership communication in Aotearoa New Zealand. Her research examines how communication constructs leadership, with a particular focus on how culture, identity, and relational dynamics influence behaviour in professional settings. At the beginning of the interview, Dr Marra explained that her work centres on *"effective communicators,"* allowing her to identify what distinguishes highly regarded leaders in New Zealand and the communication practices that underpin their success (11 November, 2025). Next, Dr Marra described New Zealand leaders as flexible, people-oriented, and highly attuned to interpersonal relationships. She emphasised that leaders tend to prioritise the team over individual achievement and often adapt their leadership approach depending on the context. According to Dr Marra, cultural awareness increasingly shapes leadership expectations in the country, because New Zealanders are placing growing value on Māori leadership principles, including egalitarianism, collective responsibility, *whanaungatanga* (relationships), and the importance of family and networks. She underscored that these values naturally influence how authority is expressed. Leadership in New Zealand, she noted, is generally subtle rather than overtly hierarchical: *"Authority is more likely to be enacted indirectly, implicitly, with an expectation that everybody shares the same understandings of who is in charge"* (Marra, 11 November 2025). This indirect style can be challenging for newcomers from more formal or explicit leadership cultures but contributes to a workplace climate grounded in approachability and relational trust. As the interview progressed, Dr Marra emphasised that trust and respect are not automatically granted; rather, they must be earned through consistent and authentic behaviour. She explained that *"it is your day-by-day actions that lead to you being seen as the trustworthy and authentic leader"* (Marra, 11 November 2025). Leaders are therefore expected to be present, engaged, and actively involved in everyday organisational life. Even minor gestures, such as acknowledging personal challenges, celebrating small successes, or participating in daily routines, play an important role in cultivating connection and community. To illustrate these dynamics, Dr Marra discussed differences between younger and older leaders. Whereas younger leaders often bring innovation, confidence, and new ways of working, older leaders draw on their experience and typically feel more secure in expressing their leadership style (11 November, 2025). She provided the example of a Māori leader, Yvonne, who co-led with a male cultural advisor to balance complementary strengths, demonstrating the collaborative and relational nature of leadership within Māori contexts. Later in the interview, Dr Marra turned to the topic of migrants and newcomers in leadership. She noted that informal communication norms and subtle expressions of authority can create uncertainty for those arriving from more structured or hierarchical cultures. However, networks play a crucial role in enabling newcomers to advance. Migrant leaders who successfully navigate New Zealand's communication norms often use their position to support others, sharing access to networks and mentoring emerging professionals. As Dr Marra observed, *"For the newcomers, equally, the informality can be a really big issue, but they need to feel empowered to make their mark as well"* (11 November, 2025). In conclusion, Dr. Marra's insights underscore the deeply relational nature of leadership in New Zealand. Leaders are expected to be flexible, culturally aware, and attentive to interpersonal dynamics, whilst, simultaneously, maintaining an egalitarian and authentic presence. Authority is exercised subtly, trust is built gradually, and networks play a vital role in shaping leadership opportunities – particularly for those entering the country's diverse and evolving workforce.

Lucia Dore: a New Zealand cross-cultural trainer

Dr. Lucia Dore is a New Zealand-based cross-cultural trainer, financial investigative journalist, and editor with extensive professional experience in Europe, the Middle East, Asia, and the Asia-Pacific region. Her career has involved leading multicultural teams, developing media intelligence reports, and training professionals to navigate cross-cultural organisational settings. At the beginning of the interview, Dr. Dore explained that much of her work centres on helping individuals understand how cultural expectations shape leadership, communication, and workplace hierarchy (28 November, 2025). Next, Dr. Dore proceeded to describe the typical leadership style she observes in New Zealand organisations as being relaxed, informal, and grounded in interpersonal connection. She noted that New Zealand workplaces can be characterised by what she referred to as a version of the *"Tall Poppy Syndrome,"* a dynamic where leaders may avoid appearing dominant or overly authoritative to maintain harmony (Dore, 28 November 2025). According to Dr. Dore, leaders are often expected to behave *"like part of the team,"* which means that authority is enacted subtly and relationally rather than through explicit displays of hierarchy. To illustrate how leadership expectations have changed over time, Dr. Dore contrasted earlier models of authority with contemporary ones. She explained that leadership in the past relied heavily on positional power, where being the manager automatically conferred respect. *"Today,"* she noted, *"people want their leader to feel like a colleague,"* and respect is earned through competence, collaboration, and approachability rather than rank alone (Dore, 28 November, 2025). Dr. Dore highlighted that newcomers from more hierarchical cultures often misinterpret this informality, sometimes assuming they hold higher status in New Zealand simply because they come from systems where hierarchy is more explicit. She contrasted this with her experience in the United Kingdom, where she was once instructed not to speak to someone *"a grade above"* her, something she stated would not occur in the New Zealand context. As the interview continued, Dr. Dore observed that this informal style of leadership can be challenging for migrants and international employees to adapt to, particularly if they come from cultures where instructions are direct, responsibilities are formally defined, and leaders are visibly distinguished from subordinates (28 November, 2025). She emphasised that New Zealand organisational culture involves *"bringing everyone into the fold,"* where leadership is tied to participation, collective contribution, and trust. There is minimal micromanagement, provided employees deliver their work effectively. This reflects wider New Zealand leadership norms centred on relational trust, autonomy, and shared responsibility. Dr. Dore further noted that effective leaders in New Zealand tend to foster informal team environments by listening actively, acknowledging diverse interests, and remaining open to employee input. She explained that empathy is central to this style of leadership, and that the low barriers between leaders and employees in New Zealand make empathetic communication easier and more natural. Later in the interview, Dr. Dore reflected on the evolving nature of leadership in New Zealand, emphasising that, as a relatively young and diverse country, leadership practices are continuing to evolve. She suggested that future shifts may involve even greater cultural integration and flexibility as workplaces become more globally connected. This perspective reinforces the idea that New Zealand leadership is both dynamic and deeply shaped by its cultural context—balancing informality, trust, and interpersonal respect within increasingly multicultural organisational environments (Dore, (28 November 2025).

In-country leadership bestseller

One of New Zealand's contemporary leadership books is *Legacy* by James Kerr (2013), a British-born writer and leadership consultant who has worked extensively with New Zealand business, sporting, and government organisations. Kerr is known for translating the high-performance culture of the All Blacks into practical insights for leaders, making his work a central bridge between sports psychology and organisational leadership in New Zealand (Kerr, 2013; Kerr, 2020). Rather than presenting the All Blacks merely as a successful sports team, Kerr argues that their sustained excellence is driven by a distinctive leadership culture centred on humility, accountability, self-discipline, and collective purpose. One of his most recognised lessons, *"sweep the sheds,"* underscores the expectation that senior players clean the locker room after matches, symbolising servant leadership and the idea that no one is above the team. This principle resonates strongly with New Zealand's egalitarian leadership norms, where effective leaders are expected to remain approachable, model humility, and contribute to collective work rather than relying on hierarchy or status. Kerr's lesson *"leave the jersey in a better place"* further reflects New Zealand's emphasis on intergenerational responsibility and long-term thinking. The idea that leaders are temporary custodians aligns both with broader New Zealand organisational culture and with Māori concepts such as *kaitiakitanga* (guardianship) and *manaakitanga* (care, generosity, and responsibility for others). These values shape many New Zealand organisations' approaches to people management, sustainability, and community engagement (Haar & Delaney, 2009). Kerr captures this sentiment when he writes, *"True leaders are stewards of the future; they plant trees they will never see grow"* (Kerr, 2013, p. 225). Several other lessons Kerr outlines, including *"go for the gap,"* which encourages innovation and strategic risk-taking, and *"keep a blue head,"* which emphasises emotional regulation, mirror qualities expected of New Zealand leaders operating in a dynamic, diverse, and relationship-oriented environment. New Zealand workplaces tend to value calmness under pressure, authenticity, adaptability, and collective decision-making. Kerr's framing helps articulate these expectations in a structured way that is accessible to both local leaders and international audiences. As a result, *Legacy* has become widely used in leadership development programmes, MBA courses, and organisational culture training across New Zealand. Its lessons are frequently adopted by businesses seeking to strengthen teamwork, employee wellbeing, and long-term strategic alignment. Fundamentally, the book's focus on humility, authenticity and purposeful leadership reflects New Zealand's belief that true success is measured not by individual achievements, but by the positive legacy leaders leave behind for their organisations, communities, and future generations.

Local leadership book	
Title	*Legacy*
Subtitle	What the All Blacks can teach us about the business of life
Author	James Kerr
Publisher	Constable & Robinson Ltd
Year	2013
ISBN	978-1-4721-0898-6

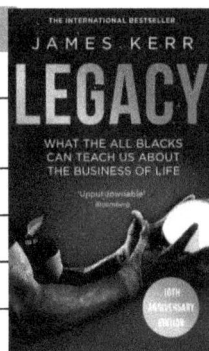

New Zealand leadership YouTube review

In the *Future of Leadership* video, Human Synergistics, a management consulting company specialising in organisational culture change, leadership development and teambuilding, features senior consultant Darren Levy discussing how leadership is evolving in New Zealand (Human Synergistics Australia & New Zealand, 2022). Levy, known for his *"dynamically challenging"* facilitation style, has worked extensively with organisations across Aotearoa and internationally, and is highly experienced in leadership development, constructive culture, high-performing teams, innovation, and change. Levy explains that as hybrid work becomes standard in Aotearoa, effective leadership in New Zealand requires strengthening four core qualities: clarity, confidence, capability, and connection. He emphasises that clear communication is essential in workplaces in New Zealand, noting that *"sending an email does not mean people know what is going on"* (Human Synergistics Australia & New Zealand, 2022, 0:54). Building confidence, both in leaders and within teams, supports strong customer engagement and overall organisational performance. Developing team capability is also crucial, especially when hybrid settings create uneven participation between remote and in-person staff. Maintaining strong connections fosters trust, inclusion, and agility across New Zealand's typically collaborative and relationship-driven workplaces. Levy underscores a broader shift towards human-centred leadership skills in New Zealand, including empathy, agile learning, facilitation and giving effective feedback – skills that increasingly outweigh purely technical expertise. He also identifies a distinctive leadership challenge: a cultural tendency towards conflict avoidance and defensiveness. Levy notes that many leaders *"tend to shy away from the tougher conversations"* (Human Synergistics Australia & New Zealand, 2022, 2:41), which, in turn, can prevent teams from addressing issues early. He emphasises the need for constructive debate, explaining that leaders must *"lean into the discomfort and have the conversations that matter"* (Human Synergistics Australia & New Zealand, 2022, 3:28). He also reminds leaders that effective communication is not just delivering a message, but ensuring understanding, stating that *"clarity builds confidence"* (Human Synergistics Australia & New Zealand, 2022, 1:32).

Next, in a Zeducation leadership class, the speaker, an experienced corporate trainer specialising in leadership, communication, and workforce capability development, explains that effective business leadership in New Zealand means recognising diversity as a strategic strength rather than just a legal obligation (Zeducation, 2024). Zeducation is a New Zealand-based training organisation that designs and delivers professional development programmes for New Zealand businesses, with a focus on leadership, diversity, culture, and performance improvement. He emphasises that Aotearoa is a multicultural society where people bring diverse cultures, upbringings, experiences, and ways of thinking to work, and that these differences shape how they make decisions, lead, and collaborate as team members. Good leaders in New Zealand, he argues, understand both visible diversity (such as age, gender, and ethnicity) and the less visible aspects (including values, upbringing, education, and life experience), instead of expecting everyone to think and act the same (Zeducation, 2024, 1:12). He links this directly to business performance, noting that inclusive New Zealand workplaces with strong leadership benefit from *"more ideas, better problem-solving, and more engaged teams"* (Zeducation, 2024, 3:04). He further explains that organisations that genuinely value diversity experience higher staff satisfaction, lower turnover, and stronger customer outcomes because employees *"feel respected, valued, and able to bring their whole selves to work"* (Zeducation, 2024, 4:10). Diversity is now *"good for business"* and essential for staying competitive, especially in global and international markets (Zeducation, 2024, 5:22). The speaker stresses that in New Zealand *"it starts at the top"*, leaders set the tone by supporting diversity, creating inclusive cultures, managing conflict respectfully, and implementing initiatives such as diverse hiring panels, employee resource groups for Māori and Pacific staff, cultural celebrations (e.g., *Matariki*), flexible work practices, cultural awareness training, and regular staff feedback (Zeducation, 2024, 6:03). He refers to examples like Air New Zealand, which has invested in female leadership, flexible work, and cultural capability programmes, and has received international recognition for its diversity efforts (Zeducation, 2024).

Understanding hierarchy in New Zealand

New Zealand prides itself on a flat organisational structure and an egalitarian approach to leadership. Cultural values emphasise fairness, inclusivity, and a preference for horizontal rather than vertical power relationships (Kennedy, 2000). Reflecting this, New Zealand's low power-distance score (PDI ≈ 22) is indicative of a strong expectation that workplace relationships remain equal and approachable (Hofstede, 2001). Managers are viewed as facilitators rather than authoritative figures, and this collaborative orientation supports openness and shared decision-making (Arrindell, 2003). Within such environments, employees typically feel comfortable engaging with managers because leaders are expected to be approachable, participative, and receptive to upward feedback (Javidan et al., 2006). A key mechanism through which New Zealanders enact this egalitarianism is linguistic and behavioural informality. Holmes (2018) shows that hierarchy is negotiated through everyday interactions rather than formal rules, with humour, especially self-deprecation and gentle teasing, often being used to reduce social distance and signal approachability. This resonates with Dr. Dore's observation that New Zealanders *"do not want hierarchy"* and often prefer leaders who feel like *"a friend,"* reflecting the broader belief that *"nobody is more important than you"* (28 November, 2025). Indeed, directness is common, but it is softened through inclusive phrasing such as "we" or "let us," which serves to enable disagreement without undermining relationships (Holmes & Marra, 2002). It is important to stress, however, that hierarchy is not wholly absent in this respect, but rather operates subtly. The so-called *'tall poppy syndrome'* discourages overt displays of superiority and encourages humility, prompting even high performers to "stay under the radar" to maintain social harmony (Dore, 28 November 2025; Kirkwood, 2007). This dynamic reinforces cultural expectations that leaders remain grounded and avoid signalling elevated status. These values are also visible in everyday leadership practices. Many New Zealand organisations use first names across all levels of staff, signalling reduced hierarchy and greater relational accessibility (Pio & Waddell, 2014). The CCBS Survey (2015-2025) also supports this aspect of organisational culture within New Zealand, insofar as the respondents noted that addressing anyone, *"even the Prime Minister,"* by their first name is normal. Such practices facilitate spontaneous "walk-about" conversations that keep leaders connected to daily operations and reinforce relational leadership (Henry & Wolfgramm, 2015). Dr. Dore's remark that even a manager *"can be your friend"* also testifies to how such informality supports openness and trust (28 November, 2025). Finally, New Zealand leadership is strongly participative, and values based. Research shows that involving employees in decisions, co-creating goals and consulting widely are viewed as effective leadership behaviours in the New Zealand context (Murphy, 2005; Pfeifer & Love, 2004). This participatory ethos aligns with broader cultural norms of collaboration and fairness. Values-based leadership, which emphasises empathy, authenticity and well-being, is increasingly prominent, supported by both Māori relational principles such as *whanaungatanga* and the wider Kiwi preference for relational integrity (Haar & Brougham, 2013; Mayes, 2019).

Overall, then, hierarchy in New Zealand is relational rather than rigid. Formal structures exist, but they are softened by cultural expectations of equality, humility, and shared responsibility. Effective leadership is therefore less about control and more about enabling others through collaboration, approachability, and values-driven practice.

How New Zealanders achieve leadership empathy

Empathy-centred leadership is increasingly visible across New Zealand organisations, where cultural preferences for inclusiveness, informality, and low power distance provide a natural foundation for relational leadership practices. Kennedy (2000) underscores that New Zealand managers often prioritise open communication and interpersonal understanding, creating favourable conditions for leadership behaviours that are grounded in care and connection. As such, empathetic leadership extends beyond interpersonal warmth and requires the establishment of environments where employees feel recognised, supported, and trusted (Kennedy, 2000). Evidence from the CCBS Survey (2015-2025) reinforces how empathy is enacted in day-to-day leadership behaviour, insofar as 80.8% of the respondents agreed that leaders actively spend time ensuring employee well-being, thus indicating that empathy is often experienced through regular check-ins, practical support, and approachable communication. Insights from the cross-cultural trainer interview also echo this observation, insofar as Dr. Dore informed us that New Zealand leaders frequently *"check in just to see how you are doing, not because something is wrong,"* highlighting the informal and relational nature of leader, employee interactions (28 November, 2025). Our other interviewee, Dr. Marra similarly emphasised that leaders *"make time to listen,"* and intentionally reduce hierarchical barriers to better understand employee needs and perspectives (11 November, 2025). Further support for this comes from the CCBS Survey (2015-2025), insofar as 62.6% of the respondents disagreed that leaders prefer to maintain personal distance from employees. These findings are consistent with academic research, which shows that many professionals in New Zealand consider their leaders to be approachable, cooperative, and willing to work alongside their teams (Holmes, 2018). These relational dynamics are especially significant in New Zealand's diverse work environments. Empathy enables leaders to navigate cultural differences, adapt to varying communication preferences, and cultivate inclusive spaces where individuals from a range of backgrounds feel heard and valued (Kennedy, 2000; Holmes, 2018). Beyond interpersonal communication, New Zealand organisations increasingly view empathy as essential to humanising work and supporting well-being. Holdsworth (2024) argues that empathetic leaders connect organisational purpose to employees lived experiences, acknowledge individual circumstances, and promote autonomy in work arrangements. This emphasis on well-being and balance was also noted by our two interviewees, who noted leaders' efforts to accommodate personal circumstances and respond to stress with understanding rather than judgement (Marra, 11 November 2025; Dore, 28 November 2025). It is also important to acknowledge that many elements of empathetic leadership in Aotearoa reflect longstanding Māori relational values. For instance, Katene (2010) identifies practices such as listening respectfully, prioritising collective well-being, and upholding the dignity of others as central to Māori leadership. These values increasingly influence mainstream leadership approaches, particularly through practices aligned with *whanaungatanga* (relationships) and *manaakitanga* (care and hospitality), which contribute to empathetic, people-centred leadership cultures. Viewed together, these insights indicate that leadership empathy in New Zealand is not merely a personal trait but a deliberate, relational, and culturally informed practice. Empathy is enacted through regular check-ins, active listening, reduced hierarchical distance, culturally sensitive communication, and genuine attention to well-being. By adopting these behaviours alongside accountability, New Zealand leaders strengthen trust, support diverse teams, and cultivate positive and sustainable organisational cultures.

Slovenia

Špela Kukovič, Lia Lačen, Lindsey Houwaard, Mare Slop, Zoi Zormpas,
Jette Arts, Mees Verkerk & Diego Muñoz

The Republic of Slovenia, which is often referred to as the "green treasure of Europe," is a small but strategically important country located at the crossroads of Central Europe and the Balkans. Just over half of its landmass is covered by forests (Plevnik & Japelj, 2023), and in recognition of its sustainability efforts, it became the first certified Green Destination in the world (Andrews et al., 2024). Since gaining its independence from Yugoslavia in 1991, the country has transformed into a stable democracy and a member of both the European Union and the Eurozone, benefiting from access to the single market and a stable currency. With just over two million inhabitants, Slovenia possesses a highly educated workforce and robust infrastructure. Its economy is strongly export-oriented, with exports of goods and services exceeding €55 billion in 2024, which is over 80% of GDP, whilst its key trade partners are Switzerland, Germany, Croatia, Italy, and Austria (SPIRIT Slovenia Business Development Agency, 2025; Trading Economics, 2024). Slovenia is amongst Europe's high-income economies, with SMEs dominating the economic landscape, accounting for more than 99% of businesses and employing nearly three-quarters of the workforce. This economic structure shapes leadership practices that emphasise pragmatism, accessibility, and adaptability, which are further influenced by cultural traditions from both Central Europe and the Mediterranean. Research suggests that there is a preference for autonomous and self-protective leadership approaches over charismatic or participative styles, although teamwork remains important (Pučko & Čater, 2011). This approach is exemplified by the former president Borut Pahor, who remarked that *"a good political leader does not underestimate the people's opinion, and especially the people themselves. A good leader is rather one who understands and respects them"* (Pahor, 2014). Overall, Slovenia's leadership culture reflects the interplay of the country's environmental identity, export-driven economy, and cultural values, combining independence with collaboration. The following chapter explores these dynamics further through both primary and secondary sources, offering insights into contemporary Slovenian business leadership skills and practices.

How Slovenians characterise leaders?

Slovenian leadership practices are shaped by the country's unique socio-historical and economic context, which is a combination of Central European traditions and Mediterranean influences. Leaders are expected to balance competence and pragmatism with careful, consensus-oriented decision-making, which is reflective of both the export-driven economy and the prevailing cultural preference for stability and social responsibility (Dimovski & Penger, 2008). Since gaining its independence in 1991, leadership has evolved; however, remnants of the previous hierarchical structures persist, particularly within the public sector and larger corporations (CCBS Survey, 2015–2020). Academic research demonstrates that Slovenian business leaders tend to be cautious and risk-averse, preferring gradual, consensus-based decision-making over bold or unilateral forms of action (Potočan et al., 2007). This tendency is grounded in broader cultural norms within Slovenia that emphasise collectivism, modesty, and social stability (Kovačič & Rus, 2014). Historically, Slovenia's experience under various political and economic systems (Austro-Hungarian, Yugoslav, and democratic) has cultivated a leadership culture that values predictability, careful planning, and shared accountability over individual assertiveness. As a result, Slovenian leaders often favour structured processes and measured progress as ways to ensure long-term trust and organisational harmony (Kovačič & Rus, 2014). This aligns with the results of the CCBS Survey (2015–2020) in which around two-thirds of the respondents reported that *"once a management decision has been made, it will not be changed very easily,"* thus reflecting a broader cultural tendency towards deliberation and accountability. Compared to some global leadership cultures, Slovenia places less emphasis on overt charisma or motivational rhetoric. As one of the survey respondents remarked, *"Especially in comparison to the US, we are a lot less prone to 'motivational speeches and BS'"* (CCBS Survey, 2015-2020). Instead, Slovenian leaders are valued for their competence, authenticity, and substance over style, qualities that align with a cultural preference for modesty and integrity in professional life. At the same time, Slovenian leadership is socially responsible: *"Leadership is sometimes very socially responsible to employees directly and by regulation."* (Arzenšek et al., 2018; CCBS Survey, 2015–2020). This emphasis on fairness and employee welfare is emblematic of both legal frameworks and cultural expectations of ethical management in the country (Dimovski & Penger, 2008). Employees tend to respect leaders primarily for their organisational experience, technical competence, and market knowledge, rather than for charisma alone (Prašnikar et al. 2014). Moreover, whilst leaders are expected to be visionary thinkers, good listeners, and decisive decision-makers, they must also maintain a respectful distance and provide feedback indirectly, due to a preference for controlled interpersonal interactions (Pučko & Čater, 2011). However, there is a noticeable divide across both sectors and generations: public institutions often maintain traditional top-down structures, whilst private companies and younger leaders are more participative and team-oriented in their approach (Potočan et al., 2007). There are also gender differences in leadership styles and practices. For example, within larger organisations, female leaders often adopt stricter, more traditional approaches like their male counterparts, whereas in smaller companies they tend to lead in a more inclusive and empathic manner (Potočan et al., 2007). With respect to the level of gender (in)equality in the country, the results of the CCBS Survey (2015-2020) suggest that access to leadership roles is broadly viewed as being the same for both men and women, thus signalling a gradual but meaningful cultural shift towards greater inclusivity. Overall, Slovenian business leadership is in a process of transition from traditional, stability-oriented management towards more open, participative, and people-centred models. Successful leaders in Slovenia are those who combine professional competence with social awareness, lead through example rather than persuasion, and balance decisiveness with empathy (Dimovski & Penger, 2008). They embody a distinctly Slovenian blend of prudence, responsibility, and authenticity, anchored in tradition yet responsive to modern organisational values (Potočan et al., 2007).

Survey results and what local respondents say

Senior managers and executives completed the Cross-Cultural Business Skills (CCBS) Survey across multiple years of data collection (2015–2025), resulting in insights from over 50 respondents. Together, these responses offer a robust and longitudinal perspective on Slovenian leadership styles, cultural norms, and organisational expectations. The most notable findings are discussed in turn below. Firstly, the findings indicate that Slovenian organisations generally exhibit relatively low hierarchical distance, insofar as 79% of the respondents stated that employees can address leaders by their first names (CCBS Survey, 2015-2025). These results are in accordance with research that shows that hierarchy in Slovenia exists but is not typically expressed through rigid interpersonal formality (Dimovski & Penger, 2008). One respondent confirmed this, when noting that *"Modern leaderhip aproaches are finally being recognised and applied in all "serious" companies"* (CCBS Survey, 2015-2025). Secondly, 64% of the respondents preferred to receive criticism privately rather than during staff meetings (CCBS Survey, 2015-2025), thus indicating an emphasis on interpersonal sensitivity and maintaining group harmony. This finding aligns with broader cultural descriptions suggesting that Slovenians favour a moderate and pragmatic communication style (Pučko & Čater, 2011). At the same time, however, 66% agreed that a manager may confront subordinates directly during meetings if necessary to achieve targeted results (CCBS Survey, 2015-2025). As one respondent opined: "[Slovenians are] *a lot less prone to motivational speeches and 'BS'*", reflecting a general preference for substance over emotional persuasion. Thirdly, the results reveal mixed tendencies with regards to decision-making and accountability. The responses to the statement that management decisions, once made, are not easily changed were divided (CCBS Survey, 2015-2025), thus indicating variation across organisational contexts. Nonetheless, a around 60% of the respondents described missing a deadline as being comparable to failure, which suggests that many Slovenian leaders maintain a strong sense of responsibility and performance orientation (CCBS Survey, 2015-2025). Several qualitative comments pointed towards hesitation in decision-making, with one respondent noting that leaders sometimes postpone decisions due to a desire to "*...find a consensus within a team and analyse all aspects in order to postpone the final decision*" (CCBS Survey, 2015-2025). This is in line with prior findings that Slovenian leaders tend to be careful and consensus-oriented in their decision-making (Potočan et al., 2007). Fourthly, 66% of the respondents agreed that maintaining a certain degree of personal distance from employees is necessary to preserve respect, underscoring the preference for professional boundaries. At the same time, the respondents were divided over whether managers should actively devote time to employee well-being, with 47% agreeing, whilst 53% disagreed with this statement (CCBS Survey, 2015-2025). This ambivalence suggests that expectations surrounding relational leadership differ across organisations, with some emphasising a supportive approach and others preferring clearer separation between personal and professional spheres. Several respondents noted that leadership is sometimes "*very socially responsible to employees*" (CCBS Survey, 2015-2025), whilst others expressed concern that such responsibility can occasionally be exploited. Next, the respondents expressed clear and consistent expectations regarding the competencies and attributes they value in leaders. An overwhelming majority (81%) selected organisational experience as the most important basis on which employees look up to their leaders, followed by technical competence, market expertise, intellect, and charismatic personality (CCBS Survey, 2015-2025). These preferences affirm that Slovenian organisations tend to value leaders who demonstrate capability, knowledge, and strategic thinking, rather than those who rely on status, appearance, or family background (CCBS Survey, 2015-2025). Finally, the survey indicated notable differences in leadership expectations and practices across sectors. Several of the open-ended responses contrasted public-sector leadership, which was described as more hierarchical, tradition-bound, and sometimes influenced by political appointments, with private-sector leadership, which was characterised as increasingly inclusive and participatory (CCBS Survey, 2015-2025). One respondent described the persistence of an *"archaic - 'because I said so'"* style in large public organisations, whereas private-sector organisations were said to embrace the view that *"every single team member is valuable and can participate in forming the strategy."* (CCBS Survey, 2015-2025). These observations suggest that Slovenia's leadership landscape is not uniform but rather shaped by organisational history, sectoral norms, and generational change.

Local leadership analysis

Mark (M.L.): a Slovenian leadership scholar

Mark is a Slovenian leadership scholar who graduated from the University of Ljubljana, School of Economics and Business and has been actively involved in leadership research and workshops for the past four years. At the beginning of our interview, he emphasised that business leaders in Slovenia are generally careful, thoughtful, and modest. He added that leaders with a lot of charisma or self-promotion are rare, and that there is a cultural preference for humility and quiet competence (Mark, 30 November 2025). From his perspective, the Slovenian leadership style has evolved over the past few decades, due, in large measure, to the country's integration into the European Union and other global connections. Today, Slovenian leaders are open to innovation, making decisions with careful consideration and often consult colleagues before finalising their choices. As he put it: *"It is not like in the US, where decisions are made quickly. Here, everything is very carefully thought through and focused"* (30 November, 2025). M.L. highlighted examples of respected leaders in the country, such as Danica Purg from the Bled School of Management, who is highly regarded for her competence and expertise. Next, he proceeded to discuss generational dynamics in leadership in Slovenia. Specifically, he opined that older leaders are valued for their experience and knowledge, whereas younger leaders are recognised above all for demonstrating adaptability (30 November, 2025). In response to a question about cross-cultural differences, he underscored that the indirect communication style which prevails in Slovenia can in some instance pose challenges for foreign managers. In his words: *"We [Slovenians] are not going to directly tell someone to clean something: we give a hint instead"* (Mark, 30 November 2025). Slovenian employees generally prefer calm, patient, and respectful leadership, he suggested, with few outbursts or dramatic displays of authority. Mark described hierarchy as expected but approachable, noting that employees can communicate with their leaders, unlike in some Asian contexts. Responsibility, fairness, and organisation are highly valued, and leaders are generally reserved, speaking only when necessary to do so. Motivation is often conveyed through practical support, opportunities for learning, and fairness rather than charisma (30 November 2025). Later, he proceeded to discuss differences between sectors and genders. Specifically, he informed us that public sector leadership tends to be more formal than private sector management. Moreover, female leaders are often more collaborative and communication-focused, whereas male leaders sometimes emphasise task completion. Finally, Mark noted that AI is increasingly integrated into leadership practices, improving efficiency but sometimes creating anxiety amongst employees (30 November 2025). In conclusion, Mark characterised Slovenian leadership as competence-driven, empathetic, and collaborative, with an emphasis on careful decision-making, fairness, and respect for employees.

Špela (Š.L.): a Slovenian cross-cultural trainer

Špela is a Slovenian cross-cultural trainer with over twenty years of leadership experience within two major organisations. She leads the team at DOLLY and manages at AutoDelta. At the beginning of our interview, she emphasised that Slovenian leaders are typically calm, thoughtful, and deliberate. Decisions are rarely made by a single individual, but rather involve consultation with multiple stakeholders. Above all, she noted, leaders value structure, order, and predictability, and tend to avoid rushing decisions, reflecting a preference for careful planning (Špela, 30 November 2025). Next, Špela moved onto discuss how Slovenian leadership has evolved in recent years, becoming more collaborative, conversational, and open to feedback. More specifically, she said that leaders today are cautious and risk-aware, often sticking to proven approaches rather than making suprising decisions. As she put it: *"A good leader is someone who can connect people"* and ensures that teams are consulted and included in decision-making processes (30 November, 2025). Later in the interview, the discussion shifted to the topic of generational differences and hierarchical dynamics within Slovenian organisations. Related to this, she proceeded to inform us that older Slovenian leaders generally command more authority due to their greater experience, which is respected across organisations. At the same time, younger employees increasingly expect clarity, feedback, and an understanding of the purpose behind leaders' decisions, which signals a shift that is driven by Generation Z (30 November, 2025). When asked about cross-cultural differences, she replied that foreign managers often struggle with the slower decision-making processes and the importance of building trust and relationships before advancing initiatives in Slovenia. When asked about the preferred leadership traits in the country, Špela emphasised fairness, responsibility, and professional distance, noting that Slovenian leaders demonstrate authority through actions rather than overt displays, and that top-level leaders maintain a certain distance whilst remaining approachable (30 November, 2025). Employees typically view their leaders as competent, clear, and sometimes reserved professionals who provide praise and support at the right moments. Leaders are expected to listen actively, remain consistent, and follow through on commitments (Špela, 30 November 2025). She also observed that Slovenian leadership in the private sector can vary depending on the organisation, whilst public sector leadership remains more formal and structured. Differences between genders are still present at the very top level, but capable women are increasingly visible, particularly in her area of expertise: finance. Leadership has become less formal and more conversational, incorporating post-hierarchical practices that encourage questions, feedback, and learning from mistakes (30 November 2025). Finally, Špela described how technology has impacted leadership in Slovenia, noting that she regularly uses AI in her accounting practice, and that it improves efficiency and supports daily work whilst allowing her to focus on team leadership and decision-making (30 November 2025). Overall, Špela characterised Slovenian leadership as thoughtful, fair, and relational, combining professional competence with careful decision-making, trust-building, and a willingness to innovate whilst, simultaneously, maintaining structured guidance.

In-country leadership bestseller

AEIOU voditeljstva: Pet pristopov k vodenju za prihodnost ("AEIOU of Leadership: Five approaches to leadership for the future") by Simona Klopčič (2019) is one of Slovenia's most influential leadership books. Klopčič is a well-respected Slovenian leadership scholar and practitioner, whose research and work focuses on organisational behaviour, management, and leadership development. The book builds on her earlier pioneering work, Voditeljstvo: Vodenje in sodelovanje, moč in odgovornost ("Leadership: Leadership and Collaboration, Power and Responsibility") (Klopčič, 2018), the first comprehensive leadership book published in Slovenia, which established her as a leading voice in the field. This book introduces the AEIOU model, which posits that Authenticity, Empathy, Innovation, Organisation, and Understanding, are the five complementary approaches to effective leadership in Slovenia. Klopčič argues that Slovenian leaders must balance these dimensions to navigate the challenges of contemporary organisations. Authenticity and empathy support trust and strong interpersonal relationships, whilst innovation and organisation ensure business objectives are met efficiently. Understanding reflects cultural awareness and sensitivity to Slovenia's consensus-oriented workplace culture, encouraging leaders to consider the collective impact of their decisions rather than focusing solely on individual gains. Like many international leadership bestsellers, Klopčič combines theory with practical examples. In this respect, the book draws on case studies from Slovenian companies and interviews with leaders in both public and private sectors. It emphasises participative leadership, showing that modern Slovenian managers benefit from encouraging team input whilst maintaining professional authority. A key feature of her approach is the integration of Slovenia's socio-cultural traditions with contemporary management practices. For example, many Slovenian firms combine formal hierarchical structures with participative leadership, which, in turn, allows employees to contribute ideas whilst final decisions remain the leader's responsibility. This reflects a broader national preference for balanced, collaborative authority that respects hierarchy yet values inclusiveness. Overall, AEIOU voditeljstva provides a practical, research-informed guide for Slovenian leaders. Along with her earlier book, it offers a critical resource for understanding leadership in Slovenia, presenting a model that blends professional competence, cultural awareness, and human-centred leadership within a uniquely Slovenian context (Klopčič, 2018, 2019).

Local leadership book		
Title	*AEIOU voditeljstva* *("AEIOU of Leadership")*	
Subtitle	Pet pristopov k vodenju za prihodnost ("Five approaches to leadership of future")	
Author	Simona Klopčič	
Publisher	AEIOU Universe	
Year	2019	
ISBN	978-961-290-109-7	

Slovenian leadership YouTube review

Insights into Slovenian leadership can also be drawn from a series of online interviews and podcasts with local experts, which shed light on how leadership practices are evolving in response to social, generational, and technological changes. The first video to be discussed is a YouTube programme titled *Moč gospodarstva*, produced by Delo and hosted by Marijana Kriston-Fazarinc. In this episode, Simona Špilak, director of the executive search agency Boc Institut, underscores that Slovenia's labour market is highly dynamic, with technological advances and AI increasing the demand for leaders who combine technical expertise with managerial and relational skills. She notes that high-demand sectors such as IT, engineering, and finance require leaders who can integrate professional knowledge with interpersonal competence to guide teams through growing complexity (Delo, 2025, 1:35). Špilak proceeds to explain that whilst AI supports leadership development and data-driven decision-making, human judgment, empathy, and strategic thinking remain irreplaceable (Delo, 2025, 14:15). The second video to be summarised is an online podcast featuring organisational consultant Simona Klopčič, who explores the psychological and relational dimensions of leadership in Slovenia. Klopčič emphasises that trust is at the core of Slovenian leadership, explaining that intentionally fostering trust creates *"chemistry in the group,"* which, in turn, strengthens organisational culture through oxytocin (Klopčič, 2020, 03:28-4:30). Her *Ikigai* model illustrates that effective leaders in Slovenia connect what they love, what they are skilled at, what society needs, and what can be monetised (Klopčič, 2020, 5:05). Klopčič argues that Slovenian leadership is gradually shifting away from traditional authority-based approaches towards more purpose-driven and human-centred models that cultivate belonging, recognition, and meaning. The third video, entitled *Vodenje v 21. stoletju* (Leadership in the 21st Century), was produced by the *Fakulteta za upravo*. The discussion features several Slovenian leadership experts, including Boštjan Kuritnik, who explains that younger employees, particularly Generation Z, respond more to competence and trust than to hierarchy. Therefore, he believes that leaders must empower autonomy, encourage experimentation, and treat mistakes as learning opportunities (Fakulteta za upravo, 2020, 09:03-13:17). Similarly, Danila Brečko stresses the importance of flexibility and continuous adaptation, which foster creativity and team development (Fakulteta za upravo, 2020, 24:35). Brečko and Kuritnik agree that technical expertise alone is no longer sufficient, as maturity, communication, and relational intelligence are equally essential qualities of successful leadership in Slovenia (Fakulteta za upravo, 2020, 19:38). Across these perspectives, a recurring idea is that of post-heroic leadership in which leaders step back to enable their employees to take ownership and initiative (Fakulteta za upravo, 2020, 36:13). This represents a clear shift from *"I lead"* to *"we grow together,"* which is emblematic of the country's movement from traditional, expertise-based management towards more human-centred and post-heroic leadership approaches.

Understanding hierarchy in Slovenia

Slovenia exhibits a moderate level of hierarchy in leadership, which is generally subtle, procedural, and grounded in competence, responsibility, and professional expertise rather than overt displays of power or status. Hofstede's Power Distance dimension places Slovenia in a moderate range, thus indicating that unequal power relations are acknowledged, but leaders are expected to act fairly, professionally, and approachable rather than authoritatively (Hofstede Insights, 2024). The GLOBE study further illustrates that Slovenia scores high on uncertainty avoidance and institutional collectivism, which reinforces structured decision-making, adherence to rules, and cautious leadership behaviour (House et al., 2004). In practice, hierarchy still exists and is clearly visible within Slovenian organisations, particularly within traditional sectors such as public administration, finance, and large state-owned enterprises, where structured decision-making, formal reporting lines, and professional distance are the norm (Dimovski & Penger, 2008). The results of the CCBS survey (2015-2025) confirm this, insofar as one respondent noted that there is: *"Still lots of attention to hierarchy,"* whilst another opined that there is *"still not enough courage to take decisions with full responsibility in the right time, when it is necessary. Too many hesitations, trying to find a consensus within a team and analyse all aspects in order to postpone the final decision."* Hierarchical practices often involve careful deliberation, formal approval procedures, and consultation with subordinates or colleagues before final decisions are taken (CCBS Survey, 2015–2025; Dimovski & Penger, 2008). At the same time, hierarchy does not mean authoritarianism; rather, research shows that Slovenian leaders are generally approachable, maintain professional credibility, and are expected to act fairly, so as to create the requisite balance between authority and accountability (Pučko & Čater, 2011; House et al., 2004). Leaders are respected for their competence and clarity of responsibility rather than their privileges or status symbols; however, formal titles such as *direktor* (director) or *gospod/gospa* (Mr./Mrs.) remain in use, and decision-making typically follows a structured, consensus-oriented process to minimise risk and uncertainty (CCBS Survey, 2015-2025). Despite the persistence of these traditional hierarchical structures, leadership in Slovenia is gradually evolving. Contemporary managers increasingly integrate relational and human-centred approaches, emphasising trust, team cohesion, psychological safety, and employee engagement (Špilak, 2025; Klopčič, 2020). Younger employees, particularly Generation Z, respond more strongly to competence, trust, and participative decision-making than to formal authority, encouraging managers to empower autonomy, support experimentation, and treat mistakes as learning opportunities (Špilak, 2025). Gender equality also shapes hierarchical dynamics, with women holding over 40% of parliamentary seats and a growing share of leadership roles across public and private sectors, thus demonstrating that competence and fairness increasingly define who occupies leadership positions rather than formal seniority or traditional privileges (European Institute for Gender Equality [EIGE], 2023; Fink-Hafner, 2021). In summary, leadership hierarchy in Slovenia exists and remains an important organising principle, particularly for clarifying responsibility, maintaining order, and ensuring accountability. It is characterised by formal procedures, respect for competence, and structured decision-making, however it is gradually being complemented by participative, post-heroic, and relational leadership practices, which is reflective of a culture that values both stability and flexibility, formal authority and human-centred engagement.

How Slovenians achieve leadership empathy

In Slovenia, leadership empathy is grounded in cultural values such as fairness, modesty, and a collaborative orientation, which, in turn, shape how managers interact with their teams. Leaders are expected to demonstrate care and understanding primarily through actions that build trust, reliability, and consistency, rather than through overt emotional displays (Lewis, 2006). Empirical research supports this approach, insofar as Slovenian managers have been shown to operationalise empathy by acknowledging employees' workload, exhibiting professional respect, and maintaining structured yet supportive relationships with employees (Kovačič & Rus, 2014). These behaviours align with employees' expectations, insofar as the CCBS Survey (2015–2025) demonstrates that Slovenian subordinates value leaders who are visionary thinkers, good listeners, and powerful decision makers, whilst the majority of the respondents also reported that leaders should actively dedicate time to ensuring the personal well-being of their team, which suggests that empathy is considered a professional responsibility embedded within organisational culture (CCBS Survey, 2015–2025). Cross-cultural research further contextualises these findings. Slovenia ranks 32nd in empathic concern, 29th in perspective taking, and 29th in total empathy across 63 countries, thus indicating moderate but meaningful levels of empathy that are expressed through practical, relational behaviours rather than dramatic emotional gestures (Chopik et al., 2017). Leadership experts reinforce this perspective. Klopčič (2019) describes authentic Slovenian leadership as being grounded in self-awareness, fairness, and trustworthiness, emphasising listening to understand one's employees rather than asserting one's dominance over them. For example, a manager might hold regular one-on-one meetings with team members, actively asking for their feedback on project decisions, and demonstrating that their perspectives are valued. Moreover, she says that leaders who cultivate belonging, recognition, and structured support foster cohesion and commitment within teams (Klopčič, 2019). For example, this could mean publicly acknowledging individual achievements in team meetings or creating mentorship opportunities for starting employees. As a result, effective Slovenian leaders combine professional competence with human-centred behaviours. They provide clear guidance, treat employees fairly, maintain open communication channels, and take concrete steps to support well-being, creating a work environment where trust and reliability underpin leadership (Lewis, 2006). Rather than relying on charisma or flamboyant gestures, Slovenian empathy is operationalised through quiet consistency, attentive presence, and structured support, which is emblematic of a culture in which leadership is as much about competence as it is about relational integrity (Chopik et al., 2017; Kovačič & Rus, 2014).

Thailand

Kanokphon Sophaphon, Eunseo Kim, Jack Maher, Joshua Tubiana,
Leandra Carsilia & Tammara Bokhorst

Thailand, located in the heart of Southeast Asia, is bordered by Laos, Cambodia, Malaysia, and Myanmar. This country, which is commonly referred to as the *"Land of Smiles"* (Smith, 2021), is widely recognised for the warmth, friendliness, and hospitality of its people. Although this moniker reflects the welcoming nature of Thai society, Thailand, which has a population of over 70 million people, is a diverse nation whose culture has been shaped by centuries of independence, robust socio-cultural traditions, and strategic diplomacy (Chanchaochai, 2017; Kittipong, 2019). In contrast to many of its Southeast Asian nations, Thailand maintained its independence and was never colonised by a European power. This allowed the country to safeguard its sovereignty and cultural heritage, which, in turn, fostered a strong national pride and a profound sense of national unity (Baker & Phongpaichit, 2014; Chan, 2018). During the nineteenth and early twentieth centuries, strategic diplomacy by Thai monarchs played a key role in protecting the nation from external pressures and ensuring continued autonomy (History State.gov, n.d.; Tuchman, 1996). These historical and socio-cultural experiences and traditions continue to strongly shape contemporary Thai business leadership skills and practices. For example, the vast majority of the Thai population are adherents of Buddhism, whose principles are deeply embedded within Thai business culture (Komin, 1990). Integrity, empathy, and respect for hierarchy are especially valued in Thai leadership, as well as the so-called *Rajadhamma ten*, which are ten royal virtues that include, amongst other things, generosity, humility, and fairness, and which serve as an important ethical framework that guides Thai leaders (Tongchangya, 2024). The following chapter sets out to understand how Thailand's rich history and socio-cultural nuances shape the prevailing leadership styles and organisational culture in the society (Anderson, 2005), by drawing upon academic research, interviews with local experts and survey data from C-level business professionals in the country.

How the Thai characterise leaders?

Leadership in Thailand is shaped by a unique blend of cultural, societal, and economic influences. Buddhist philosophy, which was introduced to the country centuries ago, is still deeply rooted within Thai business culture. Consequently, the ideal leadership approach in Thailand ordinarily involves approaching others with kindness, compassion, shared happiness, and a calm, balanced state of mind (Roongrerngsuke & Liefooghe, 2012). In practice, Thai leaders express calmness towards their employees through their behaviour and communication style. They rarely raise their voice, avoid displaying anger in public, and give instructions in a soft, measured tone. For example, during moments of workplace stress, such as a project delay. Thai leaders are more likely to reassure employees by saying *"mai pen rai"* ("it is okay, do not worry") and focus on finding a collective solution rather than blaming individuals, which, in turn, creates a sense of emotional safety and helps employees remain composed and confident (Sirilatthayakorn et al., 2020). Many Thai leaders also show concern for employee's family situations, health, or personal difficulties. A typical example would be when a manager permits flexible working hours so that an employee can care of a sick parent, or when a leader privately checks in with a staff member after noticing visible signs of stress. These small acts of kindness reflect the Buddhist value of *metta* (loving-kindness) and strengthen loyalty and trust within the team. The most distinctive feature of Thai leadership is its hierarchical and paternalistic nature. From childhood, Thais are encouraged to respect their elders and authority figures, a social pattern that subsequently extends into the workplace (Srimueangpan, 2022). Within Thai culture, education and academic credentials are seen as important markers of one's social standing. Being well-educated helps a person gain social acceptance, which, in turn, reinforces the country's hierarchical structure. According to Sirilatthayakorn et al. (2020), the cultural value of *kreng jai*, which means to be considerate, respectful, and careful about causing discomfort, remains central to Thai leaders' communication. Whilst this value helps to ensure politeness and cultivate a sense of harmony, it can also restrict direct feedback or open disagreement, as employees prefer decisions to be guided by senior leaders (Sirilatthayakorn et al., 2020). An interesting aspect of Thai businesses is that that 40 percent of them are family owned (Taksinapan (2020). The consequence of this is that it is fairly common for Thai leaders to also treat their employees like family members (Baczek, 2013). The concept of m*ong karn klai*, which means *'looking ahead,'* has also been very important in Thai culture and business leadership, historically. This is because Thailand is a long-term goal-oriented country, and therefore leaders must show a strong work ethic and strive for prosperity and longevity for an organisation (Pimpa, 2012, as cited in

Taksinapan, 2020). Modern leadership is increasingly participative and inclusive in nature, particularly within entrepreneurial and multinational contexts, with Thai leaders deriving their legitimacy from integrity, empathy, and showing respect for the social order (Taksinapan, 2020). For instance, a manager may defer to senior executives whilst still encouraging team discussions, asking for opinions, and offering guidance during decision-making. Our interview with Thai leadership scholar Dr Philip Hallinger provides concrete examples of what this looks like in practice. He explained that modern Thai leaders increasingly try to involve employees in discussions whilst still respecting seniority. For example, instead of commanding a solution, a Thai manager might say: *"Let us think about this together"* in order to calm tension and avoid confrontation but later take the final decision privately out of respect for rank (27 November, 2025). Dr Hallinger described this shift as signalling a move away from the old model in which *"leaders were the brain and everyone else was the hands,"* towards a more distributed style in which leadership *"should be everywhere in the company"* (27 November, 2025). Younger Thai leaders with international experience demonstrate this blend clearly. According to Dr. Hallinger, they encourage more open dialogue and rotate responsibilities to build confidence, which is similar to the *"geese model"* that he himself teaches managers, where team members take turns leading and supporting each other. At the same time, they continue to show sincerity (*jing-jai*) through gestures such as attending funerals, participating in staff family events, or personally checking in on employees' well-being (Hallinger, 27 November 2025). These actions reflect how Thai leaders balance global participative practices with enduring cultural norms centred on harmony, respect, and heartfelt leadership.

Survey results and what local respondents say

To gain a deeper understanding of leadership styles, practices, and business culture in Thailand, numerous C-level managers were invited to participate in the CCBS Survey (2017–2025). Drawing on several years of survey data collection enables us to provide a more reliable and comprehensive analysis of Thai business leadership skills and practices. The following section summarises the most noteworthy findings emerging out of the survey. The first major finding confirms Thailand's high-context communication style, as evidenced by the fact that more than half of the respondents identified indirect communication as a key aspect of a Thai leadership approach, reporting that they preferred to receive criticism indirectly, outside of staff meetings (CCBS Survey, 2017–2025). This finding aligns with the cultural emphasis on maintaining *'face'* (*naa*), which reflects the

151

importance of avoiding public confrontation and embarrassment to preserve harmony. It also corresponds closely with the principle of *kreng jai* (Hcli, 2023). The second theme concerns the preferred leadership traits amongst Thai professionals. Many of the respondents described themselves as leaders who emphasise empathy, approachability, and relationship-building, supporting their teams through encouragement rather than confrontation (CCBS Survey, 2017-2025). Earn Chanikan Kengluecha, a CEO from Thailand, observed that Thai leaders are *"humble, motivate employees, flexible to changes, clear communicators, smart in giving criticism, and encourage employees"* (CCBS Survey, 2022). This behaviour aligns with Buddhist-influenced values such as *mettā* (loving-kindness), which promotes compassion and caring relationships (Phontapsarn et al., 2025). Within Thai organisations, leadership is guided by *"mettā"* which fosters a sense of trust, emotional well-being, and commitment, functioning as both a spiritual ideal and a practical managerial strength (Leesmidt & Jarunratanakul, 2022). A General Manager in Thailand noted that *"taking care of employees like family members and treating colleagues with politeness and gentleness"* is a key aspect of Thai leadership, which distinguishes it from other countries (CCBS Survey, 2025). The survey data also reveals clear patterns regarding hierarchy and decision-making. Thai leaders operate in systems where authority is both expected and visibly reinforced. Many of the respondents reported that leaders receive status symbols, such as private offices or company transportation, which is reflective of their standing in the organisation (CCBS Survey, 2017–2025). These symbols correspond with the cultural role of the *"phu yai"* (respected elder), who is expected to provide direction, protection, and guidance to *"phu noi"* (juniors) (Vora & Kainzbauer, 2020). Next, the respondents rated themselves highly on setting clear expectations, taking responsibility, and providing structure, thus confirming the importance of decisive leadership in Thailand. Alongside this, they also strongly associated themselves with empathy, patience, and emotional awareness. This dual expectation reflects the Thai model of hierarchical yet compassionate leadership, where authority is exercised with fairness and relational sensitivity (Arun & Rungsithong, 2020). Overall, Thai leadership blends structure with benevolence, which is consistent with the cultural expectations of the *"phu yai– phu noi"* relationship. With respect to the level of gender (in)equality in Thai organisations, over three-quarters of the respondents reported that there were equal opportunities for men and women to attain senior roles (CCBS Survey, 2017). This finding is in accordance with other studies that show that the country consistently ranks highly with regards to women in senior management positions, and that promotion is influenced more by one's education, age, and organisational experience rather than by one's gender (Taksinapan, 2020). In conclusion, the survey results provide empirical validation for the dual nature of Thai leadership:

Thai leaders are expected to demonstrate decisive authority through clear structures and status symbols, whilst, simultaneously, embodying relational benevolence, as seen in the indirect communication style, *"kreng jai,"* and *"mettā".* This synthesis reinforces the enduring role of the *"phu yai",* a respected elder whose legitimacy derives not merely from position, but from their ability to exercise power with fairness, emotional composure, and a sincere commitment to the team's well-being.

Local leadership analysis

Dr Philip Hallinger: a Thai Leadership Scholar

Dr Philip Hallinger is widely recognised as one of the leading scholars and practitioners of leadership development in Thailand. With over forty-five years of experience in the field and more than thirty-five years of residence in Thailand, he brings both academic depth and lived cultural insight to the study of Thai organisational behaviour. Throughout his career, he has held professorships at several major Thai universities, including Chiang Mai University, Chulalongkorn University and Mahidol University, and previously served as Executive Director of the College of Management at Mahidol University. His leadership expertise is not limited to academia: *"I have done corporate training with more than 25,000 managers in Thailand... and 98% of it in Thai"* (Hallinger, 27 November 2025). When asked about the evolution of Thai leadership, Dr Hallinger emphasised that a significant shift has occurred since the early 2000s. Prior to this period, he described Thai organisations as operating through *"a very top-down hierarchical model where the leaders were at the top... they were like the brain, and everyone else was the hands"* (Hallinger, 27 November 2025). The Asian economic crisis in 1997 challenged this paradigm and created pressure for more distributed leadership systems. His collaboration with Siam Cement Group illustrates this shift vividly: he helped design a four-level leadership development programme aimed at embedding the idea that *"leadership is distributed and should be everywhere in the company"* (Hallinger, 27 November 2025). To convey this concept, he used the now-well-known metaphor of buffaloes versus geese, demonstrating the limitations of blind hierarchical following and the strength of shared vision and rotating responsibility. Later in the interview, Dr Hallinger proceed to explicate how cultural dimensions continue to shape leadership in contemporary Thailand. In particular, he informed us about the enduring importance of saving face and consensus-building, explaining that Thai leaders must protect both their own face and that of their followers. Whilst consensus can strengthen relationships, he cautioned in the interview that it can also serve as a mechanism for *"not wanting to be stuck being the one to make the decision"* (Hallinger, 27 November 2025). When asked about which traits were most valued in Thai leaders, he responded that age and seniority remain powerful forces, a fact which is exemplified in Thailand's mandatory retirement age of 60, which exists because *"age and seniority and rank are so powerful here"* (Hallinger, 27 November 2025). Next, Dr. Hallinger proceeded to explain that the most distinctive aspect of Thai leadership is that it is fundamentally heart-driven. That is to say, Thai employees expect sincerity, *jing-jai*, from their leaders, which is expressed through actions such as attending funerals, participating in rituals and walking the talk so to speak. As he explained, in Thai the verb to understand, *kao-jai*, literally means enter the heart: *"successful [Thai] leaders try to... open up their hearts, only then can you motivate them* [employees] *to change"* (Hallinger, 27 November 2025). In conclusion, he argued that this human-centred orientation is essential for building trust, respect and meaningful dialogue within Thai organisations.

Thailand Social Media Review

Social media discussions in Thailand reveal a leadership style that is rooted in cultural values of hierarchy, emotional balance, and *kreng jai*, whilst it is increasingly shaped by modern expectations of empathy and participative decision-making. These online perspectives reinforce the cultural dynamics documented by Thai scholars, who emphasise that leadership in Thailand blends authority with benevolence, face-saving behaviours, and emotional composure (Komin, 1990, 1991; Persons, 2016; Vora & Kainzbauer, 2020). One widely referenced voice is Sudkhun Khampharat, President of the Thailand Management Association, who was interviewed on the Klaoshow YouTube channel. The speaker underscores that effective Thai leadership begins with low ego, interpersonal sensitivity, and awareness of individual differences, explaining that teams respond positively to leaders who maintain harmony and avoid confrontation. This mirrors the cultural importance of *kreng jai* and indirect communication (Klaoshow, 2023, 01:41–02:23). Transformation and strategic vision are central themes in the online work of Pravit Hanutsaha, CEO and host of *Mission to the Moon*. In EP.2424 of the podcast, the speaker emphasises that contemporary Thai leaders must combine long-term vision, adaptability, and emotional intelligence to guide organisations through uncertainty. This approach reflects the expectation that Thai leaders maintain *sabai*, a calm emotional atmosphere whilst anticipating change and supporting team stability (Hanutsaha, 2025, 05:17–06:21). These ideas correspond with Buddhist-influenced leadership values emphasising *metta* and *karuna* (Leesmidt & Jarunratanakul, 2022). Practical guidance on leadership also appears on social media platforms, especially through the work of Nop Pongsatorn

Dhanabordeephat, a well-known Thai leadership coach. In the YouTube video *"How to Be a Boss Employees Love,"* the coach explains that Thai leaders often shift between four roles: visionary leader, commander, boss, and coach, to respond to team needs. This discussion emphasises sincerity (*jing-jai*), fairness, and emotional steadiness, echoing traditional *phu yai–phu noi* expectations and the moral responsibilities outlined in the *Dasavidha-rājadharma* virtues (Dhanabordeephat, 2024, 01:20–01:30; 05:56–07:24; Tongchangya, 2024). Corporate Thai platforms express similar viewpoints. KTC Thailand defines leadership as the ability to inspire, influence, and manage conflict rather than relying solely on positional authority, showing that workplace credibility depends on communication, trust, and emotional composure (KTC Thailand, 2025). Intercultural HR blogs such as Aster Lion elaborate on how *kreng jai* shapes leadership behaviour, noting that Thai leaders commonly rely on indirect communication, politeness, and relationship-building to maintain harmony (Aster Lion, 2025). These traits are consistent with long-standing observations about Thai communication norms (HCLI, 2023; Komin, 1991). The centrality of harmony is also reinforced in broader Thai social commentary. An online article by Theri (2025) analyses conflict resolution in Thailand, explaining that *kreng jai*, face-saving, and hierarchical respect influence how employees communicate concerns. This dynamic encourages leaders to adopt emotionally sensitive, private, and nuanced communication strategies to avoid disrupting relationships. Taken together, Thai social media reflects a leadership model that is hierarchical yet compassionate, indirect yet relationally intelligent, and increasingly collaborative and coaching oriented. Whilst traditional values such as harmony, respect, and calmness remain essential, contemporary online discourse shows a clear shift towards empowerment, open dialogue, and psychological safety, thus demonstrating how Thai leadership practices continue to evolve whilst staying rooted in cultural foundations.

In-country leadership bestseller
One of the most influential Thai leadership books is *The Way Thais Lead: Face as Social Capital* by Larry S. Persons (2016), an American scholar and leadership consultant who has lived and worked in Thailand for more than three decades. He earned his PhD in Leadership Studies from Bangkok's Assumption University, where his research focused on Thai cultural values and their impact on leadership behaviour. Persons is also the CEO of CQ Leadership Consulting, a Bangkok-based firm that trains Thai and international executives in intercultural management and ethical leadership. The book explores how Thai leadership is built on the cultural concept of *"face" (naa)*, which refers to the respect, honour, and social value that

a person gains in relationships. Persons argues that maintaining *face* is not only a matter of pride but rather a form of social capital that supports trust, harmony, and cooperation within Thai organisations (2016). Within Thai culture, a leader's credibility depends on how well they protect others' *face* whilst maintaining their own. This means avoiding direct confrontation, criticism, or embarrassment, as these behaviours damage harmony within the group. Effective leaders therefore use empathy, diplomacy, and subtle communication to preserve social balance. Persons describes this as *"leading through respect rather than authority"* (Persons, 2016, p. 112). The book also underscores that hierarchy and compassion coexist in Thai leadership. Leaders are expected to act as moral guardians, *phu yai* (respected elders), who provide guidance, fairness, and emotional support to their subordinates. Such leaders demonstrate empathy through acts of care, patience, and generosity, which is in alignment with Buddhist virtues such as *metta* (loving-kindness) and *karuna* (compassion). Through detailed interviews and cultural analysis, the author shows that leadership success in Thailand depends on emotional intelligence and relational awareness. Rather than enforcing rules, Thai leaders tend to motivate by creating a sense of belonging and mutual respect. Persons calls this approach *"face-giving leadership"*, where preserving the dignity of others strengthens leaders' moral authority. In conclusion, *The Way Thais Lead* presents leadership as a human-centred process deeply rooted in empathy and respect. By connecting cultural traditions with leadership practice, the book provides essential insight into how Thai leaders achieve influence through compassion, self-control, and social harmony, values that continue to define Thailand's professional culture today.

Local leadership book	
Title	*The Way Thais Lead*
Subtitle	Face as Social Capital
Author	Larry S. Persons
Publisher	Chulalongkorn University Press
Year	2016
ISBN	978-6162151163

THE WAY
THAIS LEAD
FACE AS SOCIAL CAPITAL
LARRY S. PERSONS

Thai leadership YouTube review

The first video, a studio interview on the Klaoshow channel with Sudkhun Khampharat, President of the Thailand Management Association, emphasises that Thai leadership is defined by followership rooted in respect, noting that true leadership arises when people genuinely want to follow (Klaoshow, 2023, 00:00-00:53). Inspiring others requires a clear purpose and the ability to understand oneself, others, and the organisation, which is reflective of Thai cultural values of modesty and interpersonal awareness (Klaoshow, 2023, 01:41-02:23). Khampharat's discussion of reducing ego and recognising individual differences aligns with maintaining *nam jai* (considerate goodwill) and avoiding confrontation. She further links effective leadership to openness towards organisational change, framing adaptability as a culturally grounded skill for maintaining harmony during uncertainty, whilst mindfulness supports focus, productivity, and emotional balance in line with Thai Buddhist influences (Klaoshow, 2023, 02:23-03:09; 03:55-05:15). The second video, a podcast hosted by CEO Pravit Hanutsaha on the Mission to the Moon channel, underscores visionary thinking as an essential skill for Thai business leaders, who must anticipate both market and technological shifts and convert insights into actionable strategies (Hanutsaha, 2025, 00:00-03:54). He stresses adaptability as a defining trait for navigating a fast-changing business environment, whilst emotional intelligence enables Thai leaders to manage tensions and cultivate relationships, reinforcing social harmony and *sabai* (*a comfortable atmosphere*) (Hanutsaha, 2025, 05:17-06:21; 07:36-08:34). The final video, an instructional talk by Nop Pongsatorn Dhanabordeephat on the NopPongsatorn channel, illustrates how Thai leaders wear multiple *"hats"*: visionary leader, commander, boss, and coach, adapting their style to maintain clarity and team morale (Dhanabordeephat, 2024, 01:20-01:30). The visionary leader sets long-term direction and inspires commitment by connecting daily tasks to broader organisational goals (Dhanabordeephat, 2024, 01:35-02:55). The commander role ensures clear direction in a culture of indirect communication (Dhanabordeephat, 2024, 05:56-07:24), whilst the boss role covers accountability and performance monitoring without excessive oversight (Dhanabordeephat, 2024, 08:25-09:10). The coaching role fosters growth through trust and guided thinking, reflecting Thai preferences for respectful, non-confrontational development (Dhanabordeephat, 2024, 09:25-12:40). In conclusion, Thai leadership is a culturally grounded practice that integrates personal insight, social intelligence, and organisational awareness. As delineated by Khampharat, it relies on genuine followership, self-awareness, and the maintenance of *nam jai* and *sabai*. Adaptability, which was emphasised by both Khampharat and Hanutsaha, allows leaders to guide teams through change, whilst visionary thinking supports strategic foresight. Dhanabordeephat's discussion of multifaceted roles demonstrates how Thai leaders balance long-term direction, clarity, accountability, and team growth. Together, the three videos provide a coherent view of Thai business leadership, which blends vision, empathy, and adaptability.

Understanding hierarchy in Thailand

Hierarchy is deeply embedded within Thai organisational culture and continues to influence how power, leadership, and social relations are integrated. Thailand scores high on power distance, which means that uneven power interactions are widely recognised as natural within society (Komin, 1990). Individuals are educated from a young age to respect elders, seniority, and establish social hierarchies, and these values subsequently affect organisational systems (Sirilatthayakorn et al., 2020). The cultural idea of *kreng jai*, which promotes thoughtfulness, respect, and the avoidance of behaviours that may cause discomfort to others, also shapes how Thai people communicate and follow authority. It encourages indirect speech, careful listening, and harmony over confrontation (Hanutsaha, 2025). In Thai organisations, this value influences leadership and teamwork by maintaining smooth relationships and protecting social face (*naa*) (Persons, 2016). Research shows that *kreng jai* strongly affects workplace behaviour, limiting open disagreement and reinforcing hierarchical respect (Komin, 1991). Within Thai organisations, hierarchy is not only a structural element, but rather a reflection of deep cultural values linked to *phu yai–phu noi* (senior–junior) relationships. Respect for authority is expected, and leaders are addressed with formal titles such as *Khun* or *Than*, which signal rank and dignity. Leadership status is also visibly reinforced through privileges such as larger offices, reserved parking, or personal drivers, symbols that confirm both authority and moral responsibility. These visible signs of hierarchy reflect the Thai belief that power should be exercised with care and protection for subordinates, rather than domination (Arun & Rungsithong, 2020; Komin, 1991). These material and symbolic markers, such as private offices, reserved parking, or dedicated assistants are commonly interpreted as culturally meaningful confirmations of authority and organisational structure, rather than ego-driven privileges. Our survey results support this interpretation, insofar as several Thai respondents described hierarchy as "*a natural structure that helps maintain order and harmony within the team*" (CCBS Survey, 2017–2025). Indeed, one senior manager explained that "*employees expect the leader to make the final call, but they also expect that leader to be fair, calm, and considerate*" (CCBS Survey, 2023). These responses underscore how hierarchy is accepted because it is linked to responsibility and moral conduct. However, Thai hierarchy does not imply purely authoritarian leadership. Buddhist values and the *"Rajadhamma ten virtues"* also encourage leaders to be moral, patient, empathetic, and fair (Phetchawong & Phrakhrusunthonwatcharakit, 2019). This contributes to a paternalistic leadership style that is firm but caring, directive yet supportive. This was also corroborated by the survey results, where the professionals reported that they value leaders who *"provide direction with kindness"* or who *"guide the team like a parent but still listen to opinions"* (CCBS Survey, 2024). The respondents also frequently emphasised the importance of calmness and emotional control, with one noting: *"A Thai leader must stay composed; if the leader stays calm, the team stays calm too."* This aligns with previous research showing that Thai employees prefer a consultative leadership style, where leaders solicit input but retain final decision-making authority (Yukongdi, 2010). Recent studies have demonstrated that younger professionals in urban and global business environments place greater emphasis on inclusive and collaborative leadership approaches. These developing habits, however, complement rather than replace existing expectations. Even in contemporary corporate settings, status recognition remains an important component of leadership legitimacy (Ackaradejruangsri et al., 2023). The success of leadership styles in Thailand is intimately linked to how well leaders represent the balance of power and relational warmth. Arun and Rungsithong (2020) discovered that *transformational leadership* improves job satisfaction in Thai organisations when hierarchical roles are clearly defined, implying that leadership credibility stems not only from competence but also from visible status and compliance to cultural and general expectations.

Overall, hierarchy in Thailand represents far more than a formal structure of authority: it is a cultural system that links power with responsibility, moral conduct, and interpersonal care. The survey findings and literature consistently show that Thai employees accept hierarchical differences not because they encourage domination, but because they provide clarity, stability, and a sense of protection within the workplace. At the same time, this hierarchy is softened by Buddhist values such as *kreng jai*, calmness, and compassion, which shape expectations of leaders to act fairly, remain composed, and maintain harmonious relationships. For leadership to be effective in Thailand, authority must therefore be balanced with emotional intelligence and relational warmth. In essence, Thai hierarchy functions as structured authority embedded in cultural care. Leadership succeeds when it honours status and clarity whilst, simultaneously, demonstrating empathy, humility, and moral responsibility. This blend of power and benevolence remains central to how Thai organisations operate and how leadership credibility is formed.

How the Thai achieve leadership empathy

Leadership empathy in Thailand is deeply rooted in the country's Buddhist philosophy, collectivist culture, and hierarchical social order. Empathy is not expressed through open emotion or direct confrontation, but rather through consideration, care, and respect for others' dignity. Within Thai organisations, an effective leader shows empathy by protecting relationships, maintaining harmony, and balancing authority with compassion (Komin, 1991). According to Vora and Kainzbauer (2020), Thai leadership is grounded in *a humanistic approach* that combines benevolence *(phrakhun)* and moral authority *(phradet)*. Leaders are expected to act as moral role models who support their followers' well-being whilst guiding them with calm authority. This creates what the authors call a *"father-with-a-heart"* model, which is firm but caring, and where empathy is displayed through taking personal interest in employees' lives, listening carefully, and creating an atmosphere of trust and fairness (Vora & Kainzbauer, 2020). Such behaviour reflects the Buddhist virtues of compassion *(karuṇā)* and loving-kindness *(mettā)*, which encourage patience, humility, and service to others. Empathy in Thailand is also expressed through the cultural concept *of kreng jai.* As Pimpa (2012) explains, *kreng jai* regulates communication and behaviour by promoting politeness, indirect feedback, and conflict avoidance. A good leader therefore offers criticism privately and uses soft, non-confrontational language. These behaviours protect subordinates' *face* and maintain harmony within the team, which is essential in Thailand's high-power-distance culture. At the same time, modern Thai organisations increasingly integrate global leadership ideas such as transformational and inclusive leadership. Boonchuay (2024) found that Thai school administrators who combine traditional Buddhist values with participative decision-making strengthen trust and motivation amongst teachers. By listening actively and sharing responsibility, these leaders show empathy not only through kindness but also through empowerment, encouraging followers to grow and innovate. The results of the CCBS Survey (2017-2025) also confirm that this approach extends well beyond the educational sector. Many of the Thai respondents described leaders who *"encourage employees, listen to their ideas, and support their development,"* underscoring that empowerment and open communication are becoming common expectations across industries. One Thai CEO explained that effective leaders *"give guidance but also give space for people to think and improve themselves,"* thus exhibiting a blend of traditional respect and modern participative practices (CCBS Survey, 2023). This was also confirmed by one of our interviewees, Dr. Hallinger, who noted that younger and internationally exposed managers increasingly adopt coaching behaviours, using empathy to build confidence and stimulate innovation in their teams (27 November, 2025). In one study of expatriate business leaders in Thailand, *emotionally supporting* team members and *indirect communication* were identified as distinguishing features of effective leadership (Smith & colleagues, 2018). More recently, research on young inclusive Thai leaders revealed empathy, relational trust, and interpersonal awareness as central competencies (Ackaradejruangsri et al., 2022). Even in practice at the corporate level, insurers such as Generali Thailand attribute business success to leadership rooted in listening, open communication, and an inclusive culture (Khongjitngam, 2024). Together, these findings show that *empathy* in Thai leadership is not confined to education but is indeed a core mechanism across various sectors. Additional research on inclusive Thai leaders reveals that relational sensitivity, emotional intelligence, and humility are central to bridging cultural differences and enhancing team collaboration (Ackaradejruangsri et al., 2022). The survey data lends further support to this cross-sector pattern, insofar as many of the respondents emphasised that a good leader *"listens carefully, understands team feelings, and supports employees like family,"* indicating that empathy is viewed as a practical leadership tool rather than just a moral value (CCBS Survey, 2017–2025). One senior manager stated that *"employees work better when the leader shows care and stays approachable,"* directly linking emotional intelligence to improved team performance (CCBS Survey, 2024). Dr. Hallinger also confirmed that organisations increasingly value leaders who create psychological safety by being calm, respectful, and attentive to their teams' needs, explaining that Thai employees respond most positively to leaders who *"combine authority with sincere compassion"*, demonstrating that empathy strengthens both trust and cooperation in diverse business environments (27 November, 2025). Overall, both empirical data and practitioner perspectives confirm that empathetic leadership functions as a key driver of workplace harmony and effectiveness in contemporary Thai organisations. In conclusion, leadership empathy in Thailand is best understood as a blend of cultural tradition and modern organisational practice. Rooted in Buddhist values and the principle of *kreng jai*, empathy is expressed through calmness, consideration, and respect for others. At the same time, the survey and interview data show that Thai leaders increasingly combine these traditional behaviours with participative and inclusive approaches, using empathy to empower employees, build trust, and support development.

Bibliography

Bibliography

Бизнис Лидер. (2023a). Џан Мемед: Доверба, менторство и дигитализација – рецепт за современ лидер | Бизнис Лидер S02 E03[Video]. YouTube. https://www.youtube.com/watch?v=yV3qh6GdqeM

Бизнис Лидер. (2023b). Проф. д-р Лазар Јовевски: Лидерството не е титула, туку стил на живот | Бизнис Лидер S02 E02 [Video]. YouTube. https://www.youtube.com/watch?v=Pi0kx0oXX6c

Aagaard, T., & Seibæk, L. (2025). Health worker perspectives on Greenlandic healthcare – resources, sustainability, and work-life-balance. *International Journal of Circumpolar Health*. https://pubmed.ncbi.nlm.nih.gov/40397759

Aaltoainen, E. (2025). [MS Teams] interview. 9 November.

Aarhus Universitet – Institut for Kultur og Samfund. (2023, October). Kolonialisme i Grønland: tradition, ledelse og arv [Video]. YouTube. https://www.youtube.com/watch?v=GZSqJ0QWvOI

Abrashi, G. (2023). Motivation of employees in the public sector through organisational communication: Case study Vala mobile company, Kosovo. SSRN.

Abun-Nasr, J. M. (1987). *A history of the Maghrib in the Islamic period.* Cambridge University Press.

Accelerate TV. (2022). EP 10 Bitange Ndemo, ICT Champion, Academician & Columnist Kenya. [Video]. YouTube. https://youtu.be/MnMLJCfvCls?si=38M54aQVWNoIwwyK

Ackaradejruangsri, P., Mumi, A., Rattanapituk, S., & Pakhunwanich, P. (2022). Exploring the determinants of young inclusive leadership in Thailand: research taxonomy and theoretical framework. *Journal of the Knowledge Economy, 14*(4), 3696–3723. https://doi.org/10.1007/s13132-022-01017-7

Ahtiainen, R., Hanhimäki, E., Leinonen, J., Risku, M., & Smeds-Nylund, A. (2023) Leadership in educational contexts in Finland. In *Educational governance research.* Springer. https://doi.org/10.1007/978-3-031-37604-7

Akhlaffou, M. (2020). Culture nationale et pratiques managériales au sein des organisations marocaines: Actualisation des dimensions de Hofstede. *Revue d'Études en Gestion et Systèmes (REGS).*

Alapo, R. (2017). Culture and leadership in the 21st century. *Cultural and Religious Studies,* 5(4), 179–189. https://doi.org/10.17265/2328-2177/2017.04.001

Alas, R., & Tuulik, K. (2007). Leadership style during transition in society: Case of Estonia. *Problems and Perspectives in Management,* 5(1), 50–60.

Alas, R., Vanhala, S., Elenurm, T., & Tuulik, K. (2018). Management and leadership development needs: The case of Estonia. In R. Alas & S. Vanhala (Eds.), *Business and management practices in Estonia* (pp. 51–64). Springer.

Alava, J., Kola-Torvinen, P., & Risku, M. (2024). Educational policy, governance, and leadership. In R. Ahtiainen et al. (Eds.), *Leadership in educational contexts in Finland: Theoretical and empirical perspectives.* Springer Nature, 24-35. https://doi.org/10.1007/978-3-031-37604-7

Ali, A. J., & Wahabi, R. (1995). Managerial value systems in Morocco. *International Studies of Management & Organization, 25*(3), 87–96.

Alqatan, A., Simmou, W., Shehadeh, M., AlReshaid, F., Elmarzouky, M., & Shohaieb, D. (2025). Strategic pathways to corporate sustainability: The roles of transformational leadership, knowledge sharing, and innovation. *Sustainability, 17*(12), 5547.

Amine, A., & Amine, N. (2010). Spécificités de la culture organisationnelle de la PME marocaine : Une étude empirique. *Revue Marocaine de Gestion et d'Économie (RMGE).*

Ana Maria Rocha, Santos, & Pais, L. (2024). Toxic Leadership and Followers' Work Motivation: An Angolan Study. *Universitas Psychologica, 22.* https://doi.org/10.11144/javeriana.upsy22.tlfm

Anderson, B. (2005). *Thailand: History and culture.* Thai Historical Press.

Andrews, K. D., Nikšič, M., Mladenovič, L., Cotič, B., Mušič, B., & Kerbler, B. (2024). Ljubljana—European Green Capital 2016: From Strategic spatial Planning to Governance. *Sustainability, 16*(8), 3332. https://doi.org/10.3390/su16083332

Anonymous. (2025). [MS Teams] Interview. 18 November.

Anonymous. (2025) [MS Teams] Interview. 20 November.

Anonymous. (2025). [MS Teams] Interview. 26 November.

AP News. (2024, March 10). *Greenland's economic dependence on Denmark continues amid autonomy debate.* https://apnews.com

Arctic Philosophy Network. (2021). *Arctic leadership – Defining Arctic leadership: Your story – Our future.* https://arcticphilosophy.com/arctic-leadership/

Arcticulture. (2023). *About Greenland: Culture and livelihoods in the Arctic.* https://arcticulture.com

Armanda. (n.d.-c). A Liderança em Angola - Desafios para o Futuro. https://www.portaldalideranca.pt/opiniao/convidados/2526-a-lideranca-em-angola

Arun, C., & Rungsithong, R. (2020). The influence of power distance on the relationship of leadership and job satisfaction: A case study of a Thai company in the consumer goods industry. *Executive Journal, 40(2)*, 108–129. https://so01.tci-thaijo.org/index.php/executivejournal/article/view/241756

Arzenšek, A., Franca, V., & Laporšek, S. (2018). Corporate social responsibility towards employees: Analysis of Slovenian and foreign good practices. *Journal of Contemporary Management Issues, 23*(2), 1–19.

Askarany, D. & Lam, J. (2025). The role of Māori values in corporate culture and CSR: A comparative study in Aotearoa–New Zealand's fishing industry. *Systems Research and Behavioural Science, 42*(1), 1-16 https://doi.org/10.1002/sres.3156

Aster Lion. (2025). Effective cultural communication in Thai workplaces. https://asterlion.com/effective-cultural-communication-thai-workplaces/

Baker, C., & Phongpaichit, P. (2014). *A history of Thailand* (3rd ed.). Cambridge University Press.

Balambo, M. A. (2014). National culture and the adoption of management practices: An exploratory study in Morocco. *European Scientific Journal, 10*(4), 1857–7431.

Bass, B. M., & Bass, R. (2008). *The Bass handbook of leadership: Theory, research, and managerial applications* (4th ed.). Free Press.

Bderrahman, H., Najoua, F., & Shouhail, R. (2015). Employee perception of diversity in Morocco: Empirical insights. *Journal of Global Responsibility*, 6(1), 4–18.

Belrhiti, Z., Van Damme, W., Belalia, A., & Marchal, B. (2020a). Unravelling the role of leadership in motivation of health workers in a Moroccan public hospital: A realist evaluation. *BMJ Open, 10*(1), e031160.

Belrhiti, Z., Van Damme, W., Belalia, A., & Marchal, B. (2020b). The effect of leadership on public service motivation: A multiple embedded case study in Morocco. *BMJ Open, 10*(1), e033010.

Benabdeljlil, N. (2007). Les modes de management des entreprises au Maroc : Entre contingences culturelles et économiques. *Revue internationale PME, 20*(2), 89–122.

Bethel, N. (2002). *Navigations: The fluidity of Bahamian identity.* The College of The Bahamas.

Bilgin, M. H., Danis, H., Demir, E., & Can, U. (Eds.). (2016). *Business challenges in the changing economic landscape* (Vol. 2). Springer International Publishing.

Bojadjiev, M. I., Vaneva, M., Misoska, A. T., Mileva, I., & Andonova, M. (2023). The Ninth Dimension of National Culture: Unpacking Cross-Cultural Communication Styles. *Interdisciplinary Description Of Complex Systems, 21*(5), 471–494. https://doi.org/10.7906/indecs.21.5.4

Bojadjiev, M., Hristova, S., & Mileva, I. (2019). Leadership styles in small and medium-sized business: Evidence from Macedonian textile SMEs. *Journal of Entrepreneurship and Business Innovation, 6*(2), 1. https://doi.org/10.5296/jebi.v6i2.15266

Bojadjiev, M., Kostovski, N., & Buldioska, K. (2015). Leadership styles in companies from Republic of Macedonia. *Economic Development, 17*(3), 211–222.

Boonchuay, P. K. C. (2024). Effective leadership styles in Thai educational administration: Balancing tradition with innovation. *Journal of Exploration in Interdisciplinary Methodologies.*

Botimpex. (2021). *Suksesi i menaxhimit në shitje* [Retail listing: author, ISBN 9789951784085, Albanian, 360 pp.].

Bowe, S. M. (2017). Servant leadership dimensions of Bahamian hotel industry front-line workers (Doctoral dissertation, Walden University). *Walden Dissertations and Doctoral Studies*, 4503. https://scholarworks.waldenu.edu/dissertations/4503

Brandt, T., Laitinen, E. K., & Laitinen, T. (2016). The effect of transformational leadership on the profitability of Finnish firms. *International Journal of Organizational Analysis*, 24(1), 81–106. https://doi.org/10.1108/ijoa-03-2014-0744

Brown, G. (2022). Gravette Brown - Women in Leadership (Cable Bahamas Group) [Video]. YouTube. https://www.youtube.com/watch?v=qhAp6yJoYT4

Buchan, K. C. (2000). The Bahamas. *Marine Pollution Bulletin*, 41(1–6), 94–111. https://doi.org/10.1016/S0025-326X(00)00104-1

Campbell, S. (2025, February 8). Balancing empathy and accountability in modern leadership. *The New Zealand Herald*. https://www.nzherald.co.nz

Carovska, M. [@milacarovska]. (n.d.). *Posts* [Instagram profile]. Instagram. Retrieved December 6, 2025, from https://www.instagram.com/milacarovska

CCBS Survey (2017). Global Leadership Survey. Survey Monkey. Amsterdam University of Applied Sciences.

CCBS Survey. (2015–2020). Global Leadership Survey. Survey Monkey. Amsterdam University of Applied Sciences.

CCBS Survey (2022). Global Leadership Survey. Survey Monkey. Amsterdam University of Applied Sciences.

CCBS Survey. (2017–2025). Global Leadership Survey. Qualtrics. Amsterdam University of Applied Sciences.

CCBS Survey. (2023-2025). Survey responses on leadership in North Macedonia. Amsterdam University of Applied Sciences, Cross Cultural Business Skills. Data collected using Qualtrics.

CCBS Survey. (2025). *Global Leadership Survey*. Qualtrics. Amsterdam University of Applied Sciences

Chan, S. (2018). Cultural heritage and leadership in Thailand. *Journal of Southeast Asian Studies, 49(2)*, 123–145. https://doi.org/10.1080/00224634.2018.1234567

Chanchaochai, P. (2017). Thai cultural identity and modern leadership. *Asian Cultural Studies, 22(1)*, 45–60.

Chimbunde, F., & Neneh, B. N. (2024). Linking psychological capital to organisational commitment: The moderating role of perceived aversive leadership of employees in Angola. ResearchGate.

Chongcharoen, K. (2020, June 23). Multicultural leadership and the role of Thai school leaders. In Proceedings of the 54th International Academic Virtual Conference, Prague (ISBN 978-80-87927-94-6). IISES.

Chopik, W. J., O'Brien, E., & Konrath, S. H. (2017). Differences in empathic concern and perspective taking across 63 countries. *Journal of Cross-Cultural Psychology, 48(1)*, 23–38. https://doi.org/10.1177/0022022116673915

Culture in the Workplace. (n.d.). Country comparison dashboard: Estonia. Culture in the Workplace Questionnaire™. https://cultureinworkplace.com

Cunha, M. P. E., Fortes, A., Gomes, E., Rego, A., & Rodrigues, F. (2016). Ambidextrous leadership, paradox and contingency: Evidence from Angola. *The International Journal of Human Resource Management*, 30(4), 702–727. https://doi.org/10.1080/09585192.2016.1201125

D&B Bureau. (2025, June 2). *Dr António Agostinho Neto: The first president of Angola.* Diplomacy Beyond Politics. Https://diplomacybeyond.com/dr-antonio-agostinho-neto-the-first-president-of-angola/

Davis, P. (2025, August 25). Expanding Opportunities [Video]. YouTube. https://www.youtube.com/shorts/z7VMTYe5gBU

Delo. (2025, November 3). *Vodje prihodnosti so agilni, prilagodljivi in človeško občutljivi* [Video]. Youtube. https://youtu.be/MHsFC5N98Nc?si=kM8shA7F1cgAwwIL

Devatstablee. (2021, April 11). Hofstede's cultural dimensions framework.

Dhanabordeephat, N. P. [NopPongsatorn]. (2024, 19 February). *How to เป็น "หัวหน้า" ที่ลูกน้องรัก [How to be a "boss" that employees love]* [Video file]. https://www.youtube.com/watch?v=UzLmv6S1a1M

Dhanabordeephat, N. P. [NopPongsatorn]. (2024, February 19). How to เป็น "หัวหน้า" ที่ลูกน้องรัก [Video]. YouTube. https://www.youtube.com/watch?v=UzLmv6S1a1M

Dimitrova, E., & Vesevska, I. T. (Eds.). (2020). *On the cross-path of cultural ideas: Macedonia, the Balkans, Southeast Europe – heritage, management, resources*. Skopje, North Macedonia: Faculty of Philosophy, Ss. Cyril and Methodius University in Skopje.

Dimovski, V., & Penger, S. (2008). *Leadership and management in Slovenia: Tradition and transition*. Ljubljana University Press.

Doğar, N. (2021). A cultural perspective to leadership practices in Balkans. *Academicus International Scientific Journal, 23*, 110–136. https://doi.org/10.7336/academicus.2021.23.07

Drechsler, W. (2018). Pathfinding in digital governance: The Estonian model. *Government Information Quarterly*, 35(4), 653–659. https://doi.org/10.1016/j.giq.2018.09.001

Eagly, A. H., & Carli, L. L. (2007). *Through the labyrinth: The truth about how women become leaders*. Harvard Business School Press.

Edmondson, A. C. (1999). Psychological safety and learning behavior in work teams. *Administrative Science Quarterly*, 44(2), 350–383. https://doi.org/10.2307/2666999

Einpalu, R. (2023). Kuidas pidada juhtimisvestlust? Tartu Ülikool. https://ut.ee/et/sisu/kuidas-pidada-juhtimisvestlust

Ezeorah, F. (2023). Servant Leadership: A Powerful Paradigm for Effective Leadership Servant Leadership: A Powerful Paradigm for Effective Leadership in Africa in Africa. *Journal of Vincentian Social Action Journal of Vincentian Social Action*, 7. https://scholar.stjohns.edu/cgi/viewcontent.cgi?article=1176&context=jovsa

Fakulteta za upravo. (2020, June 23). Vodenje v 21. stoletju [Video]. YouTube. https://www.youtube.com/watch?v=fJm8obtMhW8

Ferreira, M. (2025). The customary law and the traditional leadership power in Angola: Their effects on territorial planning issues. ResearchGate.

Fink-Hafner, D. (2021). Gender and political representation in Slovenia: Challenges and achievements. *East European Politics, 37*(2), 257–276. https://doi.org/10.1080/21599165.2021.1885340

Fonsén, E., Ahtiainen, R., Kiuru, L., Lahtero, T., Hotulainen, R., & Kallioniemi, A. (2022). Kasvatus- ja opetusalan johtajien näkemyksiä omasta johtamisosaamisestaan ja sen kehittämistarpeista. *Työelämän Tutkimus, 20*(1), 90–117. https://doi.org/10.37455/tt.95779

Forsha, S.K. (2017). Tikanga Māori – Lessons in leading. *Journal of Leadership Accountability and Ethics* 14 (4) http://www.na-businesspress.com/JLAE/JLAE14-4/ForshaSK_14_4_.pdf

Forster, G., & Fenwick, J. (2015). The influence of Islamic values on management practice in Morocco. *European Management Journal, 33*(2), 143–156.

Fox, L. (Trans.). (1989). Kanuni i Lekë Dukagjinit = The Code of Lekë Dukagjini. Gjonlekaj Publishing. (Original work collected by S. Gjeçov).

Franklin Covey. (2025) *The power of empathetic leadership at work*. www.franklincovey.co.nz/empathetic-leadership.

Fremtidens Ledelse. (2023, April). Fremtidens ledelse: Hvordan ser den ud og hvordan gør du dig klar? [Video]. YouTube. https://www.youtube.com/watch?v=epwxUGUcfZs

García, M., Nielsen, K., & Petersen, A. (2022). Indigenous knowledge and adaptive climate governance in the Arctic. *Arctic Review on Law and Politics, 13*(2), 45–63. https://doi.org/10.23865/arctic.v13.4567

Gentry, W., Weber, T. & Sadri, G. (2016). *Empathy in the workplace: A tool for effective leadership*. https://cclinnovation.org/wp-content/uploads/2020/03/empathyintheworkplace.pdf

Geremias, R. L. (2025). [MS Teams] Interview. 24 October.

Global Policy Unit. (2019). Country profile: Kenya. BioDev2030. https://www.biodev2030.org/wp-content/uploads/2023/01/Kenya-country-profile.pdf

Gonnah, B. J., & Ogollah, K. (2016). Effect of transformational leadership on performance of commercial banks in Kenya: Case of Family Bank Limited. *International Academic Journal of Innovation, Leadership and Entrepreneurship*, 2, 1–25. https://www.iajournals.org/articles/iajile_v2_i1_1_25.pdf

Gooden, D. J., & Preziosi, R. C. (2004). Cultural values and leadership behavior in the U.S., Jamaica, and the Bahamas. *International Business & Economics Research Journal*, 3(3), 15–23.

Government of Kosovo. (2022). Public Administration Reform Strategy 2022–2027. Kryeministri
Halili, R., & Kukovič, S. (2022). Organizational and structural approaches on administrative simplification: The case of Kosovo. *Administrative Sciences*, 12(1), 18.

Graen, G. B., & Uhl-Bien, M. (1995). Relationship-based approach to leadership: Development of leader–member exchange (LMX) theory over 25 years. *The Leadership Quarterly*, 6(2), 219–247. https://doi.org/10.1016/1048-9843(95)90036-5

Greenidge, D. (2009). Cultural mythology and global leadership in the Caribbean Islands. *In Handbook of Research on Cross-Cultural Approaches to Leadership and Management* (pp. 125–141). Edward Elgar. https://doi.org/10.4337/9781848447387.00010

Haar, J., & Brougham, D. (2013). An indigenous model of career satisfaction: Exploring the role of workplace wellbeing and relational leadership in New Zealand. *International Journal of Human Resource Management, 24*(14), 2692–2709.

Haar, J., & Delaney, B. (2009). Māori cultural values and organisational practices: A Māori leadership framework. *New Zealand Journal of Human Resource Management, 9*(1), 98–109.

Haar, J., Roche, M. & Brougham, D. (2018). Indigenous insights into ethical leadership: A study of Māori leaders. *Journal of Business Ethics* 160 (3) 621–640 https://doi.org/10.1007/s10551-018-3869-3

Hakanen, M., & Häkkinen, M. (2015). Management possibilities for interpersonal trust in a business network: Case: Health-, exercise- and wellbeing markets. *Nordic Journal of Business, 64*(4), 249–260. http://njb.fi/wp-content/uploads/2016/01/Hakanen_Hakkinen-NJB_4-15.pdf

Halili, R., & Kukovič, S. (2022). Organizational and structural approaches on administrative simplification: The case of Kosovo. *Administrative Sciences*, 12(1), 18. https://doi.org/10.3390/admsci12010018.

Hallinger, P. (2025). [Zoom] Interview. 27 November.

Hamiti, V. (2024). A transfer of language and culture: German bread and Albanian *Mikpritja. Sudosteuropa*, 72(1). https://doi.org/10.1515/soeu-2024-0014

Hansen, U. K., Hovgaard, G., Olsen, P. B., & Rasmussen, M. A. (2020). *Making sense of leadership in Greenlandic organizations. Greenland Perspective Research Paper Series*, Roskilde University. https://forskning.ruc.dk/en/publications/making-sense-of-leadership-in-greenlandic-organizations

Hanutsaha, R. [Mission To The Moon]. (2025, 4 June). *ผู้นำที่เจ๋งจริงต้องมี 10 คุณสมบัติ นี้! คุณมีครบหรือยัง? เช็กตัวเองด่วน /Mission to the Moon EP.2424 [10 qualities of a truly great leader! Do you have them? Check yourself quickly | Mission to the Moon EP.2424]* [Video file]. YouTube. https://www.youtube.com/watch?v=-MBoypjhki0

Harris, F. (2016). Māori values in the workplace: Investing in diversity. *MAI Journal: A New Zealand Journal of Indigenous Scholarship, 5*(1), 48–62. https://doi.org/10.20507/maijournal.2016.5.1.4

Hassi, A. (2019). Effect of authentic leadership on employee creativity in Morocco: The mediating role of work engagement. *International Journal of Contemporary Management, 17*(2), 23–40.

Hastrup, F. (2022). Mining for Greenlandic self-government: Fractal islands in the Anthropocene. *Island Studies Journal, 17(2), 367–384.*

HCLI. (2023, December 11). Thai Followship Kreng Jai Style - Leadership Development Training Programme Provider in Asia. Leadership Development Training Programme Provider in Asia. https://hcli.org/thai-followship-kreng-jai-style/

Helder "The Mentor". (2025, 22 juni). IMC Show_EP#07: *como vencer os desafios da liderança em Angola* [Video]. YouTube. https://www.youtube.com/watch?v=f31oD4sEvVU

Henry, E. & Wolfgramm, R. (2015). Relational leadership: An indigenous Māori perspective. *Leadership, 14*(2), 181-199. https://journals.sagepub.com/doi/abs/10.1177/1742715015616282

Hoffman, K. E. (2019). *Behind the veil of modernity: Amazigh identity and the state in contemporary Morocco.* Stanford University Press.

Hofstede Insights. (2024). *Country comparison: Denmark and global data for power distance and collectivism.* https://www.hofstede-insights.com

Hofstede, G. (2001). *Culture's consequences: Comparing values, behaviours, institutions, and organizations across nations* (2nd ed.). Sage Publications.

Hofstede, G. H., Hofstede, G. J., & Minkov, M. (2010). *Cultures and Organizations, Software of the mind. Intercultural Cooperation and Its Importance for survival.*

Hofstede, G., & Minkov, M. (2010). *Cultures and organizations: Software of the mind* (3rd ed.). McGraw-Hill.

Holdsworth, M. (2024). Humanising work: The rise of empathy-centred organisations. *HRNZ Human Resources Magazine, 29*(3), 18–21.

Holm, S. (2021). Leadership in the Arctic: Empathy and resilience in remote governance. *Nordic Public Administration Review, 7*(1), 23–38.

Holmes, J. (2018). Negotiating the tall-poppy syndrome: Humour and leadership talk in New Zealand workplaces. *Journal of Pragmatics, 134,* 167–180.

Holmes, J., & Marra, M. (2002). Humour as a discursive boundary marker in social interaction. In A. Duszak (Ed.), *Us and others: Social identities across languages, discourses and cultures* (pp. 377–400). John Benjamins.

Horta, E. (2021, 6 October). REFORMA DA ADMINISTRAÇÃO PÚBLICA, DESAFIOS e PRINCIPAL FINALIDADE. https://www.linkedin.com/

Horta, E. M. (2020). *Estrategia e gestão de pessoas em Angola: teoria e exemplos.* Mayamba Editora.

House, R. J., Hanges, P. J., Javidan, M., Dorfman, P. W., & Gupta, V. (2004). *Culture, leadership, and organizations: The GLOBE study of 62 societies.* Sage Publications.

Hristova, S., & Handjiski, V. K. (2024). Constructing success: Unveiling leadership styles in the construction industry in North Macedonia. *Business & Management Horizons, 12*(1), 1–14. https://doi.org/10.5296/bmh.v12i1.21927

Human Synergistics Australia and New Zealand. (2022). *What does the future of leadership look like in New Zealand?* [Video]. YouTube. https://www.youtube.com/watch?v=ewtg_iePmLo

Hyseni, A., et al. (2023). Internal communication in organisations: The case of the Post of Kosovo. ResearchGate preprint.

Ilies, R., Nahrgang, J. D., & Morgeson, F. P. (2007). Leader–member exchange and citizenship behaviors: A meta-analysis. *Journal of Applied Psychology, 92*(1), 269–277. https://doi.org/10.1037/0021-9010.92.1.269

Ilisimatusarfik (University of Greenland). (2022). *ILISIMATUSAAT 2022 – Leadership activities contribute to organisational development by focusing on future activities in Greenlandic organizations*. https://uni.gl/media/8438762/ilisimatusaat-2022-eng.pdf

Isopahkala-Bouret, U., Kosunen, S., & Haltia, N. (2023). University graduates' perceptions of institutional hierarchies. The case of Finnish master's degree in business administration and economics. *Scandinavian Journal of Educational Research, 68*(1), 79–91. https://urn.fi/URN:NBN:fi-fe2025082785321

Javidan, M., et al. (2006). Leadership in New Zealand: Findings of the GLOBE study. In *Culture, leadership, and organizations: The GLOBE study of 62 societies* (pp. 525–573). Sage Publications.

Jones, D. C., Kalmi, P., & Mygind, N. (2005). Choice of ownership structure and firm performance: Evidence from Estonia. *Post-Communist Economies, 17*(1), 83–107.

Jones, K. A. (2023). The role of leadership in Bahamian special economic zones. *Journal of Business & Economics Studies, 12*(2), 45–62. https://journals.sfu.ca/cob/index.php/files/article/view/383/pdf_83

Jungsberg, L., Vestergård, L., Karlsdóttir, A., & Wardekker, A. (2025). Resilience, reflexivity, and decolonization: Policy narratives in Kalaallit Nunaat (Greenland). *Frontiers in Climate, 7*, 1531036.

Kabogo, W. (2025). *[Video on collaborative success]*. Instagram. https://www.instagram.com/reel/DLcaoMttmdT/?igsh=Z3F6cHY4c2hjem1y

Kadenic, M. D. (2017). Transitioning from an economic cluster to a collaborative community: Mining projects in Greenland. *Journal of Organization Design, 6*(1). https://doi.org/10.1186/s41469-016-0011-9

Kalmus, V. (2007). Changes in young people's self-identification and value structures in transitional Estonia. *Trames: Journal of the Humanities and Social Sciences, 11*(1), 3–19.

Kamau, C., & Kamau, S. (2019). Millennial employees and changing leadership expectations in Kenyan organisations. *African Journal of Business Management, 13*(4), 134–144. https://doi.org/10.5897/AJBM2018.8675

Karlsson, V. H. (2025) [MS Teams] Interview. 28 November.

Kartallozi, I. (2025). [MS Teams] Interview. 14 November.

Katene, Selwyn. Modelling Māori Leadership: What Makes for Good Leadership? *MAI Review 2*(2) 2010, journal.mai.ac.nz/system/files/maireview/334-2540-1-PB.pdf.

Kavashe, R. (2025). *Rita Kavashe, Chairperson and CEO of Isuzu Motors Ltd.* [Video]. YouTube. https://youtu.be/JsmCofwBGSI?si=ak2hF2E6pYj1bdF!

Kennedy, C. (2000). Leadership and culture in New Zealand Lincoln University Research Archive

Kerr, J. (2013). *Legacy: What the All Blacks can teach us about the business of life.* Constable & Robinson.

Kerr, J. (2020). *The legacy mindset: How to lead for lasting success.* Constable.

Khongjitngam, S. (2024, Oct). Winning secrets: Empathy and authenticity are key in making Generali Thailand's people strategy a success.

Kibai, E. N., & Awuor, E. (2024). Leadership styles and performance of public institutions in Kenya: A case study of the county governments of Kenya. *International Journal of Management and Leadership Studies*.

Kilavuka, A. (2025). *[Comment on leadership and self-care]*. TikTok. https://www.tiktok.com/@wangari_wamae/video/7561698162612669704

Kilonzi, T. M., Atikiya, R., & Atambo, W. N. (2023). Leadership practices, stakeholder involvement and performance of national government departments in Kenya. *International Journal of Business Administration, 14*(1), 36–47. DOI: 10.5430/ijba.v14n1p36 — doi.org/10.5430/ijba.v14n1p36

Kim, A. (2024). Harambee! A triadic perspective on social impact: Organizations, evaluators, and target beneficiaries in Kenya. *Administrative Science Quarterly, 70(1)246-291*. DOI: 10.1177/00018392241303580 — doi.org/10.1177/00018392241303580

Kiplagat. (2025, April 28). Top 25 most impactful c-suite executives leading business with an edge 2025. *The Knowledge Warehouse*. theknowledgewarehouseke.com/top-25-most-impactful-c-suite-executives-leading-business-with-an-edge-2025-2/

Kirkwood, J. (2007). Tall poppy syndrome: Implications for entrepreneurship in New Zealand. *Journal of Management and Organization 13*(4) 366–382 https://doi.org/10.5172/jmo.2007.13.4.366

Kittipong, P. (2019). Political history and sovereignty of Thailand. *Asian Journal of Political Science, 27(1)*, 45–67. https://doi.org/10.1080/02185331.2019.1234567

Klaoshow. (2023, 10 March). เป็นผู้นำแบบไหนให้คนอยากตาม / คุณสุดคนึง ชัมภรัตน์ [*What kind of leader makes people want to follow | Sudkhun Khampharat*] [Video file]. YouTube. https://www.youtube.com/watch?v=ycniKWkCtwo

Klopčič, S. (2015). *Voditeljstvo: Vodenje in sodelovanje, moč in odgovornost* [Leadership: Leading and collaborating, power and responsibility]. ISBN 978-961-283-430-2

Klopčič, S. (2019a). *AEIOU voditeljstva: Pet pristopov k vodenju za prihodnost* [Book cover image]. Knjigarna Bukla. https://www.bukla.si/knjigarna/druzbene-vede/ekonomija/aeiou-voditeljstva.html

Klopčič, S. (2019b). *AEIOU vodenja: Pet pristopov k vodenju za prihodnost* [*AEIOU of leadership: Five approaches to leadership for the future*]. ISBN 978-961-290-109-7

Klopčič, S. (2020, March 23). *AEIOU voditeljstva* [Video]. YouTube. Voditeljstvo. https://youtu.be/kC9JJzEwK9Q?si=TLhTQw2iyGO6__Dh

Knowles, M. (2025). Message on leadership, grace and purpose [LinkedIn post].

Kolegji AAB. (2025, 12 augustus). Shpëtim Memishi - kolegji AAB. https://aab-edu.net/en/persons/shpetim-memishi-3/?utm_

Komin, S. (1990). Culture and work-related values in Thai organizations. *International Journal of Psychology, 25(3–6)*, 681–704. https://doi.org/10.1080/00207599008247921

Komin, S. (1991). Psychology of the Thai people: Values and behavioral patterns. National Institute of Development Administration.

Kooskora, M. (2008). Corporate governance from the stakeholder perspective in the context of Estonian business organizations. *Baltic Journal of Management*, 3(2), 193–217.

Kostov, S. (2006). *Комуницираj, преговараj, одлучуваj - биди лидер* (Communicate, Negotiate, Decide - Be a Leader). MCMS.

Kostovski, N., Bojadjiev, M., & Buldioska, K. (2015). Leadership styles and organizational culture in Macedonian companies. *Journal of Sustainable Development*, 5(13), 33-44.

Kovačič, H., & Rus, A. (2014). Leadership competences in Slovenian health care. *Zdravstveno Varstvo, 54*(1), 11–17. https://doi.org/10.1515/sjph-2015-0002

Kozo, A., Bulog, I., Wilczewski, M., Tomovska Misoska, A., Honsová, P., & Mileva, I. (2024). Culture and preferred leadership behaviors: A cross-cultural exploration of Slavic nations. *Cross-Cultural Research, 58*(4), 395–407. https://doi.org/10.1177/10693971241266282

Krsteska, K., Arikan, C. L., Mitrevski, V., & Smilevski, C. (2023). Leadership styles, organizational learning and organizational competitiveness: evidence from the Republic of North Macedonia. *Serbian Journal of Management*, 18(2), 295-314. DOI: https://doi.org/10.5937/sjm18-43019

KTC Thailand. (2025, April 8). *ภาวะผู้นำ (Leadership)* มีอะไรบ้าง ผู้นำที่ดีควรมีทัศนคติอย่างไร? https://www.ktc.co.th/article/knowledge/salary-man/leadership

KTN Entertainment. (2024). Insights from a Corporate Titan: Michael Joseph on Leadership in Kenya's Business Landscape [Video]. YouTube. https://youtu.be/pjFsf3lHUQk?si=8qyPN4klLMT7loWT

Kuokkanen, R. (2015). "To see what state we are in": The first years of the Greenland Self-Government Act and the pursuit of Inuit sovereignty. *Arctic Anthropology*, 52(2), 1–15.

Lämsä, T. (2010). Leadership Styles and Decision-making in Finnish and Swedish Organizations. In *Review of International Comparative Management*. https://rmci.ase.ro/no11vol1/Vol11_No1_Article13.pdf

Laouni, N. (2023). School principals' attitudes and level of technology integration in Moroccan public schools. *TESOL and Technology Studies, 4*(1), 1–36.

Latifi, T. (2018). The culture of relatedness in Kosovo: The role of kinship in the private and the public sphere. *Studia Ethnologica Croatica*, 30(1), 147–168. https://doi.org/10.17234/SEC.30.7

Latifi, T. (2025). [MS Teams] Interview. 13 November.

Lawrence, T. (2025). Estonia. *Institute for National Strategic Security, National Defence University*, 10(2), 18–37. https://www.jstor.org/stable/10.2307/48718171

Le Monde. (2025, March 7). *The social problems plaguing Greenland.* https://www.lemonde.fr

Leesmidt, K., & Jarunratanakul, P. (2022, May 9). View of A Comparison of Buddhist Compassionate and Transformational Leadership in Relations with Organizational Commitment: The Mediating Role of Trust in The Leader. https://so06.tci-thaijo.org/index.php/BSRI/article/view/253264/173733

Lerutla, M., & Steyn, R. (2022). Distinct leadership styles and differential effectiveness across culture: An analysis of South African business leaders. *SA Journal Of Human Resource Management*, 20.https://doi.org/10.4102/sajhrm.v20i0.1957

Lewis, R. D. (2005). *When cultures collide: Leading across cultures* (3rd ed.). Nicholas Brealey International.

Lewis, R. D. (2005). When cultures collide: Managing successfully across cultures (3rd ed.). Nicholas Brealey Publishing.

Lewis, R. D. (2006). *When cultures collide: Leading across cultures* (3rd ed.). Nicholas Brealey Publishing.

Lewis, R. D. (2006). *When cultures collide: Leading across cultures* (3rd ed.). Nicholas Brealey Publishing. https://doi.org/10.1108/01437730610709336

Libraria Buzuku. (2020, January 22). BOTIM I RI!!! Libri i vogël i lidershipit... [Promotional post]. Facebook. https://www.facebook.com/librariabuzuku/posts/2452350628351027

Lideranca Feminina Angola. (2023, 31 maart). #82 Conversas sobre Liderança com Agata Russell Ferreira [Video]. YouTube. https://www.youtube.com/watch?v=H19PuHP4gAY

Lockhart, M., & Brooks, G. (2025, October 22). Caribbean Women in Leadership [Video]. YouTube. https://www.youtube.com/watch?v=1848E56KucA

Lokaj, A. S., & Latifi Sadrija, T. (2020). Organizational culture influenced by leadership styles: The case of private businesses in Kosovo. *Problems and Perspectives in Management*, 18(3), 306–314. https://doi.org/10.21511/ppm.18(3).2020.25

Lord, R. G., Epitropaki, O., Foti, R. J., & Hansbrough, T. (2020). Implicit leadership theories, implicit followership theories, and dynamic processing of leadership information. *Annual Review of Organizational Psychology and Organizational Behavior*, 7, 49–74. https://doi.org/10.1146/annurev-orgpsych-012119-045434

Los Angeles Times (2024) *Jacinda Ardern: Leadership should not be defined by individuals* [Video] YouTube. https://www.youtube.com/watch?v=oF2qBbhJagg

Luchivisi, P. A., Egessa, R., & Odero, J. (2025). Influence of Empathy on Organisational Performance in Public Universities, Western Region, Kenya: The Moderating Role of Organisational Justice. *Research Journal of Business and Finance*, 4(2), 43-53.

M.L. (2025). [Teams] Interview. 30 November.

Marcia Gillespie (2025). [MS Teams]. Interview. 11 November.

Martela, F. (2023, November 2). How Leaders Maximize Impact by Giving Up Excessive Control [Video]. YouTube. https://www.youtube.com/watch?v=egFuBtCc6Aw

Mayes, J., Wall, G. & Cammock, P. (2019). *Value-Based Leadership in New Zealand Agri-foods Exporting Enterprises: Literature Review.* Lincoln University. https://researcharchive.lincoln.ac.nz/server/api/core/bitstreams/cf420d93-92c5-4c82-9a9f-c74d5206bd40/content

Mbigi, L. (n.d.). *The spirit of African leadership.* Google Books.

Mbithi, P. M., & Rasmusson, R. (1977). *Self-reliance in Kenya: the case of Harambee.* Nordic Africa Institute.

McCarley, N., Petersen, G., & Green, J. (2016); Stewart, J. (2006); Yukl, G. (1999). As cited in Alava, J., Kola-Torvinen, P., & Risku, M. (2024). Educational policy, governance, and leadership. In R. Ahtiainen et al. (Eds.), *Leadership in educational contexts in Finland: Theoretical and empirical perspectives.* Springer Nature, 143-145. https://doi.org/10.1007/978-3-031-37604-7

McGraw, J. (2023). Interview. 18 April.

Meda Foundation. (2024, August 11). Understanding and applying 'Ubuntu' thought process. https://meda.foundation/understanding-and-applying-ubuntu-thought-process/

Mellahi, K., & Wood, G. T. (2003). The role and potential of stakeholders in corporate governance: The case of the subsidiary. *Corporate Governance: An International Review, 11*(4), 355–366.

Memishi, S. (2021). *Suksesi i menaxhimit në shitje Kosovë dhe Ballkan*. [Author profile lists title, place and ISBN]. AAB College.

Mexhuani, B., & Mexhuani, F. (2023). Leadership styles and the legitimacy of Kosovo's leaders. *Cogent Social Sciences, 9*(1), 2242611. https://doi.org/10.1080/23311886.2023.2242611

Meyer-Sahling, J.-H., Schuster, C., Mikkelsen, K. S., Qeriqi, F., & Tóth, I. (2018). Towards a more professional civil service in Kosovo. Global Survey of Public Servants. Global Survey of Public Servants

Mileva, I., Bojadjiev, M., Stefanovska-Petkovska, M., & Tomovska-Misoska, A. (2020). Investigation of organizational culture in companies in high-rate polluted countries: Review of existing evidence and application of the new VOX Organizationis model. In M. Stefanovska-Petkovska (Ed.), *Climate change: Challenges and building resilience* (pp. 14–28). University American College Skopje. https://doi.org/10.5281/zenodo.4393515

Misoska, A. T., Mileva, I., Bojadjiev, M., Kozovik, N., & Dimovska, D. (2024). Bridging culture and leadership: Unveiling values and styles in North Macedonia. *Cross-Cultural Research, 58*(4), 408–432. https://doi.org/10.1177/10693971241262543

Mockaitis, A. I. (2007). A cross-cultural study of leadership attitudes in three Baltic states. *International Journal of Leadership Studies, 1*(1), 44–56. https://www.regent.edu/acad/global/publications/ijls/new/vol1iss1/mockaitis/cross_cultural.pdf

Mønsted, A. (2025). *Re-activating Indigenous knowledge from oral history: Landscape and intangible cultural heritage in Greenland*. Routledge.

Moore, J. R., & Hanson, W. R. (2017). Model of business ethics in Morocco: Raising honour or preserving honour. *Journal of Leadership, Accountability and Ethics, 14*(2), 62–79.

Morato, A. U. D. D. (2021). Impacto da Cultura Angolana nas Práticas de Gestão de Recursos Humanos: O Caso Pea- Projetos Educativos de Angola - ProQuest.

Mugo, M. (2022, March 9). *What ails family businesses*. MaryMugo. https://marymugo.com/family-business/

Mugo, M. (2024, December 4). *Growing a business empire – MaryMugo*. MaryMugo. https://marymugo.com/product/growing-a-business-empire/

Mugo, M. (2024a, January 30). About me – MaryMugo. MaryMugo. https://marymugo.com/about/

Mugo, M., Minja, D., & Njanja, L. (2015). The effect of succession planning on corporate growth strategy among local family businesses in the manufacturing sector in Nairobi County, Kenya. European Journal of Business and Management, 7(6). https://ir-library.ku.ac.ke/server/api/core/bitstreams/42f03d76-f2d4-4d0d-9994-8f6839ed466f/content

Muhr, S. L., Holck, L., & Just, S. N. (2022). Ambiguous culture in Greenland police: Proposing a multi-dimensional framework of organizational culture for Human Resource Management theory and practice. *Human Resource Management Journal, 32*(4), 826–843. https://doi.org/10.1111/1748-8583.12472

Mujtaba, B. G. (2010). An examination of Bahamian respondents' task and relationship orientations: Do males have a significantly different score than females? *Journal of Diversity Management, 5*(3), 1–12. https://doi.org/10.19030/jdm.v5i3.813

Mukua-Maru, J., Linge, T., & Ouma, C. (2024). Influence of communication of team leadership on team effectiveness of collaborative partnerships in international research organizations in Kenya. *Kabarak Journal of Research and Innovation, 14*(02), 146–162. DOI: 10.58216/kjri.v14i02.298 — oi.org/10.58216/kjri.v14i02.298

Mullamaa, M. (2024). Empathetic leadership and cultural consciousness in leading: Lessons from Iceland, Sweden, Estonia, Latvia, Lithuania, and Finland. *European Journal of Business and Management Research, 9*(6), 7–14. https://doi.org/10.24018/ejbmr.2024.9.6.2460

Munene, I. I. (2002). Demographic role-structure characteristics and attitudes towards merit and equity: A Kenyan case study. Higher Education Review, 34(2), 27–45. https://www.researchgate.net

Munroe, M. (2009). Becoming a leader: How to develop and release your unique gifts. Whitaker House.

Muriithi, P. N. (2020). *Impact of national cultures on global leadership in Kenya. European Journal of Business and Management, 12*(32), 1–14 https://pdfs.sema

Murphy, M.L. (2013). *Leadership in New Zealand: A qualitative exploration of local perspectives.* Paper presented at the 27th ANZAM Conference Hobart Australia.

Nduati, P. (2025). *[Leadership isn't a title; it's a responsibility]*. Instagram. instagram.com/reel/DResMnNiDB-/

Ng'ang'a, I. N., Kituku, G., Miluwi, J., & School of Business and Economics, Kenya Methodist University. (2024). Influence of strategic leadership on the performance of the Kenya Revenue Authority. *International Journal of Research and Innovation in Social Science (IJRISS),* 2954. DOI: 10.47772/IJRISS.2024.8080218

Nicolaides, A., Ndlovu, S., & Faculty of Arts, Department of Philosophy and Applied Ethics, University of Zululand, South Africa. (2023). An assessment of Harambee as an African notion towards social and educational development in Kenya. *International Journal of Educational Sciences, 40*(1–3), 76–89. DOI: 10.31901/24566322.2023/40.1-3.1251

Nooter, G. W. (1976). *Leadership and headship: Changing authority patterns in an East Greenland hunting community.* Leiden: E. J. Brill.

Norden. (2023). *Facts about Greenland.* Nordic Council of Ministers. https://www.norden.org

Northouse, P. G. (2022). *Leadership: Theory and practice* (9th ed.). Sage.

Nuttall, M. (2012). *Climate, society, and subsistence in Greenland.* Routledge.

Odari, M. H. (2020). The role of value creating education and ubuntu philosophy in fostering humanism in Kenya. *Journal of Interdisciplinary Studies in Education, 9*(51), 56-68.

Oino, P. G. (2023). Culture at the core in leadership learning and development: Experiences from Western Kenya. *Journal of African Cultural Heritage Studies, 3*(1), 183-202. https://doi.org/10.22599/jachs.126

organizational learning at the University of the Bahamas.

Pahor, B. (2014, September 1). *A good political leader forms public opinion rather than merely adjusting to it.* Bivsi-Predsednik.si. https://www.bivsi-predsednik.si/up-rs/2012-2022/pahor-ang-arhiv.nsf/pages/F3F12B707D2DBAB4C1257D57002802CB

Pakarinen, E., & Erkkilä, T. (2017). As cited in Alava, J., Kola-Torvinen, P., & Risku, M. (2024). Educational policy, governance, and leadership. In R. Ahtiainen et al. (Eds.), Leadership in educational contexts in Finland: Theoretical and empirical perspectives. *Springer Nature,* 35-36. https://doi.org/10.1007/978-3-031-37604-7

Palalić, R., & Ait Sidi Mhamed, E. M. (2020). Transformational leadership and MNCs: Evidence from Morocco community. *Journal of Enterprising Communities: People and Places in the Global Economy, 14*(2), 201–230.

Palang, H., Sooväli, H., & Printsmann, A. (Eds.). (2007). Seasonal landscapes. *Google Books.*

Pärleros, A. (2024, July 28). The success story behind Bolt - Markus Villig | Interview [Video]. YouTube.https://www.youtube.com/watch?v=azm4ygXpAjc

Pennell, C. R. (2003). *Morocco: From empire to independence.* Oneworld Publications.

Persons, L. S. (2016). *The way Thais lead: Face as social capital.* Chulalongkorn University Press.

Petkova, D. P. (2015). Beyond silence: A cross-cultural comparison between Finnish "quietude" and Japanese "tranquillity." *Eastern Academic Journal, 4*(1), 1–14. https://www.e-acadjournal.org/pdf/article_15132.pdf

Petrov, K. (z.d.). *Kosta Petrov.* LinkedIn. www.linkedin.com/in/kosta-petrov-2708789

Pfeifer, D. & Love, M. (2004). Leadership in Aotearoa New Zealand: A cross-cultural study of Māori and Pākehā perceptions of transformational leadership. *PRISM: Online Journal of Public Relations and Communication Management 2*(1) 1–15 https://www.prismjournal.org/uploads/1/2/5/6/125661607/v2-no1-a5.pdf

Phetchawong, A., & Phrakhrusunthonwatcharakit. (2019). *ภาวะผู้นำที่ดีในยุคไทยแลนด์ 4.0* [Good leadership in the Thailand 4.0 era]. *Veridian E-Journal, Silpakorn University, 12*(4), 967–990. https://he02.tci-thaijo.org/index.php/Veridian-E-Journal/article/view/167969

Phontapsarn, T., Srikruedong, S., Thitichotirattana, W. T., Sutthawarathamkit, P., & Mahachulalongkornrajavidyalaya University. (2025, April 30). *View of Brahmavihārādhammā: Buddhist Psychology for Human Resource Management in Organizations.*

Pimpa, N. (2012, October 16). *(PDF) amazing thailand: Organizational culture in the Thai Public Sector.* Researchgate.

Pio, E. & Waddell, D. (2014). Spirituality, leadership, and workplace wellbeing: New Zealand's public and private sectors. *Asia-Pacific Journal of Business Administration 6*(2) 123–138

Pirttilä, M., Hiltunen, K., Huhtala, M., & Feldt, T. (2019). Mikä johtamisessa huolestuttaa? Johtajien kokemuksia fokusryhmäkeskusteluissa. *Työelämän tutkimus – Arbetslivsforskning, 17*(1), 39–55. https://journal.fi/tyoelamantutkimus/article/view/87107

Plevnik, K., & Japelj, A. (2023). Uncovering the latent preferences of Slovenia's private forest owners in the context of enhancing forest ecosystem services through a hypothetical scheme. *Forests, 14,* 2346. https://doi.org/10.3390/f14122346

Potočan, V., Mulej, M., & Čančer, V. (2007). Influence of values, culture, ethics, and norms on economic results: Case of Slovenia. *Društvena istraživanja, 17*(3), 373–395. https://doi.org/10.1093/esr/jcm013

Prašnikar, J., Rajkovič, T., & Vehovec, M. (2014). *Competencies driving innovative performance of Slovenian and Croatian manufacturing firms* (Discussion Paper RRC VIII/14). CERGE-EI. https://www.cerge-ei.cz/pdf/gdn/rrc/RRCVIII_14_paper_01.pdf

Pučko, D., & Čater, T. (2011). Cultural Dimensions and Leadership Styles Perceived by Future Managers: Differences between Slovenia and a Cluster of Central European Countries. *Organizacija, 44*(4), 89–99. https://doi.org/10.2478/v10051-011-0009-6

Raav, I. (2025, November 26). Organisatsioonide nähtamatu vari: Kes tegelikult juhib? Visionest Institute. https://visionest.institute/2025/11/26/organisatsioonide-nahtamatu-vari-kes-tegelikult-juhib/

Radio Dukagjini. (2024, 15 mei). *Labirinth - Suzana Lutolli, Konsulente për lidership dhe menaxhment* [Video]. YouTube. https://www.youtube.com/watch?v=GEan_CdLG2I

Rannula, J. (2021, June 21). Kuidas toetab meeskonna coachingu muudatuste elluviimist? Upwise. https://upwise.ee/2021/06/21/kuidas-toetab-meeskonna-coachingu-muudatuste-elluviimist/

Rannula, J., & Nurmeots, A. (2023). Coachiv juhtimine [Blog]. Coachivjuhtimine.com. https://coachivjuhtimine.com

Rannula, J., & Nurmeots, A. (2024, August 6). Coach'iv juhtimine - kas uus imeravim juhtimises? Äripäev. https://www.aripaev.ee/raamat/2024/08/06/coachiv-juhtimine-kas-uus-imeravim-juhtimises

Rannut, M. (2023). Silence and identity in Estonian interactional pragmatics. *Pragmatics, 33*(1), 1–25. https://doi.org/10.1515/pr-2023-0003

Rasmussen, M. A. (2020). Practicing legitimate leadership in territories of interactions in Greenland. In J. Rendtorff (Ed.), *Handbook of business legitimacy: Responsibility, ethics, and society* (pp. 1479–1494). Springer. https://doi.org/10.1007/978-3-030-14622-1_106

Rasmussen, M. A. (2021). *Practicing leadership in Greenlandic organizations.* Research Portal Denmark. https://local.forskningsportal.dk/local/dki-cgi/ws/cris-link?src=ruc&id=ruc-cc13a07e-ee49-4432-8a44-61407ccc7e05

Rasmussen, M. A. (2023). 'When the boat comes in': An empirical study of leadership as emerging activities at Greenlandic fish factories. *Leadership, 19*(2), 150–166. https://doi.org/10.1177/17427150231155567

Rasmussen, M. A., & Olsen, P. B. (2022). *Ledelse i Grønland – Kaffi aassaviuk?* Ilisimatusarfik Press. ISBN 978-87-7975-160-3

Raudsepp, P. (2025). Juhtimine kiirete muutuste ajastul [Leadership in times of rapid change] [Video]. EMPOWERMENT - ettevõtete kasvukiirendi. YouTube. https://www.youtube.com/watch?v=UQOa0X6y8rY

Roche, M. A., Haar, J. M., & Brougham, D. (2015). Māori leaders' well-being: A self-determination perspective. *Leadership, 14*(1), 25–39. https://doi.org/10.1177/1742715015613426

Rodrigues, C. (2016). *ENAPTSS – Encontro Nacional sobre Administração Pública, Trabalho e Segurança Social»* Edson Horta. Maptss.gov.ao. https://enaptss.maptss.gov.ao

Roots, H. (2023, December 26). Kuidas arenguvestlus ka päriselt arendav oleks. Äripäev. https://www.aripaev.ee/saated/2023/12/26/kuidas-arenguvestlus-ka-pariselt-arendav-oleks

RTV AlbSe Official. (2022, 16 januari). *Emisioni Lidershipi dhe Inovacioni* [Video]. YouTube. https://www.youtube.com/watch?v=UH3ozeBqq-o

RTV AlbSe Official. (n.d.). *Emisioni: Lidershipi dhe Inovacioni* [YouTube channel and programme posts]. Retrieved 5 November 2025. https://www.youtube.com/@RTVAlbSeOfficial; programme announcements and guest posts.

RTV ALDI. (2021). Promovohet libri *"Suksesi i menaxhimit në shitje Kosovë dhe Ballkan"* [Video coverage of book promotion in Kosovo].

Ruru, S.M. 2016. *Māori women's perspectives of leadership and wellbeing* (thesis). University of Waikato.

Š.L. (2025). [Teams] Interview. 30 November.

Saari, T., Melin, H., Balabanova, E., & Efendiev, A. (2018). Better leadership, higher work engagement? Comparative study on Finnish and Russian private sector employees. *International Journal of Sociology and Social Policy*, 38(11/12), 922-943. https://doi.org/10.1108/IJSSP-12-2017-0181

Sahlberg, P. (2011). *Finnish Lessons: What Can the World Learn from Educational Change in Finland?* Teachers College Press.

Salin, L. (2025). [MS Teams] interview. 10 November.

Salmi, I., Pietiläinen, V., & Syväjärvi, A. (2020). The Experience Qualities Approach to Leadership and Employee Well-being. *Nordic Journal Of Working Life Studies*. https://doi.org/10.18291/njwls.122593

Samuel, M. G. (2025). Interview. 21 November.

Samuelsen, P. G. (2010). *Grønlandsk ledelseskultur* [master's thesis, *Ilisimatusarfik* (University of Greenland)]. https://www.uni.gl/media/40780/petergroenvolds-kandidatspeciale-pdf.pdf

Sarapik, R. (2023, July 8). Taavi Veskimägi õppis juhina minna laskma. Äripäev. https://www.aripaev.ee/uudised/2023/07/08/taavi-veskimagi-oppis-juhina-minna-laskma

Saunders, G. (1992). Islanders in the stream: A history of the Bahamian people (Vol. 1). *University of Georgia Press*.

Savolainen, T., & Zilliacus-Tikkanen, H. (2015). The gender divisions and hierarchies of the Finnish news organisations. *Nordicom-Information*, 37(2), 19–31.

Scarlatti. (2024). *A literature review of Māori leadership*. https://www.scarlatti.co.nz

Sequeira, M.-E., Afshordi, N., & Kajanus, A. (2024). Prestige and dominance in egalitarian and hierarchical societies: Children in Finland favor prestige more than children in Colombia or the USA. *Evolution and Human Behavior*, 45(4), 106591. https://doi.org/10.1016/j.evolhumbehav.2024.05.005

Shtepia e Librit. (n.d.). Libri i vogël i lidershipit [Retail listing: product details and ISBN]. 3 November 2025 https://www.shtepiaelibrit.com/store/en/economy-business/8956-libri-i-vogel-i-lidershipit-stefan-soederfjaell.html

Sibanda, K., & Grobler, A. (2023). Spiritual leadership within the ambit of African management philosophies using interactive qualitative analysis. *Acta Commercii*, 23(1), a1069. https://doi.org/10.4102/ac.v23i1.1069

Siljanovska, L. (2022). Theoretical Approach and Analysis of Communication as an Important Factor in Leadership in the Republic of North Macedonia. *European Journal Of Business Management And Research*, 7(2), 300–309. https://doi.org/10.24018/ejbmr.2022.7.2.1381

Silva, M. R., Roque, H. C., & Caetano, A. (2015). Culture in Angola: Insights for human resources management. *Cross Cultural Management: An International Journal*, 22(2), 166–186. https://doi.org/10.1108/CCM-02-2013-0036

Simpson, A.V., et al. (2021). Theorizing Compassionate Leadership from the Case of Jacinda Ardern: Legitimacy, Paradox and Resource Conservation. *Leadership*, 18(3), 337-358. https://doi.org/10.1177/17427150211055291.

Sirilatthayakorn, A., Chaopricha, P., Chalaechorn, N., & Joungtrakul, J. (2020). The development of Thai organisations to become learning organisations in the context of Thai culture: A grounded theory research strategy. *Research Community and Social Development Journal*. https://so04.tci-thaijo.org/index.php/NRRU/article/view/241413/166861

Smeds, L., Berlina, A., Jungsberg, L., Mikkola, N., Rasmussen, R. O., & Karlsdóttir, A. (2016). *Sustainable business development in the Nordic Arctic*. DIVA. http://norden.diva-portal.org/smash/record.jsf?pid=diva2:900150

Smith, J. (2021). The Land of Smiles: Understanding Thai culture. *Journal of Southeast Asian Studies*, 45(2), 123–145.

Smith, J., & Colleagues. (2018). Characteristics of Effective Expatriate Leaders in Thailand

Smith, K., & Boubker, O. (2014). Hofstede's model revisited: An application for measuring the Moroccan national culture. *International Journal of Business and Economic Development*, 2(3), 45–57.

Sobania, N. W. (2003). *Culture and customs of Kenya*. Greenwood Press. Sahistory.org.za

Söderfjäll, S. (2019). Libri i vogël i lidershipit (A. S. Doroci, Trans.). Pema. ISBN 978-9951-721-85-1.

Sofijanova, E., & Zabijakin-Chatleska, V. (2013). Employee involvement and organizational performance: Evidence from the manufacturing sector in Republic of Macedonia.

Soininvaara, I. (2021). The spatial hierarchies of a networked state: historical context and present-day imaginaries in Finland. *Territory, Politics, Governance*, 11(8), 1615–1634. https://doi.org/10.1080/21622671.2021.1918574

Speakersforum. (21 December, 2015). Arkistosta: Henkka Hyppönen - Mitä on hyvä johtajuus? - Speakersforum [Video]. YouTube. https://www.youtube.com/watch?v=uB643Jk9O_g

Srimueangpan, P. (2022). Guidelines for developing 21st-century leadership attributes of students at Roi Et Rajabhat University. *Journal of Organisation Management and Social Development, 2(2), 25–32.* https://so17.tci-thaijo.org/index.php/JOMSD/article/view/308/232

State Statistical Office. (2022). *Census of Population, Households and Dwellings in the Republic of North Macedonia, 2021.*

Ström, K., Wenström, S., & Uusiautti, S. (2024). Positive leadership development and leadership types in Finnish leaders' narratives. *International Journal of Research in Education and Science (IJRES)*, 10(4), 688-708. https://doi.org/10.46328/ijres.3484

Ström, K., Wenström, S., & Uusiautti, S. (2024). Positive leadership development and leadership types in Finnish leaders' narratives. *International Journal of Research in Education and Science*, 10(4), 688-708. https://doi.org/10.46328/ijres.3484

Styles, J. (2022). Organizational culture influence on the dimensions of

Styles, J. (2025). Interview. 19 November.

Styles, J. K., & Dean, D. J. (2024). Exploring the influence of organizational culture on dimensions of organizational learning at the University of the Bahamas: A structural equation modeling approach. *Journal of Higher Education Theory and Practice*, 24(11). https://doi.org/10.33423/jhetp.v24i11.7409

Styles, J., Knowles, L., & Ebron, K. (2024). Cultivating leadership: Female leaders in the Royal Bahamas Defence Force. *The Journal of Values-Based Leadership*, 17(2), Article 19. https://doi.org/10.22543/1948-0733.1519

Sutton, D.G. et al. (2007). The timing of the human discovery and colonization of New Zealand. *Quaternary International 184*(1) 109–121 https://doi.org/10.1016/j.quaint.2007.09.025

Swahili Proverbs: Methali za Kiswahili. (n.d.). Hurry – patience: Haraka haraka haina baraka. University of Illinois. swahiliproverbs.afrst.illinois.edu/hurry.html

Tafel-Viia, K., & Alas, R. (2007). Various types of Estonian top managers. *Journal of Business Economics and Management*, 8(3), 189–194.

Tahiraj, I., & Krek, J. (2022). Organisational culture in public university: A case study in Kosovo. *CEPS Journal*, 12(3), 127–147. https://doi.org/10.26529/cepsj.1198.

Tajeddini, K., & Trueman, M. (2014). Empowering leadership in hospitality and tourism management. *International Journal of Contemporary Hospitality Management, 26*(7), 1106–1125.

Takala, T. A., & Kemppainen, K. (2007). "Great Finns" – perspectives on greatness, charisma, and good leadership. *ResearchGate.*

Taksinapan, C. (2020). The study of leadership behaviour and the factors that make a leader in the organisation's culture in Thailand. *Journal of Business and Psychology.* https://so03.tci-thaijo.org/index.php/jbp/article/view/248940/167759

Tarifa, F. (2008). Of time, honor, and memory: Oral law in Albania. Oral Tradition, 23(1), 3–20.

Taylor, P. G. (2025). Thoughts on people-first leadership development [LinkedIn post].

Theri, M. (2025, June 3). Silence speaks louder: How Thais navigate conflict without confrontation. Medium. https://medium.com/@m.theri1828/silence-speaks-louder-f2b6dab29014

Thomas, A. (2017). Bahamas, The. In L. L. Lowry (Ed.), *The SAGE international encyclopedia of travel and tourism* (Vol. 4, pp. 118–120). Sage. https://doi.org/10.4135/9781483368924.n44

Thompson, A. R. (2025). Insights on leadership and the future of work in The Bahamas [LinkedIn post].

Thompson, A. R. (2025). Reflections on people-based leadership [LinkedIn post].

Tihei Mauri Ora! Māori Leadership in a Changing World. (2020). University of Auckland Executive Education. https://exec.auckland.ac.nz

Tikkanen, M. J. (2002). Long-term changes in lake and river systems in Finland. *ResearchGate.*

Time. (2014, March 19). *Thailand was never the Land of Smiles, whatever the guidebooks may have told you.* https://time.com/6597/thailand-was-never-the-land-of-smiles/

Toby. (2025, September 25). Managing In Kenya – Management Style & Workplace Culture. *Commisceo Global.* commisceo-global.com/management-guides/kenya-management-guide/

Toby. (2025a, August 8). The Bahamas – language, culture, customs and etiquette. Commisceo Global.

Tomovska Misoska, A., Mileva, I., & Bojadjiev, M. (2024). Bridging Culture and Leadership: Unveiling Values and Styles in North Macedonia. *Cross-Cultural Research, 58*(4), 322-333. https://doi.org/10.1177/10693971241262543

Tomovska Misoska, A., Taylor, L. K., Dautel, J., & Rylander, R. (2020). Children's understanding of ethnic group symbols: Piloting an instrument in the Republic of North Macedonia. *Peace and Conflict: Journal of Peace Psychology, 26*(1), 82.

Tongchangya, S. (2024). Exploring the Dasavidha-rājadhamma: A study of ancient virtues and their application in contemporary leadership. *The Journal of International Buddhist Studies, 12*(1), 45–62. https://so03.tci-thaijo.org/index.php/ibsc/article/view/278651

Tooms, A. (2010). An international effort to build leadership capacity: Insights from the first cohort of educational administration at the College of the Bahamas. *International Journal of Leadership in Education,* 13(1), 41–55.

Tuchman, B. (1996). *Thailand: A history of the monarchy and modernization.* Oxford University Press.

Tuulik, K., & Alas, R. (2010). Leadership in Estonia. Problems and Perspectives in Management, 8(1), 61–69.

Tuulik, K., Kurvits, J., & Õunapuu, T. (2013). Work-related values and leadership styles in developing Estonia. *Baltic Journal of Management,* 8(2), 200–215.

Ülavere, R. (2022, August 9). Kas Kaja on parem juht kui Jüri ehk kuidas hinnata juhi tööd? Edasi - Innustav ja hariv ajakiri. https://edasi.org/142950/raimo-ulavere-kas-kaja-on-parem-juht-kui-juri-ehk-kuidas-hinnata-juhi-tood/

Ülavere, R. (2025, March 4). Juhi oskused, millest ei rāägita/õpetata [Skills for leaders that are not discussed/taught] [Post]. LinkedIn.

University of The Bahamas. (2023). Conversation with Sir Franklyn Wilson on the Sunshine Boys and economic empowerment. https://www.ub.edu.bs/conversation-sir-franklyn-wilson-reveals-sunshine-boys-legacy-economic-empowerment/

University of Wolverhampton. (2014). *Business leadership and cultural transformation in Morocco.*

Uusen, R. (2025). Holistiline juhtimiskoolitaja Ivar Raav soovitab: 9 nõuannet, mis aitavad kasvada paremaks juhiks. Turundusraadio. https://turundusraadio1.rssing.com/chan-63908390/article543-live.html

Uusi-Kaakkuri, T. (2017). Transformational leadership and creativity: Evidence from Finnish organizations. https://www.researchgate.net/

Vadi, M., Raun, M., Õunapuu, T., Jaakson, K., Aidla, A., Leego, E., & Varblane, U. (2022). Eesti juhtimisvaldkonna uuring 2021 [Survey of the Estonian management field 2021]. Ettevõtluse Arendamise Sihtasutus; Majandus- ja Kommunikatsiooniministeerium. https://eis.ee/wp-content/uploads/2022/04/eesti-juhtimisvaldkonna-uuring-2021.pdf

Veskimägi, T. (2022, January 18). Mida sa teed siis, kui keegi ei näe? "Hea juhtimine" [What do you do when nobody is watching? "Good leadership"]. Edasi - Innustav ja hariv ajakiri. https://edasi.org/112463/taavi-veskimagi-mida-sa-teed-siis-kui-keegi-ei-nae-hea-juhtimine/

Viitala, R., (1 November, 2025). TET Talks - Jakso 3: Ihmisläheinen johtajuus [Video]. YouTube. https://www.youtube.com/watch?v=RbUGtvTFsZI

Vilakati, V. M., & Schurink, W. J. (2021, April 29). An explorative-descriptive qualitative-constructivist study of three African leaders' experiences and perceptions regarding the translation of shared African human values into leadership and business practice. *SA Journal Of Human Resource Management.*https://sajhrm.co.za/index.php/sajhrm/article/view/1433/2497

Vora, D., & Kainzbauer, A. (2020). Humanistic leadership in Thailand: A mix of indigenous and global aspects. *Cross Cultural & Strategic Management.*

Wennecke, C. W., Jacobsen, R. B., & Ren, C. (2019). Motivations for Indigenous Island entrepreneurship: Entrepreneurs and behavioral economics in Greenland. *Island Studies Journal, 14*(2), 43–60. https://doi.org/10.24043/isj.99

Williams, T., & Adams, R. (2014). Global management practices in North Africa: Comparative perspectives from Morocco. *Journal of World Business,* 49(4), 567–578.

Wilson, L. (2023). Empathy in leadership: Why understanding people drives performance. *New Zealand Management Magazine, 70*(4) 42-45

Wright, A., Inter-American Development Bank, & Felipe Herrera Library. (2018). *Development challenges in the Bahamas* (IDB Policy Brief No. IDB-PB-276). Inter-American Development Bank. http://www.iadb.org

Xu, L., Götz, F. M., Ebert, T., Silm, S., Vainik, U., Johnson, W., & Mõttus, R. (2025). Does a small country have meaningful regional personality differences? The case of Estonia. *Journal of Personality*. Advance online publication. https://doi.org/10.1111/jopy.13013

Yamamoto, K. (2000). The ethical structure of the Kanun: Is it the original source of Albanian ethics? *Design Issues of KID*, 2, 35–45.

Youssef, L., & Benkirane, A. (2024). Leadership values and cultural dimensions in Moroccan organizations: A post-pandemic analysis. *Frontiers in Psychology*.

Yukongdi, V. (2010). A study of Thai employees' preferred leadership style. *Asia Pacific Business Review, 16(1–2), 161–181*. https://doi.org/10.1080/13602380903168962

Zeducation. *Week 4 Team Leadership Class – Diversity* [Video]. YouTube. www.youtube.com/watch?v=E2qPtaSh0BY&list=PLq7pukzkGSWzLPKXi-RPru58Df-bLe1_1.

Zivkovic, S. (2022). Empathy in leadership: how it enhances effectiveness. *Economic and social development: Book of proceedings*, 454-467.

Zimmermann, A. (2022, February 7). Empathy is a business skill. *LSE Business Review*. https://blogs.lse.ac.uk/businessreview/2022/02/07/empathy-is-a-business-skill/